MUIRHEAD LIBRARY OF PHILOSOPHY

An admirable statement of the aims of the Library of Philosophy was provided by the first editor, the late Professor J. H. Muirhead, in his description of the original programme printed in Erdmann's *History of Philosophy* under the date 1890. This was slightly modified in subsequent volumes to take the form of the following statement:

'The Muirhead Library of Philosophy was designed as a contribution to the History of Modern Philosophy under the heads: first of Different Schools of Thought—Sensationalist, Realist, Idealist, Intuitivist; secondly of different Subjects—Psychology, Ethics, Political Philosophy, Theology. While much had been done in England in tracing the course of evolution in nature, history, economics, morals and religion, little had been done in tracing the development of thought on these subjects. Yet "the evolution of opinion is part of the whole evolution".

'By the co-operation of different writers in carrying out this plan it was hoped that a thoroughness and completeness of treatment, otherwise unattainable, might be secured. It was believed also that from writers mainly British and American fuller consideration of English Philosophy than it had hitherto received might be looked for. In the earlier series of books containing, among others, Bosanquet's *History of Aesthetic*, Pfleiderer's *Rational Theology since Kant*, Albee's *History of English Utilitarianism*, Bonar's *Philosophy and Political Economy*, Brett's *History of Psychology*, Ritchie's *Natural Rights*, these objects were to a large extent effected.

'In the meantime original work of a high order was being produced both in England and America by such writers as Bradley, Stout, Bertrand Russell, Baldwin, Urban, Montague, and others, and a new interest in foreign works, German, French and Italian, which had either become classical or were attracting public attention, had developed. The scope of the Library thus became extended into something more international, and it is entering on the fifth decade of its existence in the hope that it may contribute to that mutual understanding between countries which is so pressing a need of the present time.'

The need which Professor Muirhead stressed is no less pressing today, and few will deny that philosophy has much to do with enabling us to meet it, although no one, least of all Muirhead himself, would regard that as the sole, or even the main, object of philosophy. As Professor Muirhead continues to lend the distinction of his name to the

Library of Philosophy it seemed not inappropriate to allow him to recall us to these aims in his own words. The emphasis on the history of thought also seemed to me very timely; and the number of important works promised for the Library in the very near future augur well for the continued fulfilment, in this and other ways, of the expectations of the original editor.

H. D. LEWIS

MUIRHEAD LIBRARY OF PHILOSOPHY

General Editor: H. D. Lewis
Professor of History and Philosophy of Religion in the University of London

Muirhead Library of Philosophy

EDITED BY H. D. LEWIS

PHILOSOPHY AND ILLUSION

PHILOSOPHY AND ILLUSION

BY

MORRIS LAZEROWITZ

Sophia and Austin Smith
Professor of Philosophy
Smith College

LONDON · GEORGE ALLEN & UNWIN LTD
NEW YORK · HUMANITIES PRESS

PRINTED IN GREAT BRITAIN
in 11 pt Imprint Type
BY UNWIN BROTHERS LIMITED
WOKING AND LONDON

TO THE MEMORY OF MY PARENTS
MAX AND ETTA LAIZEROWITZ

This book carries on the work of *The Structure of Metaphysics* and *Studies in Metaphilosophy* and, in a way, concludes a programme. One part of the programme was to construct a hypothesis which would explain both the nonexistence of stable results in one of the oldest of the intellectual disciplines and also the undiminished preoccupation which it has attracted to itself. The other part of the programme was to apply the hypothesis to basic and representative problems in the major branches of philosophy: metaphysics, epistemology, ethics, aesthetics, philosophy of science, etc. And although a vast amount of work lies ahead, this has now been done.

The constant motivation of this book has been to improve our understanding of an enigmatic, if time-honoured, subject. As might be expected, the pursuit of understanding unhampered by serious ambivalence has brought to light facts which some people would prefer to have pushed back into their former obscurity, where they cause no uneasiness. Like Orpheus, a philosopher cannot permit his Euridyce to be brought out of the underworld into the light of day. Freud once observed that 'one cannot explain things to unfriendly people', and anyone who has the temerity to try to introduce a radical change into our way of looking at things we live with creates resistances and, if he persists, takes upon himself the labours of Sysiphos.

Most of the essays here are renewed and independent attempts to change our way of looking at philosophical thinking, in each case through a different problem. The other essays are oriented toward the same end, the correct understanding of the nature of technical, reasoned philosophy. None of the essays leans on a separate introduction, and only one, 'Paradoxes', requires a sequel, which the remainder of the book provides. The short review of a symposium on universals is included because it brings out several useful points about philosophical disagreements, and serves as an introduction for the following study, 'Understanding Philosophy'.

Four of the papers in this book have not appeared in print before: 'Empiricism and Rationalism', 'Time and Temporal Terminology', 'On Perceiving Things', 'The Problem of Justifying Induction'. For permission to reprint the remaining studies and reviews I am indebted to the editors of the following books and journals:

Metaphysics: Readings and Reappraisals, Prentice-Hall, Inc.; *British Philosophy in the Mid-Century*, George Allen & Unwin Ltd.; *Current Philosophical Issues*, Essays in Honour of Curt John Ducasse, Charles C. Thomas, Publisher; *The Philosophical Review*, *Crítica* and *Philosophy*.

To Alice Ambrose I am now, as in the past, deeply indebted for many constructive criticisms and suggestions.

Northampton, Massachusetts   MORRIS LAZEROWITZ
March, 1968

NOTE

The papers in this book which have been previously published originally appeared as follows:

'Paradoxes', in *Metaphysics: Readings and Reappraisals* (edited by W. E. Kennick and Morris Lazerowitz), Prentice-Hall, Inc., 1966.

'Wittgenstein on the Nature of Philosophy', in *British Philosophy in the Mid-Century*. A Cambridge Symposium (edited by C. A. Mace), Second edition, George Allen & Unwin Ltd., 1966.

'On Universals. A Review of a Symposium', in *The Philosophical Review*, Vol. LXVII, no. 3, 1958.

'Understanding Philosophy', in *Current Philosophical Issues*. Essays in Honour of Curt John Ducasse (edited by Frederick C. Dommeyer), Charles C. Thomas, Publisher, 1966.

'Philosophy and Illusion', in *Crítica*, Vol. 1, no. 2, 1967.

'Moore's *Commonplace Book*', in *Philosophy*, Vol. XXXIX, no. 148, 1964.

'Austin's *Sense and Sensibilia*', in *Philosophy*, Vol. XXXVIII, no. 145, 1963.

CONTENTS

B

PARADOXES

The point of wit is often to render a disturbing truth harmless, and it may be that the witticism that the philosopher's hell is Paradox Lost and his heaven Paradox Regained springs from a glimpse into the subterranean workings of philosophy. For if we look closely at metaphysical theories we find a surprisingly large number of paradoxes in unexpected places, quite apart from the explicitly formulated paradoxes such as those of Zeno and Kant. The idea which suggests itself is that a paradox or a contradiction lies hidden in every metaphysical theory, that it is in the very stuff from which metaphysical theories are woven. In our childhood we took pleasure in discovering faces and animals cleverly concealed in drawings of landscapes and the like, and it would not be surprising to learn that we take like pleasure in the contemplation of statements which contain hidden paradoxes. As will be seen in the course of this study there is reason to think that the visible theories and arguments of metaphysics teem with invisible paradoxes, contradictions, and antinomies, and that in metaphysics we are everywhere surrounded by paradox. Ancient Greek philosophers arrived at the proposition that nature works by unseen bodies. It would appear that a like proposition holds for metaphysics: metaphysics works by unseen paradoxes.

Hamlet said 'This was sometime a paradox, but now the time gives it proof'. The implication is that a statement cannot be both a paradox and a known truth, and that knowing a statement is true removes for us its paradoxical character. Science has of course put forward many paradoxical propositions which have become commonplaces. But in metaphysics it may truly be said that once a paradox always a paradox, and it would seem that metaphysics, and indeed reasoned philosophy in general, is not only the breeding ground but also the refuge of paradoxes and contradictions. There is no room for doubt that an objective investigation is called for, but very likely it will be slow to come. For the existence of a tendency to turn away from what is feared can easily be understood, as can the existence of a need to protect valued beliefs, especially those suspected of being illusions.

As strange as the fact that the known and time-honoured paradoxes have remained unsolved is the fact that so many paradoxes and contradictions have remained hidden from philosophers for so long a time. Like Poe's purloined letter, many of them are in plain view; indeed, they stand out in such pronounced relief that the only explanation of our failing to see them would appear to be a wish not to see them. To illustrate briefly, consider, in relation to the central doctrine of Parmenides, two of the small number of known statements for which Zeno argued. As is known by every philosopher, Parmenides' thesis is that something, 'being', exists and that nothing, or 'not-being', does not exist: 'It is necessary both to say and think that being is . . . and it is impossible that not-being is.' This thesis, according to reliable accounts, Zeno sought to defend against rival positions. Now, one statement for which Zeno argued is that 'there is no such thing as space' (Fr. 4). Another statement, which is one of two statements he argued for in Fr. 1, is that whatever exists must have thickness and magnitude: 'If Being did not have magnitude it would not exist at all.' It will be obvious at first glance that having magnitude entails being in space; 'x has magnitude but is not in space' is a contradiction which no one could avoid noticing. It will be equally obvious that if space does not exist and if nothing can exist without being in space, then nothing whatever exists. Thus, a plain consequence of Zeno's two statements is that nothing exists and that not-being is, a consequence which stands, of course, in contradiction to the view Zeno sought to defend. How both Zeno and Parmenides and the many acute and subtle reasoners after them up to the present day could have failed to notice this intellectual misadventure is difficult to explain except by supposing the presence of a wish not to see it. There is another, and in my opinion, better explanation: and this is that a philosophical contradiction is not a contradiction, or not a real contradiction, but something else. But this cannot be gone into here.

A further thing, as perplexing as the intellectual astigmatism for contradictions on the part of thinkers who are practised in discovering them, is the variety of interpretations which have been placed upon them. Some metaphysicians, in agreement with reports of mystics, maintain that there are self-contradictory

realities, states of affairs which make self-contradictory propositions *true*. One statement attributed to Heraclitus is the following:
'In the same rivers we step and we do not step; we are and we are
not.' And Hegel stated that 'the Absolute is Being' and also 'the
Absolute is the Naught'.[1] In agreement with these metaphysicians,
the mystic Rudolph Otto has said: 'Black does not cease to be
black nor white white. But black is white and white is black. The
opposites coincide without ceasing to be what they are in themselves.'[2] Moreover, Otto states that he has 'physically seen' the
reality which makes his contradictory proposition true. Against
this claim that there are self-contradictory propositions which
truly describe states of affairs, some metaphysicians maintain that
reality must be self-consistent but allow that appearances are or may
be self-contradictory. As against Heraclitus and Otto, a philosopher
like F. H. Bradley would maintain that when we think we see
spatial and temporal phenomena what we are actually perceiving
are self-contradictory appearances, which because they are self-
contradictory are 'mere' appearance. We do not perceive self-
contradictory realities, as there can be none. Other philosophers,
e.g. Kant, maintain that a special kind of contradictory statement
called an 'antinomy' refers to a supersensible entity, something
not in space or time, and so lying beyond the range of human
investigation. And probably every philosopher would hold with
regard to some *ordinary* self-contradictory propositions that they
are logically absurd, and refer neither to a physical reality, to a
transcandental reality, nor to a 'mere' sensible appearance.
Probably all would agree that the proposition, 'the diameter of a
circle is shorter than its radius', is a mere absurdity.

We may indeed be puzzled to know how philosophical contradictions can differ so radically from non-philosophical contradictions, and what it is in philosophical contradictions which
makes possible such different views about what their presence
shows. A contradiction is a contradiction, and it would seem
reasonable to suppose that what its presence shows in one case it
shows in *every* case in which it occurs. If in mathematics or in
ordinary non-philosophical talk, establishing a contradiction in a

---

[1] *The Logic of Hegel*, trans. by William Wallace (Oxford, at the Clarendon
Press, 1892), pp. 158–61.
[2] Quoted by W. T. Stace in *Mysticism and Philosophy* (Philadelphia,
Lippincott, 1960), p. 65.

proposition establishes the theoretical impossibility of anything making it true, then a contradiction should do this in every case. The presence of a contradiction in the concept of a supersensible reality, in the concept of a sensible reality, or in the concept of a sensible appearance, like the contradiction in the concept of an odd number which is exactly divisible by 2, will imply the theoretical impossibility of there being anything of the sort. How than are we to understand the mystic and the metaphysician? In what way are their contradictions different from those which make us dismiss propositions containing them as logical absurdities? These are important questions to ask, and in fact asking them is already a step toward answering them, and toward improving our understanding of what philosophy is.

To see something of the unorthodox character of one metaphysical contradiction, consider the view that time is not real and that its sensibly seeming to us to exist is a trick played on us by our senses. In his stadium paradox Zeno adduces an argument to show that half of a given time equals the whole of the time, $\frac{t}{2} = t$, from which the conclusion to be drawn is that the belief that there really are occurrences is a superstition induced by a delusive appearance. Zeno's demonstration of a contradiction in the concept *time* parallels a frequent form of demonstration in mathematics, i.e. the demonstration of the falsity of a proposition by *reductio ad absurdum*, with one important difference. The mathematician, unlike the metaphysician, does not explain a person's naïve belief in a disproved proposition, e.g. that it is possible to trisect an angle with straight edge and compass, by urging that he has been the dupe of the sensible appearance of something being accomplished. Why the mathematician does not resort to such an explanation is not hard to see. If there were a sensible appearance or some sort of pictorial representation of an angle being trisected with straight edge and compass, we could learn from it, as we could from the sensible appearance or representation of an angle being bisected, how to carry out the operation. But there is no doing the logically impossible, nor is there any picturing or representing in our imagination its being done. What we can represent we can, in principle, if not in fact, do. In the case of trisecting an angle with straight edge and compass, picturing the trisection is equivalent to doing it; and it is clear that any sensible appearance of my trisecting an angle with straight edge and compass, however strong the accompanying *feeling* of success might be, would not be accepted by a mathematician as *really* representing the trisection. Wittgenstein has written: 'It used to be said that God could create anything except what would be contrary to the laws of logic.—The reason being that we could not *say* what an 'illogical' world would look like.[1]' If we could say what it would look like to do the logically impossible we could say what it would be to do the logically impossible; and this means that it could be done. What is logically impossible would then be logically possible.

F. H. Bradley's version of the contradiction in the concept of *time*,[2] which is perhaps simpler than Zeno's, can, without distortion, be rendered in the following way. The existence of time implies the existence of a present moment of time, the *now*; and, plainly, if to suppose the existence of the *now* implies a contradiction, then to suppose the existence of time will also imply a contradiction. The basic divisions of time are past, present, and future, and these are mutually exclusive parts of time: the present cannot contain any part of the past, as to suppose the contrary would imply that something is happening which is no longer happening; and the present cannot include any part of the future, as to suppose the contrary would imply that something is happening which is still in the future and has not yet happened. But the present is either a time span, which is to say that it has *some* duration, however short, or it is 'simple and indivisible'[3] and is not a time span. If it is a time span then part of the present will have elapsed and still be present and part of it will not yet have been reached and yet be present. The *now*, in other words, will include some past as well as some future, which implies a contradiction. But if the present is not a time span it cannot be a part of time, which is absurd. Hence the proposition that time exists has either of two logically impossible consequences and is false. Therefore time is unreal and exists only as a delusive appearance.

It is not to be denied that an interesting and baffling difficulty in the notion of time has been brought to light by metaphysicians,

[1] *Tractatus Logico-Philosophicus*, trans. by Pears and McGuinness (London: Routledge, Kegan Paul Ltd., 1961), 3.031.

[2] *Appearance and Reality* (London: George Allen & Unwin Ltd., 1920), Ch. IV.

[3] Bradley's expression.

although the question as to whether it is a contradiction has been argued at length and with the inconclusiveness we have come to expect in philosophy. One paradoxical consequence of the claim that time exists only in appearance throws it into an unexpected light, and shows that the metaphysical contradiction on which it is based has not been properly understood. This consequence has somehow been overlooked although it is direct and plain, requiring no complicated chain of reasoning. The proposition that time only appears to exist, and that there only appear to be occurrences, implies quite plainly that there are certain occurrences: it implies that there occurs a succession of sensible appearances of various happenings taking place. And the proposition that there are certain occurrences implies, obviously, the existence, or reality, of time. It might be urged that the metaphysician has allowed the existence of temporal appearances because of an intellectual oversight, i.e. by failing to see the consequence of what he allows, and that it is open to him to retract his admission. But anyone who urges this is making no more than a 'move', to use a word which has become popular in contemporary philosophy, in order to extricate the metaphysician. But this is a move which the metaphysician cannot accept. For apart from the absurdity of denying that time *appears* to exist, metaphysicians have recourse to the 'appearances' in explanation of the common belief that time exists.

Bertrand Russell has remarked that modern philosophy from Descartes on has been infected by 'subjective madness', and Hume's frequently quoted description of his feelings on looking back at his philosophizing while playing backgammon with friends would seem to bear out Russell's observation. Hume wrote: '. . . and when after three or four hours' amusement I . . . return to these speculations, they appear so cold, and strain'd, and ridiculous, that I cannot find in my heart to enter into them any farther'.[1] More important than Hume's confession of his feelings are the implications which lie just below the surface of his views, and also of the views of Descartes, Locke, Berkeley, Kant, and more recent philosophers. But before examining any specific theories, one of the basic traditions of philosophy, rationalism, which reaches from the present back to the earliest days of philosophy, should be looked at. For if modern philosophy suffers from subjectivity, the outcome of which is solipsism, ancient as

[1] *The Treatise of Human Nature*, Bk. I, Pt. IV.

well as modern philosophy has been haunted by the spectre of nothingness, which is the hidden outcome of rationalism. One philosopher has said that rationalism 'suffered shipwreck...because its fruits lacked nourishing value'.[1] It may be pointed out that many philosophers are still sailing the rationalist ship in the metaphysical seas, and it is not unlikely that the passenger list will increase. But despite the many spectacular theories rationalist philosophers have produced, it can easily be shown that the consequence of rationalism, like that of Zeno's pieces of reasoning, is Gorgias' proposition that nothing exists.

I

It has been denied by many philosophers that thinking alone can 'bring us information of any fact in the world',[2] but many of the very greatest philosophers have certainly thought the contrary and have imagined themselves to have constructed and demonstrated by reason alone world-views, systems of propositions about the existence and nature of things. This includes at least some philosophical empiricists, e.g. Berkeley and Hume. Generally speaking, rationalism, as opposed to empiricism, is the view that by the use of pure reason, without the help of the senses, it is possible to determine the nature of reality, the material or materials of which it is constituted, its structure, and how it operates. In the *Phaedo* Socrates is made to say, 'I was afraid that my soul might be completely blinded if I looked at things with my eyes, and tried to grasp them with my senses. So I thought that I must have recourse to conceptions, and examine the truth of existence by means of them ... I am scarcely prepared to admit that he who examines existence through conceptions is dealing with mere reflections, any more than he who examines it as manifested in sensible objects.'[3] Even before Socrates Parmenides had said: 'Let not the habit engrained by manifold experience force you along this path, to make an instrument of the blind eye, the echoing ear, and the tongue, but test by reason my contribution to the great debate.'[4] The title of the oldest known mathematical treatise,

[1] Hans Hahn, 'Logic, Mathematics and Knowledge of Nature', in *Logical Positivism*, ed. by A. J. Ayer (Glencoe, Ill.: The Free Press, 1959), p. 150.
[2] *Ibid.*, p. 159.   [3] F. J. Church's translation,
[4] Quoted by Benjamin Farrington in *Greek Science* (Pelican Books, 1944), Ch. IV.

the Ahmes Papyrus, sums up the essence of rationalism and also gives something of the grandiose psychology underlying it: it is, 'Rules for Enquiring into Nature, and for Knowing All That Exists'.[1] This title expresses the ideal which lies behind Leibniz's dream of a *Characteristica Universalis*, about which he said: 'If we had it we should be able to reason in metaphysics and in morals in much the same way as in geometry and analysis.' His claim in his own quaint words is that 'If controversies were to arise, there would be no more need of disputation between two philosophers than between two accountants. For it would suffice to take pencils in their hands, to sit down to their slates, and to say to each other (with a friend as a witness if they liked): Let us calculate.' It is instructive also to note Descartes' remark in his *De Mundo*: 'Whoever examines carefully the rules I have laid down and the truths thereby reached, will be able to proceed to demonstrations *a priori* of everything that occurs in the world.'

A. J. Ayer has described rationalism in the following words: '. . . the fundamental tenet of rationalism is that thought is an independent source of knowledge, and is moreover a more trustworthy source of knowledge than experience; indeed some rationalists have gone so far as to say that thought is the only source of knowledge.'[2] And Brand Blanshard has spoken of '. . . the conviction held unanimously by rationalists from Plato to McTaggart that reason can supply us with knowledge of the world. . . .'[3] The following is a more detailed description of this doctrine: '. . . start anywhere in experience, develop what is implied in what is before you, and you will find yourself committed, on the principle of the flower in the crannied wall, or of the widening circles in the pool, to an all-comprehensive system in which everything is bound by necessity to everything else. To judge that this is a flower is to use a universal. But the universal, when you attend to it, burgeons. It is necessarily connected through genus and species with a hierarchy above it. Its appearance at this spot and moment is connected spatially, temporally, and causally with every other event in the universe. And these relations, if we saw clearly enough, would turn out to be necessary also.'[4]

---

[1] T. E. Peet's translation.

[2] *Language, Truth and Logic*, second edition (London: Victor Gollancz Ltd., 1948), p. 73.

[3] 'The Philosophy of Analysis', *Proc. of the British Academy*, Vol. XXXVIII, p. 41.   [4] *Ibid.*, p. 40.

If we read with care the rationalists, and also at least some of the empiricists, that is to say, if we look at what they *do* in philosophy rather than at the surrounding talk about what they are doing, we can see that they all operate on the idea that 'thought is the only source of knowledge'. This holds true not only for the avowed rationalists from Parmenides to F. H. Bradley, but also for others, and even for those who wave the empiricist banner. If we can detach ourselves for a moment from the *picture* philosophy presents to most of us, its ontological face, so to speak, and soberly think on the matter, we easily come to realize that *no* proposition of philosophy can properly and truly be introduced with such words as 'Experience shows that . . .'. The findings of our senses play no role whatever in establishing or rejecting a philosophical theory. Be that as it may, however, it is clear that many important philosophers have the notion that secure knowledge of reality is to be arrived at only by 'recourse to conceptions' or by 'recourse to the mind',[1] and they give every appearance of erecting their impressive and reasoned theories on the basis of this notion. In fact, the impression gained from reading many rationalist philosophers is that they think the senses stand in the way of our arriving at truth and even that they are diseased and should be 'quarantined'.

The usual formulations of the fundamental tenet of philosophical rationalism, by employing such phrases as 'world-hypothesis established by recourse to the mind', dramatize the power of thought and draw our attention away from equivalent and more manageable formulations of the tenet. One historian of philosophy wrote about Parmenides that '. . . his mind was imaginative and poetical, and [he] was thus protected from the logical consequences of his premises'.[2] Undoubtedly many of us naturally use language in a way which plays into our deeper needs rather than into our scientific curiosity: and it would not be surprising if the poetical ways of stating rationalism have a comparable function. The less beguiling way of formulating the general claim that the 'truth of existence' can be known by reasoning on concepts alone is to say that *all* propositions are *a priori*, i.e. are either true by logical necessity or false by logical

---

[1] Jowett's translation of the same phrase.
[2] Theodor Gomperz, *The Greek Thinkers*, Vol. I, trans. by Laurie Magnus (London: John Murray, 1949), p. 178.

necessity. The truth of an assertion, p, is determinable without resorting to observation or an experiemnt if it satisfies either of the following two conditions: (1) its negation, $\sim p$, is internally inconsistent, i.e. either is a self-contradiction or directly implies, by itself alone without involving any other proposition, a self-contradiction; (2) p is a deductive consequence of one or more propositions whose negations are or directly imply self-contradictions. This is to say that a proposition is *a priori* if its truth-value can be determined either by some sort of examination of the proposition *itself* or if it can be calculated from propositions whose truth-values can be established by such an examination. If now, as rationalism claims, knowledge of reality can be obtained by unaided thought, or, to put it equivalently, if propositions about the existence and nature of things can be established or confuted solely by reasoning on them, then *all* propositions without exception are *a priori*. Wittgenstein once wrote, in a Spinozistic vein: 'The great problem about which everything I write turns is: Is there an order in the world *a priori*, and if so what does it consist in?'[1] The notion that the world has an *a priori* order, or that reality is a system of things standing in logically necessary relations to each other, is equivalent to the notion that the world is delineated by a set of *a priori* truths. If this notion is correct, the appropriate procedure to resort to in attempting to answer the question, 'What does the order consist in?', is reasoning on propositions.

A first reading of the rationalist metaphysicians may make us think that they take into account two kinds of propositions about reality, those which are contingent and cannot be affirmed or denied by 'recourse to the mind', and those which are *a priori*. Thus, Leibniz ostensibly distinguishes between truths of reason and truths of fact. The former, according to his claim, hold for all possible universes, as against the latter which are true only for particular possible universes, and hence cannot be established or confuted without the help of experience. This distinction between propositions would also seem to be involved in Spinoza's distinction between *natura naturans* and *natura naturata*, and it would seem to be implied by most, if not all, rationalistic systems of philosophy. The ins and outs of the various rationalistic doctrines cannot of course be gone into here. Little more can be done

[1] *Notebooks*, 1914–16 (Oxford: Basil Blackwell, 1961), 53e.

beside remarking that if we look with care at what philosophers *do* rather than at how they *talk* about what they do we see that the premise on which they erect their theories is the proposition that the universe down to its smallest detail can, *in principle*, be known *a priori*, by reasoning alone.

It is instructive, in this connexion, to see how Leibniz, apparently without realizing it, abolishes the distinction he explicitly draws between *a priori* and contingent propositions. Truths of reason, he tells us, are 'identical enunciation[s], whose opposite[s] involve an express contradiction'.[1] Their opposites can be made true by no possible state of affairs, and are thus true of all possible worlds. Contingent propositions, on the other hand, are those whose opposites are possible; they therefore are such as can be made true by some state of affairs and false by others. Despite making this distinction, however, it turns out that Leibniz holds a view about the relation between contingent and necessary truths which implies that so-called contingent propositions are necessary. He holds that they are really analytic but to see that they are 'requires an infinite analysis, which God alone can accomplish'. Necessary truths and truths of fact '. . . differ from each other almost as rational numbers and surds. For necessary truths can be resolved into such as are identical, as commensurable quantities can be brought to a common measure; but in contingent truths, as in surd numbers, the resolution proceeds to infinity without ever terminating. And thus the certainty and the perfect reason can be known to God only, who embraces the infinite in one intuition. And when this secret is known, the difficulty as to the absolute necessity of all things is removed, and it appears what the difference is between the infallible and the necessary.'[2] The difference between the necessary and the infallible, on Leibniz's explanation, is a difference in complexity, not a difference in their logical character. To us some propositions appear to be contingent, but only because their subjects are infinitely complex, which prevents us from seeing that affirming their subjects while denying their predicates involves a self-contradiction. God sees what we are prevented from seeing by the limitations of our minds, and He sees that all true propo-

[1] *Leibniz: The Monadology and other philosophical writings*, trans., with introduction and notes, by Robert Latta (Oxford, 1898), p. 236.
[2] *Die philosophischen Schriften von G. W. Leibniz*, herausgegeben von C. J. Gerhardt, Berlin, 1875–90, Vol. VII, p. 309.

sitions are really truths of reason. *Every* true proposition, thus, is to be construed as being analytic and as holding for all possible worlds. This directly and plainly implies that there is only one possible world, which therefore is necessary and has an '*a priori* order'. For suppose there to be two different possible universes, $U_1 \neq U_2$. Then there would be at least one proposition p which was true of U_1 and not of U_2. Hence p would not be true for all possible universes and would not be necessary. A further consequence of Leibniz's claim about contingent propositions is that knowledge of the world is, in principle, obtainable by reasoning on concepts alone. Leibniz erects his metaphysics on the principle that truths of fact are really analytic, and therefore on the principle that the truth-values of propositions about the world could be arrived at by a sufficiently extended analysis of their subjects. Parenthetically, it may be noted that philosophers who adopt the formula that the contingent is 'grounded' in the necessary also do their theorizing on the Leibnizian principle that all true propositions are true by logical necessity. Leibniz gives us the picture of God contemplating various world-plans and bringing one of them into existence. 'The whole universe', he writes, 'might have been made differently; time, space, and matter being absolutely indifferent to motions and figures; and God has chosen among an infinity of possibles what he judged to be most suitable.'[1] But the picture he gives us of a titanic world-builder is a deceptive piece of window dressing, a spurious empirical front, for a non-empirical view. For the claim that all true propositions are analytic is equivalent to the claim that all false propositions are self-contradictory; and this comes to the claim that whatever is possible is necessary and what is not necessary is not possible. A necessary proposition has no possible, non-contradictory, alternatives; hence, on the present claim, there can be no alternative possibilities. It is easy to see now why the God of Leibniz created the world that He did. Being necessary it is the only logically possible world and was the *only* one He could create! He had no choice, because no alternatives were open to him. Paradoxically, it also follows that God could not have created the world, for what exists by logical necessity cannot fail to exist and so cannot be brought into existence. Spinoza said that not even God could

[1] *The Philosophical Works of Leibnitz*, with notes by George Martin Duncan, 1890, pp. 223–4.

bring it about that from a given cause no effect should follow; and we say that just as God cannot bring about what is logically impossible so he cannot bring about what is logically necessary. More paradoxically still, it follows from the rationalistic premise that nothing exists, not even an Omnipotent Being who is capable of bringing about various things.

To show first that things cannot exist. It will be clear that objects and occurrences, such as inkwells, grains of sand, mountains, rainbows, clouds, volcanic eruptions, planets, in short, all the objects and occurrences constituting nature, are, for one thing, such that their nonexistence is logically possible. For another thing, their changing in some respect or other is logically possible. Horses in fact do exist and centaurs in fact do not exist, but it is logically possible for there to be centaurs and no horses. Similarly, those amongst things which change are such that it is logically possible for them not to have changed or to have changed in a way different from the way in which they actually did change; and those amongst things which have remained unchanged are such that it is logically possible that they should have changed. If it were in fact the case that nothing in nature changed in any particular, if, to put it figuratively, the universe were in a state of frozen immobility, it would nevertheless be logically possible for the various things in it to change. And if, to consider the opposite extreme, things were in a state of constant and bewildering change, it would nevertheless be possible for them not to change. Now, the existence of things whose nonexistence is conceivable, i.e. things of a kind that could, logically, fail to exist, implies that there are propositions which are true but which could in principle be falsified. And the existence of things that undergo change or, if they remain the same, could change in some way or other, implies that there are propositions whose truths could conceivably be upset and could be denied without contradiction. In short, the existence of a world of things and occurrences implies the existence of propositions whose actual truth-values are not their only possible truth-values. It implies that there are propositions that are neither analytic nor self-contradictory. Hence if all propositions were *a priori*, either not possibly true or not possibly false, if contingent propositions were, so to speak, crowded out of logical space, things the existence of which would entail there being non-*a priori* propositions would be logically crowded out of the cosmos.

Mountains, planets, grains of sand, rivers, etc. could not, logically, exist.

In an equally simple and direct way it can be seen to follow from the rationalist thesis that the sensible appearances, which metaphysicians urge us to discount or put aside in the investigation of reality, also cannot exist. Not only does the thesis logically crowd out of existence things like trees, the moon, and Niagara Falls, it also crowds out of existence sensible appearances of there being such things. There is no more room for the one than there is for the other. The position which many metaphysicians, according to their own explicit words, have adopted is that while reality cannot be self-contradictory there can be, and there are, self-contradictory appearances. It is puzzling, to say the least, to be told the if there really were cows then a self-contradictory proposition would be *true*, but that there are self-contradictory cow-appearances, which of course also implies that a self-contradictory proposition is true. We well may wonder what makes it possible for anyone to hold a view according to which the proposition that there are cows is self-contradictory and therefore false, and the proposition that there are appearances of there being cows is self-contradictory and true. It would seem natural and correct to think that what the presence of a contradiction shows in the one case it shows in the other case, and that if being self-contradictory is what logically prevents there really being cows, being self-contradictory must also prevent there really being the self-contradictory appearances of cows. Ordinarily, and removed from philosophy, we should say that what is logically impossible, e.g. my wearing a pink tie which is uniformly grey, cannot be, and we should also say that it cannot be pictured in a painting, mirage, or dream: both the picture and the pictured cannot exist. But for some reason which is hidden from us it would appear that what it is proper and correct to say away from philosophy is not proper and correct to say in philosophy.

It is not, of course, to be doubted that a great many people find a kind of enchantment in metaphysical contradictions and that they somehow solace themselves with the rejection of the appearances, whatever doing this may come to. We may hazard the guess that one thing behind this philosophical rejection is an important psychological rejection, caused by the unsatisfactoriness of life itself. In our sojourn here 'One woe doth tread upon another's heel, So fast they follow', as Hamlet says; and it would be understandable if some people detached their interest from the world and sought psychological refuge elsewhere, if they 'fled from the confusion of the senses' and found comfort in the 'heaven above the heavens'. Freud has said that 'Really we never can relinquish anything; we only exchange one thing for something else. When we appear to give something up, all we really do is adopt a substitute.'[1] In metaphysics, to which we cannot help but bring our emotional problems, we discover substitute objects for our wishes or substitute ways of gratifying our wishes, and we do this in such a way as to make the substitutes unrecognizable to others as well as to ourselves. This may be part of the reason why the metaphysical rationalist fails to discern the consequences of his basic tenet, viz. that the sensible appearances do not exist, that there is not even the illusion of a world. For perhaps the consequence is in a substitutive way bound up with a forbidden, nihilistic wish. John Wisdom has described the case of a man who, under hypnosis, saw a blank on a printed page wherever the word 'the' occurred. We may say that the metaphysician works under a spell which makes him blot out some things from his conscious awareness; for the consequence comes out of his tenet with stark clarity. The consideration that brings to view the consequence is the same as the consideration which shows that the nonexistence of a world of things is directly implied by the tenet.

Any actual sensible appearance, e.g. the appearance of there being a teacup or of there being stars in the night sky, is the kind of thing which has come into existence but might, conceivably, not have. And this implies that some proposition could, logically, have a truth-value other than its actual truth-value. It implies that there is a true proposition whose denial is not a self-contradiction, or that it has a truth-value which is not certifiable *a priori*, by reasoning alone. A sensible appearance is, furthermore, the kind of thing which could, theoretically, change in various ways, ways in which in fact it does not change. For example, the sensible appearance of a crimson square, even though static, is such that it could go through a change of colour or shape; and this also implies the existence of a proposition which has a possible truth-value

---

[1] 'The Poet and Day-dreaming', *Collected Papers* (Hogarth Press and The Institute of Psychoanalysis, 1925), Vol. IV, p. 175.

C

other than its actual truth-value. But clearly, if all true propositions are analytic, or to put it perhaps more generally,[1] if all true
propositions are *a priori* true, then there is no logical room for what
metaphysicians count as 'the appearances'. The appearances of
there being buildings, shadows, rivers, then, could no more exist
than can the things and occurrences themselves. It needs no
depth of perception to see that, psychologically speaking, the
underlying tenet of rationalism contains within itself the complete
emotional rejection of the phenomenal world.

Leibniz said in his essay *On the Radical Origin of Things*
'. . . that we may explain a little more distinctly how temporal,
contingent or physical truths originate in eternal, or essential or
metaphysical truths, [whose 'contrary implies contradiction or
logical absurdity'[2] we must first know, that, by the very fact
itself that something rather than nothing exists, there is some
demand for existence in possible things or in possibility itself or
essence, or (so to speak) a stretching forth to existence, and, to
sum it up in a word, that essence *per se* tends to existence.'[3] On the
view that all propositions are either true or false by logical necessity,
there is indeed the problem of explaining how 'something rather
than nothing exists', for the opposite proposition that 'nothing
rather than something exists' follows. There can be no 'demand
for existence' in the possible, no 'stretching forth to existence', for
there is nothing that might not be and nothing that might be:
there is no room for 'possible things'. Matters are not helped in
the least by distinguishing between temporal, contingent truths
and eternal, essential truths whild holding that the former 'originate' in the latter, i.e. that we 'have physical necessity from metaphysical'.[4] For the consequences of *a priori* truths are themselves
a priori truths. The reason for this is short and plain: In general,
if q is a consequence of p, such that it is logically impossible for
q to be false when p is true, then the only condition under which
q could be false is that p be false. If this condition is removed
by p's being necessarily true, there will be no condition which
would make possible the falsity of q. This means that q must itself
be a necessary truth. A 'temporal' truth which originates in an

---

[1] In order to take into account Kant's claim that there are synthetic *a priori*
propositions.
[2] *New Essays Concerning Human Understanding*, trans. by A. G. Langley,
p. 694.
[3] *Ibid.*, p. 693.   [4] *Ibid.*, p. 694.

eternal truth is itself an eternal truth; and a supposedly contingent truth which is a consequence of a necessary truth is itself a necessary truth, not contingent. Rationalist philosophers who appear to acknowledge the usual distinction between necessary and contingent statements make only nominal obeisance to it. For the claim that so-called contingent statements have their logical ground is *a priori* statements has the effect of denying that any statement is contingent.

It is a simple matter now to show that minds cannot exist, that there is no more room in the rationalists' universe for psychological phenomena than there is for physical phenomena or for their sensible appearances. There is of course a considerable variety of philosophical theories about the nature of minds and how they are related to animal bodies. Some rationalists, e.g. Plato and Descartes, have argued that minds are immaterial substances which animate some or all animal bodies; others, e.g. Leibniz, have put forward considerations for the view that the only substances are minds, and that animal bodies as well as all other things are composed of them; still others, e.g. Hume, have argued that a mind is just a connected succession of psychological occurrences; and there are further theories which have been put forward and defended by philosophers. In general and independently of any particular philosophical theory about the ultimate nature of mind, it is clear that the existence of a mind involves the occurrence of changing psychological states, whether they are only rudimentary sensations or developed mental processes of various sorts. And even if it is supposed that a mind might be in a state of total sleep during which no psychological changes or processes were taking place, it will nevertheless be granted that a mind is the sort of thing in which it must be possible for changes and processes to take place. The existence of a mind implies the possibility of psychological changes going on, coming to an end, being succeeded by others, and so on, even though none in fact occur. Thus, the existence of a mind implies that there are propositions which, if true, could nevertheless be false, and if false, could nevertheless be true, i.e. propositions which would be made true by the occurrence of certain events and made false by their non-occurrence. Hence, if no statement could, logically, have a truth-value other than the one it has, it would be impossible for there to be psychological events, and so impossible for there to be minds.

Finally, to complete the inventory of what, on the rationalistic tenet, cannot exist, the Absolute Being of metaphysical theology is also logically crowded out. The central notion in all or most metaphysical systems is the notion of a perfect Being, one who is all-good, omniscient, omnipotent, etc. Kant stated that the main problems of metaphysics revolve around God, freedom, and immortality; and it is of particular interest that rationalists who try to prove the freedom and immortality of the soul have failed to see that the basic premise on which they construct their proofs implies the nonexistence of the thing whose properties they endeavoured to demonstrate. But most remarkable of all, the greatest paradox is that the Being which saturates the most impressive of the metaphysical systems can be demonstrated, from their basic premise, not to exist. One cannot in this connection help but think of Achilles' heel which was left vulnerable by the mental lapse of his anxious mother, and also of the explanation of her lapse.

The consideration again is elementary and direct. Amongst the attributes of the supreme Being is omnipotence, the property which makes Him the Creator and Ruler of all that is. This property is sufficient for the present purpose. There is the classical argument against God, attributed to Carneades, which takes the existence of evil to show that God is either not all-good or not all-powerful. But it should be pointed out that anyone who construes the argument in this way, as John Stuart Mill and others seem to have done, is unconsciously shifting from one meaning of the word 'God' to another meaning of the word. For the existence of evil certainly cannot be taken to show that an all-good, all-powerful Being is either not all-good or not all-powerful. It does not show that a Being than which a greater is inconceivable is less great than it could conceivably be. Instead it shows, if it shows anything at all, that if there is a creator of the universe, He is not a perfect Being, than which a greater is inconceivable. There is, in other words, a shift in the meaning of the word 'God' from that of 'omnipotent, omniscient . . . Being' to that of 'maker of the world'. Without this shift of meaning, it could only be viewed as a consideration against the existence of a perfect Being. And the argument against God from the rationalistic premise has to be construed in the same way, as demonstrating His nonexistence, and as doing this without bringing into the consideration appeal to matter of fact. It will readily be seen that the argument from the fundamental proposition of rationalism for the nonexistence of a greatest possible Being holds also for a lesser Being. An Omnipotent Being is, of course, one that is capable of bringing to pass any theoretically possible state of affairs, on a cosmic or lesser scale. The existence of such a Being implies the possibility of things being brought into existence, being changed, and being annihilated. But on the principle that all propositions are necessarily true or necessarily false, whatever exists, exists necessarily, and can neither be changed nor be brought into existence, nor can it be annihilated. Similarly, what does not exist is logically impossible and cannot be brought into existence. The principle prohibits *a priori* the possibility of acts of creation and annihilation, and so logically bars from existence a Being whose existence would imply the possibility of such acts. A number of additional arguments come to mind, arguments furthermore connecting up with other attributes of God, and it is an engaging occupation to formulate them. The general consideration behind them all is that the existence of a Perfect Being implies that some propositions could have a truth-value other than the one they have. It implies, in other words, that some propositions are not *a priori*.

II

According to ancient sources Gorgias attempted to demonstrate three paradoxical propositions: (1) Nothing exists; (2) If there is anything we cannot know it; (3) Even if we knew it we could not communicate our knowledge to anyone else.[1] The first proposition has already been seen to be the outcome of the rationalistic tradition in philosophy. The second two propositions, surprisingly enough, appear instead to be the outcome of the empiricist tradition in philosophy, the tradition most closely allied with the natural sciences. It is a remarkable feature of both of these propositions that they could have been (as they still can be) earnestly urged on his students by an educator. The apparent disregard of the realities of the situation involved in an instructor saying to his class, 'The following argument should convince you, as it has me, that communication by means of language is impossible',

[1] John Burnet, *Greek Philosophy* (London: Macmillan & Co., Ltd., 1928), p. 120.

brings back to mind Hume's description of how he felt on looking back at philosophy. It is of course not beyond the possibilities (although it does seem beyond the reasonable possibilities to nearly all philosophers) that there is no actual disregard of the realities of a situation and that Gorgias' words do not imply that there is a grave obstacle to communication. However that may be, Gorgias' second statement, namely, that it is impossible to know the nature or existence of material things, is implied by philosophical views according to which sense experience is not only relevant to but required for determining their nature and existence. Solipsism is a direct consequence of the second proposition; and Gorgias' third claim that a person cannot know that others understand his words as he understands them, or that language is private to its users, is a direct consequence of solipsism.

Gorgias' argument for his second proposition is conjectural but it may, perhaps, be briefly reconstructed in the following way. In order to determine whether my perception of a physical object is veridical I have to compare my perception of the thing, how it looks to me at the time, with the thing as it actually is. But when I try to do this I find myself in the egocentric predicament of only being able to compare one of my perceptions of the thing with another of my perceptions of it. Try as I may, I never succeed in comparing any of my perceptions of the thing with the thing itself. Therefore I can never know, never be sure beyond the shadow of a doubt, what the properties of the thing are, nor even, for that matter, that there is a thing. Solipsism follows directly, quite apart from the more usual considerations leading to it. Locke expressed the equivalent of Gorgias' second proposition in these words: 'Since the mind, in all its thoughts and reasonings, hath no other immediate object but its own ideas, which it alone does or can contemplate, it is evident that our knowledge is only conversant about them.'[1] As is well known, he abandoned this position for the view, which seems to be more consonant with common sense, that we have knowledge of the external world 'by sensation, perceiving the existence of particular things',[2] while at the same time holding that 'The mind knows not things immediately, but only by the intervention of the ideas it has of them'.[3] According to this view, our knowledge of things is based on

---

[1] *Essays Concerning Human Understanding*, Bk. IV, Ch. I.
[2] *Ibid.*, Bk. IV, Ch. III, sec. 2.   [3] *Ibid.*, Bk. IV, Ch. IV, sec. 3.

inferences from our ideas, or sense data. In Locke's own words, 'The notice we have by our sense of the existence of things without us, though it be not altogether so certain as our intuitive knowledge, or the deductions of our reason employed about the clear abstract ideas of our minds; yet it is an assurance that deserves the name of knowledge.'[1]

A first reading of the two Lockeian positions leaves the impression that they are poles apart, but if we look at them with greater care a puzzling likeness between them begins to emerge. The first view amounts to the claim that we do have knowledge of the truth-values of propositions which are exclusively about our ideas but that we cannot know the truth-values of propositions which go beyond our ideas and refer to material things. The second view is equivalent to the claim, advocated by many important contemporary philosophers, that the truth-values of propositions referring to material things, which the mind is unable to 'contemplate', can be rendered more or less probable by the occurrence of ideas, but cannot in principle be made certain. Now it is quite plain that an empirical inference regarding the existence of an object, whether supported by scant or considerable evidence, is such that it could, logically, be checked, not by collecting more evidence, but independently of the collected evidence. It is open in principle to checking by what does not count as more *evidence*, i.e. by confrontation of the thing itself. For example, when on hearing what I recognize as violin playing by Heifetz coming from a house in my neighbourhood I infer that a record is playing, I can check my inference that it is not Heifetz himself but a record by going into the house and looking. And empirical inferences to the existence of less accessible objects than a record player in someone's house, e.g. Klamm in Kafka's *Castle*, are *by their nature* subject to confirmation independently of the evidence from which they are made. No matter how inaccessible to confrontation an object or state of affairs may be, if its existence can be believed on evidence, its existence can in principle be known apart from the evidence which points to it. Where there is no logical possibility of directly checking the existence of a thing there is no making an inference to its existence, there is only talk which pantomimes genuine inference-talk. The only thing that could preclude the logical possibility of independent checking, by confronting the object

[1] *Essays Concerning Human Understanding*, Bk. IV, Ch. XI, sec. 3.

itself, would be the logical inaccessibility of the object. But what rules out the logical possibility of getting at the object itself at the same time rules out the logical possibility of making an inference to its existence from evidence.

Locke's view is not that physical objects are very difficult to get at; rather his view is that there is no conceiving what it would be like to get at or confront them, which is to say that physical objects are logically inaccessible. His view thus implies that it is logically impossible to check a putative inference that a physical object exists or that it has a certain property independently of the occurrence of the ideas on which it is based. This in turn implies that it is a pseudo-inference, made in what G. E. Moore has called a 'philosophic moment'. It does no more than verbally ape an actual inference from evidence. It can be seen that only in appearance is Locke's view that 'we have an assurance that deserves the name of knowledge' more consonant with common sense than his view that 'Knowledge consists of the perception of the agreement and disagreement between two ideas'.[1] His second position, like the first, offers no 'way of escape from the individual to the world';[2] it offers no exit from subjective and private sense experience to the world of public objects. The solipsism which is the plain outcome of his first position is also the less visible consequence of his second position.

There are at least two forms of solipsism, which, expressed in what might be called 'the language of private soliloquy', are: (1) 'I cannot know that anyone else exists', and (2) 'I alone am real'. A close look at these variants of solipsism will show, as in the case of Locke's two views, that behind the delusive manœuvring with terminology, they come to the same thing. A careful look at empiricist doctrines after Locke, including the doctrines of Kant and various phenomenalists, will also show that the 'subjective madness' of solipsism is a consequence they have in common. Recently an important philosopher has pleaded the cause of phenomenalism in the following words: 'One is inclined to say, therefore, that phenomenalism must be true, on the ground that the only alternative to it, once we have agreed to use the sense-datum terminology, is the iron curtain theory of perception: that physical objects are there sure enough

---

[1] *Essays Concerning Human Understanding*, Bk. IV, Ch. I.
[2] Bertrand Russell's phrase, *A History of Western Philosophy* (London: George Allen & Unwin, 1945).

but we can never get at them, because all we can observe are sense-data: and surely this theory at least can be shown untenable.'[1] If we can, for a moment, free our thinking from the need which makes one wording of a theory more attractive than another wording, it is not difficult to see that between the iron curtain theory of perception and the phenomenalist theory of perception, which lays down as a condition for knowing that a physical object exists the completion of an infinite number of sense observations, there is only a difference of linguistic façade, not of theory. No curtain can be more iron than the curtain of logical impossibility. It is just as unrealistic to think that the consequence of the iron curtain theory of perception, namely, that 'physical objects are there sure enough but we can never get at them', is avoided by phenomenalism as it is to think that it is avoided by Locke's second theory. On phenomenalist theory, too, we can 'never get at' things. Our knowledge is confined to the perception of agreement and disagreement between ideas; and no inference, theoretically capable of independent checking, can be made from sense-data to things.

This brings us to the point where an important if surprising paradox lying in philosophical empiricism becomes discernible. It is most easily elicited from the introductory part of sense-datum theory, but it can be brought out in other parts of the doctrine as well. Apart from the interest attaching to it because of its connection with empiricism, the importance of the paradox resides primarily in the fact that it can in its general features be reproduced over and over again in a great variety of philosophical contexts. There can be no doubt that its investigation would in the end lead to an improved understanding of how technical philosophy works, what its underlying mechanics are. The specific paradox which emerges is that the argument for the statement that we are conversant only with our ideas, or that our senses reveal only sense-data to us, never material things, cancels out a distinction which the statement rests on or implies. Let us consider briefly an example removed from sense-datum theory: take the Hobbesian claim that all desires, of saints and sinners alike, are really selfish, that, despite all appearances to the contrary, none of our desires is unselfish. If this proposition is the factually informative asser-

[1] A. J. Ayer, *Philosophical Essays* (London: Macmillan & Co. Ltd., 1954), p. 143.

tion it appears to be and does actually tell us something about the baseness of our desires, it involves a distinction between selfish and unselfish desires, a distinction which implies the conceivability of there being unselfish desires. But, to put it shortly, the Hobbesian philosopher who argues that a person who satisfies any of his desires thereby satisfies *himself*, that the satisfaction of any of his desires is necessarily a *self*-satisfaction, and consequently that his desire is selfish, implies by his line of reasoning that it is inconceivable for a desire to be unselfish. His argument thus can be seen to cancel the distinction which the proposition it supports requires, if the proposition is to be construed as telling us something important about the nature of our desires. The argument,[1] by implying that the concept *unselfish desire* is self-contradictory, implies that the concept *selfish desire* is identical with the concept *desire*, and that to say that someone has a selfish desire is to say *nothing more* than that he has a desire. If the argument is taken to back the proposition that all desires are selfish, the proposition must be construed as saying nothing more startling or informative about desires than that they all are desires. But this is not what a Hobbesian would be anxious to advance as part of his philosophical creed. What he wishes to assert with his words 'All desires are really selfish' is not an empty tautology. Nevertheless his argument destroys the distinction implied by the natural, non-tautologous interpretation of his utterance.

A sense-datum philosopher who maintains that physical objects, such as match boxes, pens, sheets of paper, are perceived only 'indirectly', by the 'intervention of ideas', wishes to show two things. The first thing he wishes to show is that there are such objects as illusory sense-data, say of touch and sight, sense-data which are not parts of the surfaces of material things. The so-called argument from illusion is given to show that there are sense-data which we 'tend' to take to be parts of the surfaces of material things but about which we should be mistaken if we did take them to be parts of things.[2] Consider a simple instance of the illusory perception of a thing, e.g. a white sheet of paper looking yellow to us in a special light. It is argued that in such a case we

---

[1] The question as to whether it contains a mistake is not to the point in the present consideration.

[2] H. H. Price, *Perception* (New York: Robert M. McBride & Co., 1933), Ch. II.

must be seeing something that is yellow, an object which has the colour the sheet of paper only appears to have. And this object, for obvious reasons, cannot be a part of the surface of the physical sheet of paper. In the case of a non-veridical perception, it is contended, the object our senses 'reveal'[1] to us is not physical nor part of a physical object; it is a sense-datum that is 'directly' perceived, without the intervention of anything else. A physical object, e.g. the white sheet of paper, or a stick partly immersed in water, of which we have a non-veridical perception, is perceived only indirectly, through the intervention of directly perceived sense-data.

The second of the two things the sense-datum philosopher wishes to show is that in the case of a veridical perception, just as in the case of a non-veridical perception, the object our senses reveal to us is also a sense-datum, itself not part of a physical object. Thus, even when we see the white sheet of paper *as* white, i.e. when it looks white to us, what sight reveals to us is not the white sheet of paper itself. Instead it reveals a white object which is not identical with part of the surface of the sheet of paper. To establish this, the phenomenalist philosopher tries to show in various ways that veridical and non-veridical perceptions of material things are 'qualitatively' indistinguishable or that they are the 'same in nature'. G. E. Moore, for example, once wrote, 'Double images have convinced me that the sense-datum of which I am speaking when I say "That's a sofa" is not identical with any part of the surface of the sofa'[2]. The underlying consideration, given its clearest expression in Plato's *Theaetetus*, is that any veridical perception could in principle be duplicated by an exactly similar delusive perception. The inference from this is that the object of a veridical perception is 'generically the same', or 'the same in nature', as the object of a non-veridical perception; and since the object revealed to us in a non-veridical perception of a material thing is a sense-datum which cannot be part of its surface, the sense-datum revealed by our senses in a veridical perception of the thing cannot be part of its surface either. The conclusion is that both in veridical and in non-veridical perception material things are only indirectly perceived: 'all that a person's senses reveal to him is the presence of sense-data',[3] they never reveal to

---

[1] A. J. Ayer, 'Phenomenalism', *Philosophical Essays*, p. 141.
[2] *Commonplace Book* (London: George Allen & Unwin, 1962), p. 78.
[3] A. J. Ayer, *op. cit.*, p. 141.

him the presence of things nor of parts of the surfaces of things. The end result is that no sense-datum is part of the surface of a physical object.

It will undoubtedly have been noticed that, as in the case of the Hobbesian proposition about the selfishness of all desires, the phenomenalistic proposition makes a declaration about *all* sense-data in relation to the surfaces of material things. The proposition is not an inductive generalization: it is not arrived at in consequence of an inspection of instances, although Moore's way of describing what it was that convinced him that sense-data are not parts of the surfaces of physical objects might create the impression that his general conclusion is based on an examination, or on a series of examinations, of the contents of sense experiences. A person who attempts to establish or render probable a general proposition to which an examination of cases is relevant must be able to say what a counter-instance would be like. For his procedure is appropriate to showing or tending to show the non-existence of possible counter-instances: the procedure is carried on under the condition that he could identify such an instance if he encountered one. But philosophers who advance the proposition that no sense-datum is ever part of a physical surface are *prevented* by their line of reasoning from being able to say what it would be like for a sense-datum *to be* part of the surface of a material thing. It is not hard to see that Moore is also put into this position: like Hume, who could not say what it would be like to discover the 'principle' within himself, i.e. the simple and continued self which he introspectively looked for and failed to find,[1] Moore could not say what it would be like for any of his sense-data of the sofa to be identical with a part of its surface. The argument from generic sameness purports to demonstrate something about the *intrinsic* nature of sense-data, namely that they belong to the class of objects which are of such a kind that it is *logically impossible* for them to be parts of material things. A philosopher who argues for the proposition that all that we can observe are sense-data and that our senses never reveal to us the presence of material things, cannot say what it would be like for us to observe

---

[1] It will be remembered that the outcome of his search was that he had no idea of a 'simple and continu'd substance', which is to say that he did not know what it would be like for there to be one. In Hume's philosophical dictionary 'simple and continu'd self' was a senseless expression.

anything but sense-data. Nor can he say what it would be like for a sense-datum to be part of the surface of a physical thing. Parenthetically, this explains what was behind Prof. O. K. Bouwsma's complaint that following Moore's directions for picking out a sense-datum did not enable him to pick one out:[1] there is no more picking out a sense-datum from amongst the objects disclosed to us by our senses than there is picking out a green thing in Emerald City. In Emerald City where everything is green, to ask someone to point to a green thing is simply to ask him to point to a thing.

If there is no saying what it would be like for one's senses to reveal anything other than sense-data, then to say that all that our senses reveal are sense-data comes to saying nothing more about what our senses reveal to us than that all they reveal to us is what they reveal to us. Obviously and undeniably, however, a sense-datum metaphysician does not wish to state a proposition which says no more about what his senses reveal to him than that they reveal to him what they reveal to him. Nor in declaring that no sense-datum is part of the surface of a material object does he wish to state a proposition as factually uninformative about sense-data as the proposition that they are all sense-data. The proposition he unquestionably wishes to hold implies a distinction between sense-data which are or may be parts of the surfaces of physical things and sense-data which are not parts of their surfaces. This distinction is clearly implied by his inviting us to consider a white sheet of paper which looks yellow or a straight stick which looks bent. But the arguments he produces for his conclusion cancel this distinction. They imply that it is logically impossible for a sense-datum to be part of the surface of a material thing, which in turn implies that *being part of the surface of a physical thing* does not set off some actual or possible sense-data from other actual or possible sense-data. A philosopher who arrives at the conclusion that a sense-datum is never part of the surface of a material thing gives us the picture of himself as correcting the popular belief that our senses frequently reveal to us the presence of parts of the surfaces of things, or that some of our data are parts of their surfaces. He certainly does not think that his statement has the same *factual content* as the statement that every sense-

---

[1] 'Moore's Theory of Sense-Data', *The Philosophy of G. E. Moore*, Library of Living Philosophers, ed. by P. A. Schilpp, Vol. IV (Open Court Pub. Co., 1942).

datum is a sense-datum. But his argument prevents his statement from having more than the null factual content of a tautology. Here, as in the case of the Hobbesian view, and as in the case of a vast number of other views in philosophy, the paradoxical fact emerges that the arguments adduced for a proposition imply the invalidity of a distinction which the proposition requires.

This paradox is a sphinx whose riddle must have an answer, and undoubtedly an answer will someday be forthcoming. It might be remarked that one explanation leaps to nearly everyone's mind, and this explanation is always accompanied by the feeling that it is conclusive and original. The explanation is that philosophers have simply made the *mistake* of arguing for one proposition while thinking themselves to be arguing for a different proposition. But those who find this explanation appealing push out of their minds the fact that philosophers have made this sort of 'mistake' so often and in so many different connections, and they continue to make it, even after their mistake has been pointed out to them. In his discussion of Hobbes' ethical theory C. D. Broad has written: 'Butler makes a very true observation about this theory of Hobbes. He says that it is the kind of mistake which no one but a philosopher would make.'[1] The kind of mistake attributed to philosophers in explanation of our paradox would seem to be one which no one but a philosopher would make; but this suggests the idea that it is not a mistake, but something else, something in the very nature of philosophy. For philosophers are not worse reasoners than others.

III

Anyone who reads the writings of the great metaphysicians cannot avoid the notion that philosophy requires a special gift for unravelling concepts and bringing to light unsuspected contradictions in them. He must soon come to think that metaphysics is the native home and even the sanctuary of paradoxes and contradictions. Its contradictions, quite apart from the puzzling variety of interpretations placed on them, have the mystifying property of being in a permanent state of acceptance and rejection, a permanent Est et Non. Unlike mathematical contradictions, metaphysical contradictions are the kind of constructions about which it is

[1] *Five Types of Ethical Theory* (New York: Harcourt Brace & Co., 1930), pp. 64–5.

possible permanently to disagree as to whether they are contradictions. To mention one instance of such a durably controversial contradiction, lines of reasoning have been adduced by philosophers to demonstrate a contradiction in the notion of an uncaused occurrence: from Empedocles, who stated that 'from what does not exist it is impossible that anything come into existence', to F. H. Bradley, who wrote that 'a happening and a change without any cause at all . . . is a self-contradiction and impossible'.[1] Other thinkers have, as might be expected, rejected the claim that the concept of a happening without a cause is self-contradictory. Thus, A. J. Ayer writes: 'But why should it be supposed that every event must have a cause? The contrary is not unthinkable.'[2] This intellectual deadlock, and a great number of others encountered in philosophy, make inescapable the thought that perhaps every philosophical statement is one side of an antimony. Kant developed only a small number of the special contradictions he called 'antinomies', but it takes no great amount of ingenuity to devise further ones.

Historically the theses and antitheses of the Kantian antinomies appeared as rival theories and were espoused by philosophers who were under the impression that one of each pair of theories would eventually be established to the satisfaction of all and the other would be disestablished to the satisfaction of all. Anaxagoras, for example, held that there was no 'least of what is small, but there is always a less', while Democritus adopted the position that there is a least of what is small, that 'division stops at the indivisible substances and does not continue to infinity'. Kant thought he had shown that the two antithetical propositions were so related logically that each could be demonstrated by reasoning which reduced the other to an absurdity. On this he rested his claim that it was an illusion to imagine that eventually one proposition would be established for all time and the other disestablished for all time. It may very well be an illusion to think that any metaphysical theory could be established and rival theories permanently eliminated. For no metaphysical theory, regardless of whether it refers to what transcends sense experience or to such non-transcendent things as space, time, motion, material objects, has yet been either established or confuted to the satisfaction of all metaphysicians. And it *may* be the case, therefore, that all meta-

[1] *Appearance and Reality*, p. 65.   [2] *Philosophical Essays*, p. 272.

physical theories, those referring to non-transcendent phenomena as well as those referring to transcendent phenomena, stand to their rival theories much as a thesis stands to its antithesis in a Kantian antinomy. If this is the case, as the entire history of philosophy gives reason to think, then the philosopher's labours are indeed the labours of a Sisyphus who eternally rolls a rock up a hill only to have it roll down. His labours are heroic but his achievements, reckoned in terms of established theories, must forever be nil.

How an antinomy is to be understood, how it works and what it shows, is an important question which has not received the attention it deserves. Constructing antinomies is certainly easier than understanding them, and in this essay only the easier thing will be done. Kant's second antinomy, the thesis of which is that every composite substance in the world is composed of simple parts and the antithesis that none can be, may be viewed as an antinomy about space, to the effect that space must be composed of simple spaces, space infinitesimals, and also that it cannot be. A closely similar antinomy can easily be devised about time, namely, that time, in the words of one metaphysician, 'must be, and yet cannot be, made of pieces'[1]. By way of an aside, it may be observed that in Kant and Bradley we encounter a curious division of opinion as to what an antinomy shows: one holds that it points to a transcendent world into which the human mind is not privileged to enter; the other holds that it implies the unreality of a sensible phenomenon. Now the antinomy of time consists of the thesis that the existence of time implies the occurrence of a smallest possible interval of time, an indivisible moment, and the antithesis that the existence of time implies that no smallest time interval occurs. The antinomy is that a smallest unit of time must and yet cannot occur. The argument for the thesis is the following. Assume that the existence of time implies that no smallest time interval occurs. Now time consists of time intervals, and any time interval is such that half of it must first elapse before the whole interval elapses, which means that it consists of a geometric series of time intervals of decreasing length. A time interval, e.g. a minute, comes to an end, after which the passage of a new time interval begins; therefore the series of decreasing time intervals making it up will have to come to an end. But it could not come to

[1] F. H. Bradley, *Appearance and Reality*, p. 61.

an end if, under our assumption, there cannot be a smallest time interval, the occurrence of which would bring the series to an end. Since it is absurd to say that a minute has no end, there must, contrary to our assumption, be a smallest possible unit of time, an indivisible moment. Assume now the thesis, namely, that the existence of time, which involves the passage of periods of time, implies that a smallest possible time interval occurs. It is clear that, as before, for the whole of any time interval, such as a minute or an hour or a day, to elapse, half of it has first to elapse; and the half which has yet to elapse is itself a time interval half of which has first to elapse before it elapses, etc. without end. But on our assumption it follows that the series has a smallest member, a last term. This implies that an unending series has an end, or that a series which can have no smallest term yet has a smallest term. Hence the existence of time implies that no smallest time interval occurs.

Before bringing this essay on metaphysical paradoxes to a conclusion, it will be interesting and also instructive to devise an antinomy that comes out of a recent disagreement between important philosophers. The disagreement, which has its roots in Anselm's ontological argument for God's existence, is over the question whether existence is a property of things. The two rival answers, one, that existence is not a property of things, advanced by Bertrand Russell, the other, that it is a property of things, advanced by G. E. Moore, can with equal cogency be argued for as thesis and antithesis of an antinomy. In *Principia Mathematica* Russell wrote: 'When, in ordinary language or in philosophy something is said to "exist", it is always something *described*, i.e. it is not something immediately presented, like a taste or a patch of colour, but something like "matter" or "mind", or Homer (meaning "the author of the Homeric poems"), which is known by description as "the so-and-so" ... It would seem that the word "existence" cannot be significantly applied to subjects immediately given.'[1] It can be seen that how a subject is given to us, whether directly or by means of a description, is not to the point with regard to the question whether existence, like weight, can be a property of things. A consideration which shows that existence cannot be an attribute of a subject that is immediately given also shows that it cannot be an attribute of a subject that is given in some other

[1] Vol. I, pp. 174-5.

D

way, or not given to anyone at all. What Russell wishes to argue for is that existence is not a property either of physical things or of sensations or of sense-data but of 'propositional functions'. Kant held that existence is not a characterizing property of things, while Russell wishes to hold that it is not a property of things at all, neither a characterizing property nor a non-characterizing property. Bringing in talk about how subjects are or may be given has primarily the purpose, apart from gratuitously importing a piece of sense-datum metaphysics, of simplifying the consideration for the view that existence is not a property of things by confining it to statements of the form 'This x is ϕ'.

Consider the statement 'This blade of grass is green' (or the statement 'This visual patch is green'), which makes an attribution to a subject whose presence is required by the demonstrative 'this'. The negation of the statement, 'It is not the case that this blade of grass is green', or 'This blade of grass is not green', implies no contradiction and is itself capable of being true. This is to say that the statement 'This blade of grass is green' can be denied without implying a contradiction. It is contingent. The statement 'This blade of grass exists (or is existent)' is however in a different case. Its denial 'This blade of grass does not exist' implies a contradiction: it implies 'This blade of grass exists' and it also tautologously implies itself, 'This blade of grass does not exist'. The denial thus implies the self-contradictory statement, 'This blade of grass exists and does not exist'. It follows that if existence is a predicate of things, such a statement as 'This blade of grass exists' makes an *a priori* true claim. It follows in general that all things which exist exist by logical necessity, which is absurd. The conclusion to be drawn is that existence is not a property which is attributable to things.

Against this conclusion and in favour of the proposition that existence is a property of things, Moore has presented an equally cogent argument. His reasoning is that it is 'plainly true that, in the case of every sense-datum I have, it is logically possible that the sense-datum in question should not have existed—that there simply should have been no such thing. If, for instance, I am seeing a bright after-image with my eyes shut, it seems to me quite plainly conceivable that I should have had instead, at that moment, a uniform black field, such as I often have with my eyes shut; and if I had had such a field, then that particular bright after-image simply would not have existed.'[1] It is easily seen that this consideration applies equally to what counts in philosophy as being immediately given and to objects referred to by phrases like 'this blade of grass' and 'this sheet of paper'. Now, to continue Moore's argument, a statement such as 'This sheet of paper might not have existed' implies the statement 'This sheet of paper does in fact exist';[2] hence a true statement of the first sort implies a true statement of the second sort. The conclusion to be drawn is that existence is a property attributable, without logical absurdity, to things, and not only to propositional functions.

The antinomy of existence can now be briefly stated in the following manner. To prove the thesis that existence is a property attributable to things, assume the antithesis that it is not. It then follows, by *modus tollens*, that statements such as 'It is logically possible that this sheet of paper should not have existed' and 'It is logically possible that this patch of colour should not have existed' are false and, therefore, that the corresponding statements 'It is logically impossible that this sheet of paper should not have existed', etc. are *true*. But this is absurd in itself, and it directly implies the absurd proposition that whatever exists exists necessarily. Hence the assumption is absurd, and the thesis is demonstrated. The antithesis may be similarly demonstrated from the assumption of the thesis. To put it shortly, the assumed proposition that existence is a property of things implies that whatever has existence has it by logical necessity. This implies that existing sheets of paper, blades of grass, patches of colour, etc., exist by logical necessitation, which is to say that their nonexistence is inconceivable. But this is absurd. The antinomy is of the general form

$$\text{Suppose } p, \text{ then} \qquad\qquad \text{Suppose } \sim p, \text{ then}$$

$$\frac{\begin{array}{c} p \to q \\ \sim q \end{array}}{\therefore \quad \sim p} \qquad\qquad \frac{\begin{array}{c} \sim p \to q \\ \sim q \end{array}}{\therefore \quad p} \ .$$

It is hardly necessary at this point to observe that metaphysics is a strange subject which stands in sharp contrast to other intellectual disciplines in which reasoning plays a central role. Locke

[1] *Philosophical Papers* (George Allen & Unwin Ltd., 1959), p. 126.
[2] *Ibid.*, p. 125.

remarked, 'God has set some things out in broad daylight',[1] and it certainly can with truth and without exaggeration be said that metaphysics is not one of them. Some philosophers have in fact said as much. Hegel wrote: 'When philosophy paints its grey in grey, then has a shape of life grown old. By philosophy's grey in grey it cannot be rejuvenated but only understood. The owl of Minerva spreads its wings only with the falling of the dusk.'[2] And Bradley wrote: '. . . when the sense of mystery and enchantment no longer draws the mind to wander aimlessly, and to love it knows not what: when, in short, twilight has no charm—then metaphysics will be worthless.'[3] It would seem that metaphysical thinking is an activity which flourishes in the dusk. It is to be hoped that the torch of Prometheus will some day capture the owl of Minerva in its light, without blinding it altogether. Lest this happen, some philosophers will wish to leave the bird of wisdom undisturbed in the murk that is natural to it. Gorgias said with regard to stage illusion that 'the deceived is wiser than the not-deceived'; and some philosophers will feel that it is wiser just to go on doing metaphysics than to pause and look at the doing of it. One philosopher has said: 'Certainly philosophy must be either a search after attainable truth or a solemn game played with words to the advantage of those who are paid in our Universities for playing it, but of nobody else.'[4] Having expressed a strange and disconcerting alternative to the accepted notion of what philosophy is, he dropped the matter. The striking thing is not that the alternative was dismissed without any investigation whatever, but that it should have been stated at all. The impression created is that an unwelcome voice for a moment made itself audible, but so muted as to prevent our paying any attention to it. Perhaps, like the child in the fairy tale who cried 'But the emperor has no clothes', the muted voice speaks the truth. This is a possibility; for philosophy is a strange subject and must have a strange explanation. But this is a possibility that is not likely to invite the curiosity of philosophers.

[1] *Essay Concerning the Human Understanding*, Bk. IV, Ch. XII, sec. 1.
[2] *Philosophy of Right*, trans. by T. M. Knox (Oxford University Press, 1945), Preface, pp. 12–13.
[3] *Appearance and Reality*, pp. 3–4.
[4] A. H. Armstrong, *An Introduction to Ancient Philosophy* (Boston: Beacon Press, 1963), p. 1.

WITTGENSTEIN: THE NATURE OF PHILOSOPHY

I shall light a candle of understanding in your heart which shall not be put out. II *Esdras*

Ludwig Wittgenstein was one of the most original philosophers of this century and there can be no doubt that the impact of his perceptions into the nature of philosophical problems will radically and permanently change the course of philosophy in the future. Unfortunately, the influence of his thought has been retarded. Apart from a paper in the *Proceedings of the Aristotelian Society* and his famous *Tractatus Logico-Philosophicus*, he did not permit any of his work to be published during his lifetime, although some of his lectures were privately circulated in mimeographed form among a selected group of his students. According to all accounts, Wittgenstein was a man of compelling personality and tended to gather a circle of favoured students around himself. An aura of mystery, not untinged with religion, was thus created around his work as well as around the special group of students. Understandably, such an atmosphere might well, and in fact did, have consequences somewhat less than desirable from an intellectual point of view. Fortunately time has already begun to disperse the emotional mists and clear up the air; and now that Wittgenstein's work is being made publicly available, now that it belongs to the public domain, so to speak, it should make itself felt widely and objectively in the doing of philosophy. Without stretching a metaphor unfairly, philosophy up to the present may be described as an expanding museum of exhibits, a sort of Madame Tussaud's to which new figures are constantly being added but from which no figures are ever removed. But some things that Wittgenstein said will plant a seed in the minds of philosophers which will in time develop into an improved understanding of the workings of philosophy, enable us to look at it in a new way. And the explanations of theories and arguments flowing from this understanding will not become just further exhibits: they will instead place the exhibits in a light which will enable us to see them for what they are. Professor John Wisdom's observation in a letter to me[1] is worth quoting here: 'What Wittgenstein and others following him said did not by any means make everything as clear as one would wish. There was plenty of room for improvement. And a renewed look at what went before Wittgenstein can be a help in going forward from Wittgenstein. But one may recognize this without trying to do philosophy like one blind to the change Wittgenstein made.' It may be that a philosopher *must* do philosophy like a person who is blind to what Wittgenstein saw.

Philosophy over the years presented itself in a number of different guises to Wittgenstein, some of them the usual ones all of us know, others not. It is, of course, the later ways in which he saw philosophy that are so enlightening and helpful, but to realize how enlightening these are some of the earlier ways need to be looked at. Before considering these, however, it is important to notice a connection between some things G. E. Moore did and insights into philosophy Wittgenstein arrived at later. As is well known, Moore brought philosophical theories (or some of them, at least) down to earth from the Platonic 'heaven above the heavens' where they were protected against our understanding. Placed in the light of the ordinary sun they could be scrutinized under less distorting conditions. Such a general philosophical view as Bradley's, that physical things are not real, or are mere appearance, which casts a spell over the intellect, he would translate into (and perhaps it would not be far off to say, *deflate* into) its concrete implications, for example, that he was not really wearing a waistcoat or that he was mistaken in believing that there was a sheet of paper on which he was writing with a fountain pen. Moore's ostensible purpose in effecting his translations into the concrete was to force on our attention the consequences of an abstract philosophical theory, consequences which we apparently tend to avoid noticing. The point of doing this was, frequently if not always, to refute a theory by subjecting it to 'trial by example'. But what could not fail to emerge, whether grasped consciously, or unconsciously, was that construed as having Moore's translations, the theories were altogether too plainly false for anyone to have failed to see *for himself* that they were false. A further puzzling feature attaching to Moore's translations is that many

[1] February 1966.

philosophers who became acquainted with them did not give up their views. The idea which inevitably suggests itself is that a philosophical view like 'physical things are unreal' is not what it has been taken to be. The question could not but arise whether the view is actually *incompatible with* a factual proposition such as that Moore is wearing a waistcoat and is writing with a fountain pen. Surprising as it might seem, Moore's translations into the concrete, if they showed anything, tended to show that the theories were not open to his translations. The problem then becomes one of understanding rightly how a philosopher is using language who says, 'Physical things are not real', or 'Physical things exist but are mere appearance'. Wittgenstein's later work shows us the way to a correct understanding of such statements.

In one place Moore observed that it would seem that language, ordinary everyday language, was 'expressly designed to mislead philosophers'.[1] With the same complaint apparently in mind Wittgenstein said that 'Philosophy is a battle against the bewitchment of our intelligence by means of language',[2] and 'A philosophical problem has the form "I don't know my way about" '.[3] Moore resorted to one procedure, that of careful analysis of the meanings of words, to free philosophers from their bewitchment. Wittgenstein also used this procedure to help them find their way through the maze of language. According to him 'A main source of our failure to understand is that we do not *command a clear* view of our use of words.—Our grammar is lacking in this sort of perspicuity'.[3] To express the matter with the help of a metaphor of his that has captured the imagination of many philosophers, what will help the fly escape from the fly-bottle is analysis of usage, getting straight about how we ordinarily use words. There is, however, a difference in their procedures which it will be useful to look at. This difference might very well have led Wittgenstein to say that a philosopher of Common Sense ('and that, *n.b.*, is not the common-sense man'[4]) is himself captive in the fly-bottle but favours a special corner in it, that in trying to refute positions

[1] *Philosophical Studies* (London: Routledge & Kegan Paul, 1922), p. 217.

[2] *Philosophical Investigations* (Oxford: Basil Blackwell, 1953), p. 47.

[3] *Ibid.*, p. 49.

[4] L. Wittgenstein, *Preliminary Studies for the 'Philosophical Investigations', Generally known as The Blue and Brown Books* (New York: Harper & Row, 1958), p. 48. Subsequent references to this work will be designated *The Blue Book*.

which go counter to Common Sense he also 'does not know his way about'. For Moore's disagreements with philosophers result in *philosophical* stalemates, stalemates as old as those between Parmenides and his opponents.

It will be recalled that Moore's defence of Common Sense against the attacks of philosophers, attacks sustained throughout the long history of philosophy, has been rejected as begging the question, and Moore has been criticized as being dogmatic about the 'truisms' he lays down. And in bringing them, unsupported by chains of reasoning, against the counterclaims of philosophers who back their own propositions with analytical arguments, he has, in the opinion of many thinkers, begged the very questions that are in debate. Moore's familiar expletives, 'nonsense', 'absurd', 'obviously false', etc. may momentarily silence a philosopher who goes against Common Sense, but it does not affect the way he continues to think about the 'errors' of Common Sense. Long ago Parmenides said, 'Heed not the blind eye, the echoing ear, nor yet the tongue, but bring to this great debate the test of reason'. We might restate this philosophical recipe to the following effect, without antecedent prejudice to the question as to whether our senses are reliable sources of information or not: Disregard the eye, the ear, and the tongue (for we all pretty much hear the same, taste the same, and see the same), but bring only reasoning to a philosophical investigation. Moore's defence does not do this. Thus, e.g., Moore allows that he neither gives nor attempts to give an argument for *the premises* of what he puts forward as proofs for the existence of external things; and a philosopher who does give arguments against the Common Sense claim that we have knowledge of the existence of things like waistcoats and pens might, with the appearance of justification, charge that Moore is dogmatic and begs the question. And, indeed, Moore does need to explain why calling philosophers' attention to truths of Common Sense does not bring them back to it nor make them give up their wayward attacks on it. But perhaps an explanation can be found only by looking at philosophy from a vantage point outside it, that only from an external standpoint will it be possible to see the nature of philosophical stalemates.

It can with justice be said that Wittgenstein has been read with too much haste recently and that some of his ideas have been slid over and others have been put into the service of the private needs of philosophers, with consequent gaps and distortions in our understanding of his later work. In the present connection it is important to read with particular care one of his passages on what happens when we philosophize and how we are to be brought back from philosophy to Common Sense without at the same time being brought back to philosophy. The passage also shows how his procedure differs from Moore's. Moore, on the whole, represents the philosopher who departs from Common Sense as having made an error of fact; Wittgenstein frequently represents him as having made an error of language, and identifies the mistake, with the aim of effecting a cure. The following is the passage:

'When we think about the relation of the objects surrounding us to our personal experiences of them, we are sometimes tempted to say that these personal experiences are the material of which reality consists. How this temptation arises will become clearer later on.

'When we think in this way we seem to lose our firm hold on the objects surrounding us. And instead we are left with a lot of separate personal experiences of different individuals. These personal experiences again seem vague and seem to be in constant flux. Our language seems not to have been made to describe them. We are tempted to think that in order to clear up such matters philosophically our ordinary language is too coarse, that we need a more subtle one.

'We seem to have made a discovery—which I could describe by saying that the ground on which we stood and which appeared to be firm and reliable was found to be boggy and unsafe.— That is, this happens when we philosophize; for as soon as we revert to the standpoint of common sense this *general* uncertainty disappears.

'This queer situation can be cleared up somewhat by looking at an example; in fact a kind of parable illustrating the difficulty we are in, and also showing the way out of this sort of difficulty: We have been told by popular scientists that the floor on which we stand is not solid, as it appears to common sense, as it has been discovered that the wood consists of particles filling space so thinly that it can almost be called empty. This is liable to perplex us, for in a way of course we know that the floor is solid, or that, if it isn't solid, this may be due to the wood being rotten but not to its being composed of electrons. To say, on this latter ground, that the floor is not solid is to misuse language. For even if the particles were as big as grains of sand, and as close together as these are in a sandheap, the floor would not be solid if it were composed of them in the sense in which a sandheap is composed of grains. Our perplexity was based on a misunderstanding; the picture of the thinly filled space had been wrongly *applied*. For this picture of the structure of matter was meant to explain the very phenomenon of solidity.

'As in this example the word "solidity" was used wrongly and it seemed that we had shown that nothing really was solid, just in this way, in stating our puzzles about the *general vagueness* of sense-experience, and about the flux of all phenomena, we are using the words "flux" and "vagueness" wrongly, in a typically metaphysical way, namely, without an antithesis; whereas in their correct and everyday use, vagueness is opposed to clearness, flux to stability. . . .'[1]

Looking at a philosophical utterance in this way is enormously helpful, but it is not enough. And Wittgenstein did go beyond this point of view to deeper insights into the way philosophy works, as is shown, for example, by his characterizing a philosophical problem as one which arises 'when language goes on holiday',[2] or 'when language is like an engine idling, not when it is doing work'.[3] The plain implication of these observations and of many other things he has said is that a philosophical problem is not a mere verbal muddle to be cleared up by analysis of usage, but is rather the expression of a special kind of game that can be played with language. On this construction of what doing philosophy consists in, to solve a philosophical problem is just to understand the game that is being played with terminology.

To go back to his earlier work, in the *Tractatus* Wittgenstein states a number of views about the nature of philosophy or of some of its parts. The following statements give the most important of the views he advanced:

(1) Most of the propositions and questions to be found in philosophical works are not false but nonsensical. Consequently we

[1] *The Blue Book*, pp. 45–6. [2] *Philosophical Investigations*, p. 19.
[3] *Ibid.*, p. 51.

cannot give any answer to questions of this kind, but can only establish that they are nonsensical. . . . And it is not surprising that the deepest problems are in fact *not* problems at all. (4.003)

(2)   Philosophy is not a body of doctrine but an activity.

A philosophical work consists essentially of elucidations.

Philosophy does not result in 'philosophical propositions', but rather in the clarification of propositions. (4.112)

(3)   All philosophy is a 'critique of language'. . . . (4.0031)

(4)   The totality of true propositions is the whole of natural science (or the whole corpus of the natural sciences). (4.11)

Philosophy is not one of the natural sciences.

(The word 'philosophy' must mean something whose place is above or below the natural sciences, not beside them.) (4.111)[1]

The inconsistencies among these different things that Wittgenstein said about philosophy are not inconspicuous, and their going unnoticed must have an explanation. But bringing out inconsistencies is not important in the present connexion. What is important to see is that philosophy could present such different faces to him. About his own statements in the *Tractatus*, presumably those which concern philosophy, he said: 'My propositions serve as elucidations in the following way: anyone who understands me eventually recognizes them as nonsensical, when he has used them—as steps—to climb up beyond them. He must, so to speak, throw away the ladder after he has climbed up it. He must transcend these propositions, and then he will see the world aright.' (6.54)

This pronouncement, which many people have found exciting, is odd, to say the least; and the excitement it arouses must derive from some sort of hidden message it conveys. Perhaps, like the Delphic oracle, it 'neither speaks nor conceals, but gives a sign'. On the surface the pronouncement seems to imply that his own statements are nonsensical *elucidations*, and also, according to his own words, that nonsensical elucidations can lead to one's seeing the world aright. The underlying implication would seem to be that philosophers do not see the world aright, and that they can be led by nonsense to see it aright. It must be granted that

[1] From the translation by D. F. Pears and B. F. McGuinness.

nonsense seems at times to have remarkable curative powers, but it is hard to think that it could be a 'specific' for philosophers. However that may be, the series of views he advanced, either explicitly or by implication, about philosophy are the following. (*a*) Most philosophical utterances are devoid of literal intelligibility, in the way in which 'The good is more identical than the beautiful' is without literal intelligibility. (*b*) No philosophical proposition is true. This follows directly from (4), and parallels something he said at a later time: 'What the philosophers (of whatever opinion) say is all wrong, but what the bedmaker says is all right.'[1] He also seems to have held, (*c*), that some philosophical propositions are true. Thus, he came out for one of Hume's views about causation: 'Belief in the causal nexus is *superstition*.' (5.1361); and he also came out for the view that a proposition about the future is a hypothesis: 'It is an hypothesis that the sun will rise tomorrow: and this means that we do not *know* whether it will rise.' (6.36311). (*d*) He held, furthermore, that in philosophy no propositions are advanced. According to one way philosophy presented itself to him, it was just clarification analysis and had no propositions of its own to put forward: there are no 'philosophical propositions' as there are scientific ones.

The claim, (*a*), that most philosophical utterances are devoid of literal intelligibility is usually linked with the so-called Verifiability Principle, which requires some comment. Moritz Schlick formulated in the following words the principle for determining whether an indicative sentence which does not express an *a priori* proposition has or lacks literal significance: 'Stating the meaning of a sentence amounts to stating the rule according to which the sentence is to be used, and this is the same as stating the way in which it can be verified (or falsified). The meaning of a proposition is the method of its verification.'[2] This version of the principle is usually attributed to Wittgenstein and probably it originated with him. It has commonly been understood, by those who have adopted it as well as by those who have rejected it, to eliminate metaphysical sentences from the class of literally meaningful sentences constructible in a language, and in this

---

[1] From notes taken by A. Ambrose and M. Masterman in the intervals between dictation of *The Blue Book*. These notes will be referred to subsequently as *The Yellow Book*.

[2] *Gesammelte Aufsätze*, 1926–36 (1938), p. 340.

way to rid philosophy of its most spectacular if also its most unsatisfactory branch. This understanding of what the job of the criterion is fits in with a number of statement in the *Tractatus*, but a careful reading of the wording of the criterion brings to light the curious fact that it does not eliminate metaphysics and certainly contains within itself the possibility of the return of the rejected. For the criterion, as it is worded, does not preclude the possibility of there being supersensible verification, which would be the kind of verification appropriate to a statement referring to a non-sensible reality. That is, as phrased (and the phrasing cannot be supposed the result of a merely accidental lapse), the criterion is open to the specification, 'The meaning of a metaphysical proposition is the method of its verification'. The criterion does not rule out of court the claims of a philosopher like Husserl, who wrote: 'Under the title of "A Pure or Transcendental Phenomenology" the work here presented seeks to found a new science—though, indeed, the whole course of philosophical development since *Descartes* has been preparing the way for it—a science covering a new field of experience, exclusively its own, that of "Transcendental Subjectivity".'[1]

In the present connexion, it is particularly interesting to notice that one idea about philosophy expressed in the *Tractatus* (4.113) is that it 'settles controversies about the limits of natural science'. This would seem to imply the view that at least one task of philosophy is to settle territorial disputes between science and religion. The underlying idea, from which perhaps Wittgenstein never completely freed himself, is that the metaphysician is able to survey reality in all of its parts, supersensible as well as sensible, and, like the guide at the maze in Hampton Court, is able to help those who get lost in the cosmic labyrinth. This idea may have considerable connection with the fact that a number of Wittgenstein's later students have returned to metaphysics. It should be mentioned, however, that at least one follower of Wittgenstein has taken a different course, also consonant with the criterion. According to him one task of philosophy, perhaps its only task, is to bring to light modes of verification appropriate to different sorts of propositions. Interestingly enough, logic has a similar function, according to Aristotle. Ross describes Aristotle's con-

---

[1] Edmund Husserl, *Ideas, General Introduction to Pure Phenomenology*, trans. by W. R. Boyce Gibson (New York: The Macmillan Co., 1931), p. 11.

ception of logic as not being 'a substantive science, but a part of general culture which everyone should undergo before he studies any science, and which alone will enable him to know for what sorts of proposition he should demand proof and what sorts of proof he should demand for them'.[1]

To return to the four different and incompatible views of philosophy to be found in the *Tractatus*: (*a*) Most philosophical utterances are senseless, (*b*) Philosophical propositions are not truths, (*c*) Some philosophical propositions are truths, (*d*) There are no philosophical propositions. These lie comfortably enough alongside each other, and there is no evidence that Wittgenstein ever attempted to sort them out and select from among them. Nevertheless, it cannot be supposed that in Wittgenstein's active and original mind they could continue indefinitely to live in amity with each other. And their existence shows unmistakably that one of his main preoccupations, perhaps his central one, was to get clear about the nature of philosophy. In his later thinking Wittgenstein did not completely free his mind from his earlier views about philosophy. A few examples will be enough to show this. In *Philosophical Investigations* he writes: 'The results of philosophy are the uncovering of one or another piece of plain nonsense and of bumps that the understanding has got by running its head up against the limits of language'[2] and also, 'My aim is: to teach you to pass from a piece of disguised nonsense to something that is patent nonsense'.[3] In *The Blue Book* he sometimes seems to represent philosophers as making false empirical claims, although in this connection he disagrees with Moore as to how they are to be corrected. He wrote:

'There is no common sense answer to a philosophical problem. One can defend common sense against the attacks of philosophers only by solving their puzzles, i.e. by curing them of the temptation to attack common sense, not by restating the views of common sense. A philosopher is not a man out of his senses, a man who doesn't see what everybody sees; nor on the other hand is his disagreement with common sense that of the scientist disagreeing with the coarse views of the man in the street.'[4]

At times he represents philosophers as making mistaken claims

---

[1] W. D. Ross, *Aristotle* (London: Methuen & Co., 1930), p. 20.
[2] P. 48.   [3] *Ibid.*, p. 133.   [4] *The Blue Book*, pp. 58-9.

about the uses of terminology, claims which his own investigations are designed to correct. He describes what he does in the following words:

'Our investigation is therefore a grammatical one. Such an investigation sheds light on our problem by clearing misunderstandings away. Misunderstandings concerning the use of words, caused, among other things, by certain analogies between the forms of expression in different regions of language.—Some of them can be removed by substituting one form of expression for another; this may be called an "analysis" of our forms of expression, for the process is sometimes like one of taking a thing apart.[1]

He also wrote:

'When philosophers use a word—"knowledge", "being", "object", "I", "proposition", "name"—and try to grasp the *essence* of the thing, one must always ask oneself: is the word ever actually used in this way in the language-game which is its original home?—
What *we* do is to bring words back from their metaphysical to their everyday usage.'[2]

At times he seems to represent the philosopher as making two different kinds of mistake simultaneously, one a factual mistake, to be removed by looking or introspection, the other a linguistic mistake, to be removed by noting what an expression is normally applied to. Thus in *The Blue Book* he said: 'Examine expressions like "having an idea in one's mind", "analysing an idea before one's mind". In order not to be misled by them see what really happens when, say, in writing a letter you are looking for the words which correctly express the idea which is "before your mind".'[3] We may gather from this that the Platonist, for example, is led by a common form of words into holding a false factual belief about what is before one's mind; he is misled by a linguistic analogy into forming a wrong notion of the actual application of the expression, 'analysing an idea before one's mind' (compare with 'analysing a substance before one's eyes'). This in turn results in a false belief regarding what *is* before one's mind when one conducts an analysis. The impression gained is that

[1] *Philosophical Investigations*, p. 43.   [2] *Ibid.*, p. 48.   [3] P. 41.

both errors are to be corrected by looking at the facts, both the erroneous idea about usage and the erroneous idea about what takes place when we 'have an idea before our mind'. But plainly the 'linguistic mistake' of the Platonist, who appears to think that there are special refined objects designated by the phrase 'idea before one's mind', is not like that of a person who thinks the word 'horse' is normally used to apply to cows or like that of a person who sees a horse but thinks he sees a cow or thinks he sees what in fact does not exist. Wittgenstein could not have failed to realize this, and, indeed, a new insight into philosophy had begun to develop in his mind.

The direction of his thinking became more and more oriented toward the notion that philosophical problems are muddles, verbal tangles which are to be straightened out by recourse to ordinary usage, with the help of a special device he called 'language games'. A philosopher develops a 'mental cramp', and the therapy for removing it is to bring him back to ordinary usage. The following passage from *The Blue Book* will make this clear. In considering the question as to whether I can know or believe that someone else has a pain, he wrote:

'But wasn't this a queer question to ask? *Can't* I believe that someone else has pains? Is it not quite easy to believe this?— . . . needless to say, we don't feel these difficulties in ordinary life. Nor is it true to say that we feel them when we scrutinize our experiences by introspection. . . . But somehow when we look at them in a certain way, our expression is liable to get into a tangle. It seems as though we had either the wrong pieces, or not enough of them, to put together our jig-saw puzzle. But they are there, only all mixed up; . . .'[1]

The thing to do to get straightened out, to cure our verbal malady, is 'to look how the words in question *are actually used in our language*'.[2] When Wittgenstein observed that to call what he did 'philosophy' was perhaps proper but also misleading, and that what he did was one of the 'heirs' of philosophy, he certainly had in mind the technique of examining the actual usage of expressions in the language for the purpose of 'dissolving' philosophical problems. It is worth noticing, in passing, that he conceived his work as beneficially destructive. 'Where does our

---

[1] P. 46.   [2] *Ibid.*, p. 56.

investigation get its importance from, since it seems only to destroy everything interesting, that is, all that is great and important? (As it were all the buildings, leaving behind only bits of stone and rubble.) What we are destroying is nothing but houses of cards and we are clearing up the ground of language on which they stand.'[1]

To return to the question as to whether what he did might appropriately be called philosophy, he had in mind not only the procedure of attempting to settle controversies by examining usage—so as to bring philosophers down to the linguistic realities —but also, possibly, the new notion that was beginning to take form. It must be allowed that he did not give very much expression to the insight into the linguistic structure of philosophical theories which gave rise to this notion, nor did he elaborate and develop it; but he did give *some* expression to it and he did make some application of it. In *The Blue Book* there occurs this important paragraph:

'The man who says "only my pain is real", doesn't mean to say that he has found out by the common criteria—the criteria, i.e., which give our words their common meanings—that the others who said they had pains were cheating. But what he rebels against is the use of *this* expression in connection with *these* criteria. That is, he objects to using this word in the particular way in which it is commonly used. On the other hand, he is not aware that he is objecting to a convention. He sees a way of dividing the country different from the one used on the ordinary map. He feels tempted, say, to use the name "Devonshire" not for the county with its conventional boundary, but for a region differently bounded. He could express this by saying: "Isn't it absurd to make *this* a county, to draw the boundaries *here*?" But what he says is: "The *real* Devonshire is this". We could answer: "What you want is only a new notation, and by a new notation no facts of geography are changed." It is true, however, that we may be irresistibly attracted or repelled by a notation. (We easily forget how much a notation, a form of expression, may mean to us, and that changing it isn't always as easy as it often is in mathematics or in the sciences. A change of clothes or of names may mean very little and it may mean a great deal.)'[2]

---

[1] *Philosophical Investigations*, p. 48.   [2] P. 57.

The idea that quite unmistakably comes through from this passage is that a philosophical theory is a misleadingly phrased introduction of an altered piece of terminology. The form of sentence in which a philosopher presents his remodelling of conventional language is the form of sentence ordinarily used to state a matter of fact; and in presenting his renovated terminology in this way he makes himself dupe to what he does, as well as anyone who either sides with him or opposes him. The philosopher imagines himself to be expressing a matter of fact or a theory, i.e. to be delivering himself on what really is the case or on what exists or on what cannot exist; and his mistake lies in the construction he places on what he is doing, not in his understanding of the actual use of terminology. He is mistaken about what he does with conventions of usage and is not mistaken about what the accepted conventions are: 'The fallacy we want to avoid is this: when we reject some form of symbolism, we're inclined to look at it as though we'd rejected a proposition as false. It is wrong to compare the rejection of a unit of measure as though it were the rejection of the proposition, "The chair is 3′ instead of 2′ high". This confusion pervades all philosophy. It's the same confusion that considers a philosophical problem as though such a problem concerned a fact of the world instead of a matter of expression.'[1]

This view as to the nature of philosophical statements and of what might be called the 'fallacy of philosophy' quite plainly has great explanatory power. The position that philosophical utterances are about states of affairs, about reality, does not, for one thing, square with the analytical arguments with which philosophers support their theories; neither does it explain, for another thing, how a philosopher can hold his views while not being, to use Wittgenstein's words, 'a man out of his senses, a man who doesn't see what everybody sees'. The position that philosophical utterances use language improperly or are misdescriptions of actual usage does not explain why a philosopher is not corrected by bringing terminology back to its 'original home'. It does not explain why a philosopher who is made to feel embarrassed by being shown the correct use of language nevertheless does not give up his claim, or if he does give it up is able to return to it later. The view which makes philosophical utterances out to be pronouncements embodying covertly revised criteria for the use

[1] *The Yellow Book.*

of expressions explains both these things, and it also explains other eccentricities attaching to philosophical theories. To use Wittgenstein's imaginative metaphor, it explains why the fly cannot be shown the way out of the fly-bottle. The fly cannot be led out because it does not want to be led out. The fly-bottle is only superficially its prison. At a deeper level, the fly-bottle is its home which it has built for itself out of language.

A somewhat extended passage from *The Yellow Book* would seem plainly enough to indicate that this was the direction his thinking took about the nature of philosophical theorizing, i.e. about what goes on when we think in a 'philosophic moment', to use Moore's expression. It should be remarked immediately that the passage does not indicate this direction unambiguously and in so many plain words, without indications of other directions. But Wittgenstein's mind does not seem to have worked in straight lines. The following is the passage, and it is well worth a careful reading:

'Suppose now I call my body by the name of Wittgenstein. I can now say, "Wittgenstein has toothache", just as I can say, "Shaw has toothache". On the other hand I should have to say, "I feel the pain", and I might feel it at a time when Wittgenstein had not toothache; or when Shaw had. It is only a matter of fact that Wittgenstein has the toothache when I feel the pain.

'If I use "I" and "Wittgenstein" thus, "I" is no longer opposed to anything. So we could use a different kind of notation. We could talk of pain in the one case and of behaviour in the other. But does this mean the same as saying that I have real toothache and the other person has not? No, for the word "I" has now vanished from the language. We can only now say "There is toothache", give its locality and describe its nature.

'In doing this we are keeping the ordinary language and beside it I am putting another. Everything said in the one can, of course, be said in the other. But the two draw different boundaries; arrange the facts differently. What is queer about an ordinary notation is that it draws a boundary round a rather heterogeneous set of experiences. This fact tempts people to make another notation, in which there is no such thing as the proprietor of a toothache. But without the people realizing it, or even realizing that there are two, the two notations clash.

'Put it another way. To the person who says, "Only I can have real toothache", the reply should be, "If only you can have real toothache there is no sense in saying, 'Only I can have real toothache'. Either you don't need 'I' or you don't need 'real'. Your notation makes too many specifications. You had much better say, 'There is toothache', and then give the locality and the description. This is what you are trying to say and it is much clearer without too many specifications. 'Only I have real toothache' either has a common sense meaning, or, if it is a grammatical (philosophical) proposition, it is meant to be a statement of a rule; it wishes to say, 'I should like to put, instead of the notation, "I have real toothache", "there is real toothache", or "I have toothache".'" Thus the rule does not allow "only I have real toothache" to be said. But the philosopher is apt to say the thing which his own rule has just forbidden him to say, by using the same words as those in which he has just stated the rule.

' "I can't know whether another person has toothache" seems to indicate a barrier between me and the other person. I want to point out to you that this is a pseudo-problem. It is our language which makes it seem as though there were a barrier.

'I talked before of the differences which our language stresses, and the differences it hushes up. Here is a wonderful example of a difference hushed up. It is not entirely hushed up for, of course, all the notations must have the same multiplicity. Nothing can be said in the one which can't also be said in the others. But a notation can stress, or it can minimize; and in this case it minimizes.'

Even a cursory reading of these words exposes a number of different tendencies in Wittgenstein's thinking about philosophy. Thus, he describes the question as to whether it is possible to know that another person has a pain as a 'pseudo-question'. There is also the hint that a philosophical problem is some sort of mix-up, the linguistic symptom of a mental cramp. There is further the notion that philosophical theories, or anyway some philosophical theories, introduce alternative forms of expression which translate into expressions in ordinary use, i.e. 'keeping the ordinary language and beside it . . . putting another, the difference between the two being that they 'arrange the facts differently'. It may be remarked, to bring into connexion what

Wittgenstein says here with other things he says about philosophy, that it is hard to see how an alternative notation could in any way be an attack on common sense, to be cured by bringing philosophers back to ordinary language. And it is equally hard to see how a notation which uses 'the words "flux" and "vagueness" wrongly, in a typically metaphysical way, namely, without an antithesis' could translate into ordinary language where 'in their correct and everyday use vagueness is opposed to clearness, flux to stability. . . .' Indeed, it is not hard to see that a notation which translates into the language of common sense cannot be *an attack* on common sense; and it is not hard to see that a notation in which ordinary words occur without their antitheses *cannot translate into*, have 'the same multiplicity' as, a language in which they occur with their antitheses. All this only goes to show that on different occasions and in somewhat different connections Wittgenstein tried out different ideas to explain the enigma that is philosophy.

If we do not let ourselves be diverted by the different ideas in the above passage as to what a philosopher does and how he gets himself into difficulties, we are led to the notion, not that the philosopher fails to 'command a clear view of our use of words', but that the perception he has into the uses of words makes him wish to modify or in some way alter those uses. It is evident that the alterations he institutes do not have any of the jobs alternative forms of expression usually have, e.g. to say the same thing with greater economy or with improved efficiency for calculating or with greater vividness or just to avoid monotony of expression. The picture of the philosopher which begins to come into focus is that of someone who scans the intricate map of language, and, unlike the grammarian and the thesaurus compiler, is not satisfied merely to report rules imbedded in the language, but in various ways changes the rules. Differences in the uses of expressions which ordinary language does not perspicuously display, differences which it 'hushes up', he is sometimes impelled to try to bring out in sharp relief; and differences in the uses of expressions ordinary language 'stresses' he is sometimes inclined to mute. The reasons, in the form of arguments, that he gives for the changes he introduces quite obviously make negligible or no connexion with the everyday kinds of work language does for us. The conclusion which is at least latent in a good many things he said is that a philosopher alters ordinary language or 'puts another language beside it' for the remarkable effects doing this creates. In the passage above, ordinary language is represented as responsible for the idea that a barrier exists between people which prevents one person from knowing that another has a pain. But it should be realized at once that the sentence 'I cannot know whether another person has a toothache', i.e. the sentence which creates the idea of a barrier, is *not* an ordinary sentence. Wittgenstein was, of course, aware that ordinary language does not put this idea in the mind of 'the man in the street': in his words, 'we don't feel these difficulties in ordinary life'. The sentence is a philosophical production whose job is not at all like that of a sentence such as 'I cannot know whether Socrates has a toothache; he endures pain with stoicism'. To describe what is happening in Wittgenstein's way, a philosopher who says, 'I cannot know whether another has a pain' is objecting to the conventional use of 'has a pain' but is not aware that he is objecting to a convention. His sentence announces the academic deletion from language of such phrases as 'knows that another person has a pain', 'knows that another person sees red', and in this way he brings out the great difference between the use of 'has a pain' and the use of 'has a tooth'. But he introduces his re-editing of language conventions in a way which creates the idea that there is some sort of barrier between people. It is not everyday language, but the manner in which he announces changes in everyday language which is responsible for the inappropriate idea.

When Wittgenstein said, 'What we are destroying is nothing but houses of cards and we are clearing up the ground of language on which they stand', quite possibly what he intended to convey was that like the pretence use of cards as building materials a philosophical theory is constituted by a pretence use of language. Quite possibly he wanted to convey that to give utterance to a philosophical theory is not to use language to express a theory but is only to use language to create the false idea that a theory is being expressed. And when he observed that 'we may be irresistibly attracted by a notation', he may have been referring to deeper things in our minds that philosophical utterances link up with. It is not easy to know where one is reading too much and where too little into the mind of an original thinker.

3

ON UNIVERSALS

REVIEW OF A SYMPOSIUM

This brochure[1] consists of three papers which were read at the Aquinas Symposium sponsored by the Department of Philosophy of the University of Notre Dame on March 9 and 10, 1956. The first paper is 'Propositions and Sentences' by Professor Church: the second, by Professor Goodman, is 'A World of Individuals'; and the third, by Professor Bochenski, bears the title 'The Problem of Universals'. In an explanatory introduction these papers are described as 'literally' making up a symposium and as being 'papers that converge on the Problem of Universals from three different philosophic positions'. Apparently they are a selection from the papers given at the two-day meeting and were not prepared with the intention of making contributions to a connected discussion of a specified problem relating to universals, one which normally would attempt to canvass differences of opinion between the participants. The convergence which the writer of the explanatory introduction finds in the three essays is invisible to me. It is possible, for example, both to be a nominalist in Goodman's sense of 'nominalism' and to reject nominalism in Church's sense, and it is possible consistently to reject nominalism in Goodman's sense while being a nominalist in Church's sense. This can hardly be taken to indicate convergence on *the* problem of universals.[2]

Church in his essay gives a brief account of the historical background, from the Stoics to the present, of two current senses

---

[1] *The Problem of Universals*. A Symposium, by I. M. Bochenski, Alonzo Church, Nelson Goodman.

[2] It is instructive to compare the lack of convergence in this symposium with philosophical disagreements centering on the concept of time. See p. 141. In important respects, disputation that goes on in philosophy is like disagreements which are based on verbal misunderstandings. William James was apparently beguiled by this resemblance into thinking that the answer to the question about whether the man went around the squirrel depends on what a person who offers an answer means by 'go around'. For a useful discussion of the William James puzzle, see John Wisdom's *Philosophy and Psychoanalysis*, Basil Blackwell, pp. 95–7.

of the term 'proposition' in philosophy: (1) the traditional sense of declarative sentence together with its meaning, and (2) the abstract sense of 'content of meaning' of a declarative sentence (p. 5). The first sense implies that there are as many propositions as there are translations of a given declarative sentence into other languages, whereas the second sense implies that there is only one proposition which is expressed by the sentence and its various translations. Church thinks than many logicians find the traditional sense awkward or unsatisfactory and that there is a definite need for the abstract notion, at least for some purposes. It is not easy to see why logicians should find the first sense awkward; for if they do not wish to use the word 'proposition' in that sense and wish to use it in the abstract sense they are at liberty to do so, as that sense exists and is available. A reasonable construction to be placed on Church's plea for the abstract sense is that he wishes it to be made the *exclusive* sense of the word 'proposition'. The puzzling thing is why he did not proceed directly and without ado to his point, and also why he did not abandon the word to its two present senses and introduce a new term which would have only the abstract sense. What is the aura[1] about the word 'proposition' which should make it a battleground for exclusive possession? Church goes on to give Leibniz's considerations in *Dialogus de connexione inter res et verba* for the view that whatever is the 'subject of truth' is *something* which is neither a thought nor a thing nor yet an actual sentence, but is a *possible* thought or a *possible* proposition, or perhaps even a possible sentence (p. 9). The expressions 'possible thought' and 'possible proposition' are construed to mean proposition in the abstract sense; and Church contends that interpreting Leibniz's 'possible thought' to mean possible sentence does not play into the nominalist position, as possible sentences are 'not particulars but universals' (p. 8). This supplements his contention, developed elsewhere, that there is something other than a sentence which is the subject of an assertion and of a belief.

Professor Goodman attempts, in 'A World of Individuals', to make clear his position, which he identifies as nominalistic, and to defend it against a number of criticisms. His version of nominalism is that it consists in the refusal to countenance classes: '. . . the nominalist rejects classes as incomprehensible, but may take

---

[1] See p. 91 *et seq.*

anything whatever as an individual', where this rejection 'does not involve excluding abstract entities' (p. 17). It is clear, then, that Goodman's nominalism is compatible with Church's Platonism. For it is possible consistently to hold that there are 'contents of meaning' which are the subjects of truth and belief, actual or possible, and at the same time to reject classes as incomprehensible; and it is possible to reject Goodman's nominalism and accept classes as perfectly comprehensible while disavowing abstract entities, in particular, propositions in the sense of G. E. Moore and Church. However unlikely it may be that Church would accept Goodman's view about the incomprehensibility of classes, the specific views they advance in their papers are not incompatible despite terminological appearances. But what is the reason for rejecting classes as incomprehensible? It is that classes go against Goodman's maxim that two different entities cannot be 'made up' of the same entities (p. 18). Given k initial elements or individuals, Goodman allows that there exist $2^k - 1$ 'wholes' or 'individual sums' of the elements, where a condition for anything being a whole is that it consist of one or more elements and only of elements (p. 19). The use of 'whole' is thus very different from the use of 'class': there cannot be a null whole nor a whole of wholes, as there can be a null class and a class of classes, a class of classes of classes, 'and so on ad infinitum, climbing up through an explosively expanding universe towards a prodigiously teeming Platonic heaven' (p. 19). Goodman thinks that his position is 'virtually unassailable' (p. 31), and it must be admitted that it is indeed unassailable. For his arguments against classes do no more than bring to our attention features of the logical use of the word 'class' which have for some reason become distasteful to him; and he cannot of course be prevented from rejecting this use of the word. But the position that classes exist and are perfectly comprehensible is equally unassailable; logicians who accept classes are not unaware of their features which Goodman highlights. Instead of inducing semantic agoraphobia in them, the fact that classes generate an 'explosively expanding universe' is accepted as a desirable feature.

Bochenski in his paper, from which the symposium under review takes its name, states 'provisionally' what he considers to be *the* problem of universals, namely, 'Are there universals?' He declares at the outset that he takes the position that 'every extra-mental thing in the universe is singular, not universal' (p. 35). And on the next page he writes, 'When we know things, we form in our minds certain images, concepts, etc. It must be stressed that those subjective entities are *real*, consequently individual, being parts of an individual mind.' It would seem that with these two declarations (and, indeed, with the second alone: '*real*, consequently individual') Professor Bochenski gives us his answer to the question, 'Are there universals?' His answer, by obvious and direct implication, is that there are no universals. Nevertheless, he states that he will not attempt to arrive at the solution of the problem. According to his own account he confines himself to restating some of its aspects 'in the frame of recent logical semiotical techniques, and in face of some new ontological doctrines' (p. 35), a restatement which requires the investigation of five 'levels or realms of reality' (p. 36).

I must confess to being puzzled by a number of things in the three papers. To touch on only one of them: if one question as to whether there are universals is the question as to whether declarative sentences have meanings, 'contents of meaning', it is not easy to see how there could be any disagreement over it. Nor is it easy to see why one philosopher should think it necessary to produce *arguments* for the existence of universals or 'contents of meaning', and why another should think that special 'logical semiotical techniques' are needed to help determine this.

4

UNDERSTANDING PHILOSOPHY

'Philosophy is certainly an activity which needs constantly to be defended. Indeed, it is hardly conceivable at all except as a constant struggle against sophistry.' Peter Winch, *Mind*, Vol. LXXIII, p. 608.

'Metaphysics has a long and distinguished history, and it is consequently unlikely that there are any new truths to be discovered in descriptive metaphysics. But this does not mean that the task of descriptive metaphysics has been, or can be, done once and for all. It has constantly to be done over again. If there are no new truths to be discovered, there are old truths to be rediscovered.' Peter Strawson, *Individuals*, Introduction.

'Time and again I have emerged from a course of reading in philosophy with the conviction that the authors were really avoiding specific problems by converting them into tenuous sophistries that have very little real meaning.' Ernest Jones, *Free Associations*, p. 60.

'What is your aim in philosophy?—To show the fly the way out of the fly-bottle.' Ludwig Wittgenstein, *Philosophical Investigations*, p. 103.

Professor Ducasse once said that the ills of philosophy are chiefly due to the lack on the part of philosophers of 'a clear realization of the nature of the problem to be solved, on the one hand, and, on the other, knowledge of the sort of method appropriate to the solution of the problems of the nature given'.[1] He also pointed out that philosophical divergences of opinion are not occasioned by 'inadequate observation or description'.[2] And Wittgenstein, in a similar vein, has remarked: 'Philosophical problems are, of course, not empirical problems; they are solved, rather, by looking into the workings of our language.'[3] These are useful things to say about a field of intellectual endeavour which is highly prized and at the same time is characterized by continuous anarchy that resists scientific discipline. For they tend to sharpen our awareness

---

[1] *Philosophy as a Science: Its Matter and Its Method* (New York: Oskar Piest, 1941), p. xviii.
[2] *Ibid.*, p. 142.　　　　[3] *Philosophical Investigations*, p. 47.

of the condition of total drouth in philosophy; and they heighten the need to seek for an explanation of this condition. It will be the aim of this essay to improve our understanding of philosophy by looking at it through the eyes of an important thinker, Freud, who was interested in philosophy but turned away from it in disappointment.

Aristotle said in his *Metaphysics* that 'All men by nature desire to know'. As a generalization his statement appears to be an exaggeration of the actual state of affairs; but it cannot be doubted that those who enter into the sciences are motivated by a desire to know. It would seem that those who take up technical philosophy, or to use Freud's term 'philosophy proper', are also moved by a wish to know, for philosophy looks like science, and has, indeed, been conceived of as the most fundamental of all sciences. As is natural enough, Freud viewed it as a field of human endeavour from which important and useful things may be learned. In a letter he wrote in 1907 to a Viennese publisher he included Theodor Gomperz's *Griechische Denker* in his list of ten books, to which, as he said, 'a man owes some of his knowledge of life and his *Weltanschauung*; books which one has enjoyed and gladly recommends to others, but do not evoke awe or dwarf one by their great stature'.[1]

Freud's words seem to be a plain enough indication that he held philosophy in high esteem, that he looked on it as a subject whose cultivation would certainly be far from a waste of time. A number of years later, however, he underwent a change of mind about the worth of philosophy. In his *Autobiographical Study*, when touching on his later speculative works, he wrote: 'I should not like to create the impression that during this period of my work I have turned my back on patient observation and have abandoned myself entirely to speculation. I have on the contrary always remained in the closest touch with the analytic material and have never ceased working at detailed points of clinical or technical importance. Even when I have moved away from observation, I have carefully avoided any contact with philosophy proper. The avoidance has been greatly facilitated by constitutional incapacity.[2]

[1] Quoted in Ernest Jones' *The Life and Work of Sigmund Freud*, Vol. 3 (London: Hogarth Press, 1957), p. 422.

[2] *An Autobiographical Study* (the Hogarth Press and the Institute of Psycho-Analysis, 1946), p. 109, authorized translation by James Strachey.

The reason why Freud was concerned to avoid contact with philosophy while engaged in theoretical psychoanalytic work would appear to be that philosophy, as he conceived it, was a wholly speculative field and that contact with it might stimulate a tendency within him to abandon himself 'entirely to speculation'. His former warm recommendation of a well-known history of Greek philosophy as a 'good friend' suggests that he felt an attraction of some strength to philosophy, and his later remark indicates that the needs of his professional work required resisting this attraction, even when (perhaps we should say, especially when) he 'moved away from observation'. I do not think, however, that we need take as more than a *façon de parler* his self-declared constitutional incapacity for philosophy. For it he had had such an incapacity, he could hardly have feared infection by philosophy or seriously felt a need to avoid it. More important than this, the weight of his continuous practice makes unrealistic the notion that Freud had anything to fear from highly speculative fields. No one who has read his theoretical writings, including his analytical studies of historical figures, could fail to be impressed by how much his conclusions were governed by observations made in his clinical practice. In view of this fact it might even be natural to think that his former recommendation was just an expression of good will towards a field which to him consisted of theories having only the value of an intellectual diversion.

It can fairly be said that philosophy played only a negligible role in Freud's thinking, but not too negligible for him to record his discontent with it. And perhaps his change of mind came about not simply because philosophy seemed to consist of theories which are never brought down to earth by observation or experiment, but because he suspected that they are the kind of theories which cannot, *in principle*, be linked with scientific procedures. The overtones of his comments about the philosophical rejection of the possibility of unconscious mental processes point to such a suspicion. In his *Autobiographical Study* he wrote that 'the study of pathogenic repressions and of other phenomena which have still to be mentioned compelled psycho-analysis to take the concept of the "unconscious" seriously. Psycho-analysis regarded everything mental as being in the first instance unconscious; the further quality of "consciousness" might also be present, or again, it might be absent. This of course provoked a denial from the philosophers, for whom "conscious" and "mental" were identical, and who protested that they could not conceive of such a monstrosity as the "unconscious mental". There was no help for it, however, and this idiosyncrasy of the philosophers could only be disregarded with a shrug.'[1] He goes on to remark that 'Experience (gained from pathological material, of which the philosophers were ignorant) . . .' compelled the acknowledgement of the existence of the unconscious. Being made acquainted with pathological material has not won from many philosophers the admission of the possibility of unconscious thoughts, which suggests that evidence does not now, as it did not then, count against the *philosophical* identification of the mental with the conscious.

To put the matter shortly here, a philosopher wo says, 'All thoughts are really conscious thoughts', or with Locke says, 'Consciousness always accompanies thinking', can in all sincerity maintain his position in complete disregard of any sort of observational evidence. And the reason why he can do this is that his view is *philosophical*, which is to say that it is the kind of view that is not linked to evidence. About a certain Aristotelian view, which has never been without its advocates, one commentator has said, 'The modern reader cries out for evidence, not argument'.[2] Unlike the modern reader (who is not without his own idiosyncrasies), the philosopher has what might be called a *defining* idiosyncrasy. This is that he can, and does, hold views in disregard of all evidence, and that he can, and does, rely on argument instead of on observation. The philosopher is able to do this because his view is not the kind of view in whose acceptance or rejection observation plays a role. The philosophical words 'No mental process is unaccompanied by consciousness' do not express a proposition which goes against Freud's empirical claim about the existence of unconscious mental processes, however much they may seem to do so. Some sort of awareness of the *verbal* nature of the philosophers' 'identification' of *mental* and *conscious*, and the difference between what Freud was concerned with and what philosophers were concerned with, might have been responsible for his dismissing with a shrug the philosophical contention.

Sensing that a philosophical statement is the sort of statement

[1] *An Autobiographical Study* (the Hogarth Press and the Institute of Psycho-Analysis, 1946), pp. 55–6.

[2] Benjamin Farrington, *Greek Science* (Pelican Books, 1944), p. 110.

which is supported by an argument rather than by observation is a step toward glimpsing the inner workings of philosophy. It brings us nearer to a clear perception of the verbal character of philosophical utterances, which makes disagreements between philosophers, as well as between philosophers and others, 'degenerate into unfruitful disputes about words.'[1] It is conjectural but not out of the question that Freud had a disconcerting perception of the way philosophy actually works, and that it was this which, underneath, prompted his disavowal. A letter he wrote about a book by the Russian philosopher, Chestov, lends plausibility to this idea. In it he said, 'Probably you cannot imagine how alien these philosophical convolutions seem to me. The only feeling of satisfaction they give me is that I take no part in this pitiable waste of intellectual powers. Philosophers no doubt believe that in such studies they are contributing to the development of human thought, but every time there is a psychological or even a psycho-pathological problem behind them.'[2]

Somewhere Freud says, 'No, science is not illusion. But it would be an illusion to suppose that we could get anywhere else what it cannot give us'. It goes without saying that philosophers have had, as indeed they continue to have, the idea that their subject is a kind of science and that it seeks to discover the truth about various matters, about space, causation, mind, beauty, goodness, etc. And they of course think that they can get from philosophy the kind of thing we expect from science. Like many others, Freud could not avoid the idea that philosophy endeavours to discover facts about reality but does not go about its task in a scientifically responsible way. A widespread impression of philosophy is that it is a theoretical science. But there are features of philosophical theories, demonstrations, and disagreements that are out of joint with the idea that philosophy is a discipline in which truth is sought—features which, like Poe's purloined letter, are in plain view but arouse little or no curiosity. These features make it at least probable that any similarity between science and philosophy is delusive and that it is an error to think that we can get from philosophy the *kind* of thing we get from science, knowledge or reasonable hypotheses about the existence, nature, and causes of things. Freud may well have had a perception of

---

[1] *An Autobiographical Study*, p. 57.
[2] Quoted by Ernest Jones, *op. cit.*, p. 140.

the great difference between the two, may have seen through their superficial similarity; and what he referred to as his 'constitutional incapacity' for philosophy might have been the feeling of antipathy, to which he gave expression in his letter, against 'philosophical convolutions', the verbal twistings and turnings ('moves' is the current term) which are the stuff from which philosophy is made. Like many intellectuals, he turned away from philosophy, instead of bringing it under his scrutiny.

Freud has described the blows which astronomy, biology, and psychoanalysis have struck at the self-esteem of educated mankind, and if the hypothesis to be presented in these pages about the nature of philosophy is, in essentials, correct, the narcissism of a special group of intellectuals will receive still another blow. For this hypothesis transforms a familiar and valued friend into a stranger who, moreover, is 'repulsive', to use an adjective applied by one philosopher[1] to the hypothesis. If correct, it places a class of thinkers with a long and respected tradition into the unwelcome position of being the dupes of an intellectual activity in which they constantly engage but whose true nature has remained effectively veiled from their understanding. It should be said at once that it is desirable to link an assumption which has destructive import with something positive and constructive, something which will replace what is destroyed. But when this turns out not to be possible, the improvement of our understanding of a human creation has, nevertheless, a value of its own which it does not lose when achieved at the cost of a sacrifice. Perhaps this is part of the underlying meaning of the tale that Odin was permitted to look into the well of wisdom only by paying for it with one of his eyes.

The hypothesis to be developed here is that the philosopher does not use language for the expression of conscious thoughts; unwittingly he uses language only to give expression to unconscious thoughts. The philosopher does special kinds of things to language, without being aware of what he is doing, and at the same time he uses the language to express forbidden thoughts which are hidden from him. In a metaphor, language is the philosopher's plasticene which he moulds in various ways and into which he impresses his deepest phantasies. Freud has remarked that there is an underlying psychological identity between poetry, religion,

[1] *Psychoanalysis, Scientific Method and Philosophy*, A Symposium, edited by Sidney Hook (New York University, 1959), p. 178.

and philosophy. He wrote: 'The delusions of paranoics have an unpalatable external similarity and an internal kinship to the systems of our philosophers. It is impossible to escape the conclusion that these patients are, in an *asocial* fashion, making the very attempts at solving their conflicts and appeasing their primary needs which, when these attempts are carried out in a fashion that is acceptable to the majority, are known as poetry, religion and philosophy.'[1] Nowadays it will come as a surprise only to very few to be informed that the underlying purpose of poetry, religion, and philosophy, the psychological role they play for us, is the same. Here, however, it is necessary to remark on a difference between poetry and religion on the one hand and philosophy on the other hand. By and large, and without going into exceptions, it may be said that lines of poetry and religious utterances have a descriptive use, i.e. a use to describe occurrences, states of affairs, things, etc. For the most part, poets and prophets employ language for the expression of conscious thoughts, independently of the unconscious thoughs that may be associated with them. Philosophical utterances, however akin they may be to poetic and religious statements in psychological respects, are a different sort of linguistic breed. Philosophical statements do not have the descriptive use they appear to have. They are not about occurrences, states of affairs, or things. For example, Zeno's implied claim that time is self-contradictory and does not exist and Hobbes' *philosophical* proposition that all desires are really selfish are not about the existence of time and the nature of desire. But they are not, as some philosophers might be inclined to hold, senseless. A philosophical statement, apart from the unconscious thoughts of which it is the bearer, does not have the kind of job to perform that it is natural to attribute to it, and which if not performed renders it literally unintelligible. Its job at the upper level of our minds is not to express thoughts; the work it performs is linguistic, not descriptive. Whatever descriptive import it has is confined to the unconscious phantasies it expresses. To put the matter incautiously, but in a way which brings out a point of dissimilarity as well as a point of similarity between poetry, religion, and philosophy, the *descriptive sense* of a philosophical sentence is nothing in addition to the unconscious thoughts it is made to express.

It is difficult to come to terms with the idea that, for example,

[1] *Collected Works* (Hogarth Press Ltd., 1964), Vol. XVII, p. 26.

F

Hobbes' or Zeno's words are not to be taken at face value, as being about time and about desire, but instead, like dreams, stand in need of interpretation. That philosophical utterances have been constantly misconstrued and that in order to understand them we require an explanation of their linguistic structure and their unconscious purport is attested to by the strange fact that in its twenty-four hundred years of existence technical philosophy has not produced a single uncontroverted proposition.[1] Only a weakened sense of reality, produced by a powerful need, could make it possible for anyone to dismiss this fact as of little significance and as having an obvious explanation. Two common explanations may be noted in passing. One is that philosophy is not a demonstrative science and that we cannot expect from it what we expect from a demonstrative science; but this explanation leaves us puzzled as to why philosophers give arguments in demonstration of their views. The other is that philosophical problems are so complex and difficult that they have resisted solution and have therefore left room for debate; but this leaves us in the dark as to why philosophers have for so long been able to advance their solutions with the greatest assurance, as indeed they continue to do. Philosophers who give these reasons forget them the moment they begin doing philosophy: they argue as if they thought that philosophy is a demonstrative science, and they advance their views as if they did *not* think that the complexity of philosophical problems rendered proposed solutions uncertain. It is evident that the explanations are thin rationalizations, sops to the feeble demands of a weakened sense of reality. One well-known philosopher wrote in a recent review of a book: 'The book leaves us with two cheering impressions, first, that there is progress in philosophy, second, that there is no shortage of problems for philosophy to make progress in.'[2] It is hard to imagine anyone being made hopeful about a field which in its history of twenty-four hundred years has produced only flourishing anarchy. If the sense of reality this philosopher shows does not recommend itself to us, we can at least admire his patience and sustained optimism.

[1] This is true despite the remarkable claim that in philosophy there are 'old truths' which need to be rediscovered. If we substitute 'views' for 'truths' in Strawson's statement quoted at the head of this paper, we have a description of what actually goes on in philosophy.

[2] *Philosophical Books*, Vol. IV, no. 3, p. 6.

The unfruitful history of philosophy is sufficient reason for assuming that it is the nature of the subject which permits its propositions to be permanently debatable and its arguments permanently open to assured acceptance as well as to assured rejection. The historical fact, which philosophers have managed so far to keep at a safe distance from themselves, strongly indicates that a philosophical theory is not the kind of theory which has a truth-value and that a philosophical disagreement is not the kind of disagreement that can in principle be resolved by evidence of some sort. It certainly makes permissible the inference that we have all along been looking at philosophy through the wrong kind of spectacles. This is only an inference, of course, and, as might be expected, has been rejected by those who are entrenched in the subject and seek by every means to protect their investment in it. After all, which philosopher can tolerate the thought that he has been deluded about his subject, which has become his intellectual home, and has been mistaken in believing that the aim of his investigation is to discover truth. Few will be able to bring themselves to make the unwelcome inference; but in any case, it can be replaced by considerations which show, without reference to the history of the subject, that a philosophical view is not what it has always looked to us to be. It can be shown that a philosophical disagreement exists under a condition which, in the normal case where the truth-value of a proposition is at issue, would rule out its continuation, if not its existence from the very beginning. For it can be shown that a philosophical dispute is carried on with all the parties knowing everything that is required for knowing who is right and who is wrong, if there is a right and a wrong.[1] To put it in other words, the dispute is maintained while there is no piece of relevant evidence missing, no incompleteness of data, to leave room for a divergence of opinion. The remarkable conclusion from this is that if one party to the dispute is mistaken he knows that he is mistaken but nevertheless thinks he is not, and also thinks to be wrong the position he knows to be right.[2] This

---

[1] See *The Structure of Metaphysics* (London: Routledge & Kegan Paul, Ltd., 1955), especially Ch. IX.

[2] Philosophers by a kind of inadvertence admit this when, as happens frequently, they characterize each other's 'mistakes' as obvious. In this connexion the words of one philosopher are worth quoting: 'The philosophical positions that Moore opposes can, therefore, be seen to be false *in advance* of an examination of the arguments adduced in support of them. We can know that

conclusion presents us with an absurdity. But with its rejection must also go the notions that a philosophical view is either true or false, and that the work of a philosophical argument is to establish the truth-value of a proposition. If we reflect with detachment on the matter, we can see that these notions must be incorrect. We can see that a dispute which is carried on with all the relevant facts known is not about the facts, however vivid the appearances to the contrary may be. The lady who before our very eyes is sawed in half by the magician but comes out whole was just not sawed in half. What might be called the 'illusion of philosophy' is the idea, which has the strength of an *idée fixe*, that philosophical utterances have truth-values.

Consider a typical, and current, philosophical dispute, one which lends itself to a relatively brief examination. This dispute can be conveniently examined in relation to a nonphilosophical statement that no one, either philosopher or nonphilosopher, would dream of denying or doubting or arguing about in any usual circumstance. In his *The Great Mathematicians* H. W. Turnbull makes the following statement: 'There are the well-known propositions that a circle is bisected by any diameter, or that the angles at the base of any isosceles triangle are equal, or that the angle in a semicircle is a right angle, or that the sides about angles in similar triangles are proportional. These and other like propositions have been ascribed to Thales.'[1] It is hard to think that anyone could find anything in the form of words Turnbull uses to which to take exception; but as is well known some able philosophical thinkers have been able to do so in certain circumstances. They have denied that there are such things as propositions. Other able philosophical thinkers have, of course, maintained that there are propositions. The disagreement has the air of centring on a question of existence, comparable to the question regarding the existence of the Loch Ness monster, which continues to excite disagreement. Its likeness to the question about the Loch Ness monster vanishes, however, when we attempt to identify what sort of information the philosophical question asks for and what the

something is wrong with Prichard's reasoning before we study it.' (Norman Malcolm, *Knowledge and Certainty*, p. 181.) The 'we' cannot fail to include Prichard, the implication being that Prichard must have held his view while knowing it to be false. The writer offers the remarkable explanation that 'philosophical reasoning has a peculiar power to blind us to the obvious' (p. 180).

[1] (New York University Press, 1961), p. 5.

disagreement is about. For on the assumption that the question and disagreement are about the facts, every possible identification of the subject in dispute yields the paradox of a disagreement going on with everyone knowing who is right and who is wrong.

It is quite clear that philosophers who would not dispute that there is, for example, the theorem that a diameter of a circle bisects it, may, and in fact do, divide over whether there are propositions. Now if the *philosophical* view that there are no propositions implies that there is no such theorem as that a diameter bisects its circle then the paradox obtains. For the disputing philosophers would all know a given theorem, i.e. a certain proposition, while disagreeing over whether there are any propositions. However the debate is in the end to be construed, it is evident that it cannot be over the existence of theorems, axioms, assertions, etc. A new attempt to identify the subject of debate has to be made.

The term 'proposition' has, as it is used in philosophy, a number of senses. Without going into qualifications and refinements, we may say that the special sense involved in the dispute is given by the phrase 'literal meaning of a declarative sentence'. Thus, the word 'proposition' is used to refer to the meaning of a declarative sentence, or to what it says. One argument that has been given for the view that there are propositions, as distinct from sentences which express them, is that we can be aware of a sentence without knowing its meaning, so that in learning what it means we are made aware of something over and above and in addition to the sentence itself. Another argument, used against those who deny that there are propositions, is that different indicative sentences, in the same language or in different languages, have the same meaning, which again is taken to show that the literal meaning of a sentence, the proposition it expresses, is something distinct from the sentence. The picture that these arguments conjure up of what is involved in understanding a sentence is that two processes are involved, seeing and thinking, each process having its own proper object: by sight we are made aware of a sentence and by thought we are made aware of a proposition.

We may now seem to have identified what it is the existence of which philosophers are debating; but to suppose this is a mistake. They cannot, in arguing about whether propositions exist, be disagreeing about the existence of theorems, assertions, and the like—although we may remain mystified about what makes it possible to disagree over the former without at the same time disagreeing over the latter. But the puzzle as to what the dispute is about remains, if we take it to centre on the question whether indicative sentences have literal meanings. Construing the dispute to be over the correct answer to this question does not enable us to circumvent the paradox of people disagreeing about the answer to a question while knowing what the answer is. For a philosopher who maintains that there are no propositions, equally with a philosopher who maintains that there are, knows perfectly well that there are indicative sentences which have literal meanings, and so knows that there are propositions. The philosopher who insists that there are propositions knows that his opponent is aware of the fact that many indicative sentences have literal meaning and so knows that his opponent in debate is aware of the fact that there are propositions, but continues to argue with him, as if trying to correct his lack of knowledge. The situation we are confronted with is baffling, to say the least. And indeed we can make no sense of it so long as we take the dispute about the existence of propositions to be over whether in fact indicative sentences have literal meaning. If the paradox is to be avoided, the only recourse is to suppose that the existence of literally meaningful indicative sentences is not involved in the dispute about whether there are propositions.

A further interpretation of the dispute, construed as a factual disagreement of some sort, suggests itself at this point. This is that it is about whether the meanings of indicative sentences are *entities*, or objects. There are features of the dispute, such as choice of terminology and the way certain arguments are framed, which make plausible this interpretation. Some philosophers who advocate the view that there are propositions go so far as to maintain that indicative sentences are *names*, which suggests that propositions are being thought of as objects or entities that are named by sentences, objects for which the sentences 'stand'. On this construction, a philosopher who maintains that there are propositions is really asserting that propositions are entities; and a philosopher who says that there are no propositions is not denying the existence of propositions but instead is maintaining that propositions are not entities, that they are not a kind of thing. But avoiding one difficulty, as this interpretation enables us to do, lands us in another. For there is no process of examining a proposition to determine whether it is an entity or is not an entity. This is not to say that a procedure is lacking at present which might in the future be discovered. Rather, it makes no literal sense to speak of a process of examining the meaning of a sentence in order to determine whether it is an entity: the phrase 'examines the meaning of a sentence in order to ascertain whether it is a thing' describes nothing. By drawing closer we can determine whether what we see is a shadow or a thing, but there is no drawing closer to determine whether a shadow is a thing. In the same way there is no drawing nearer to and scrutinizing more carefully the meaning of a sentence: the words 'Plato examined the literal meanings of indicative sentences and found that their meanings are really entities', and also the words 'Roscelin examined their meanings and came to the opposite conclusion', do not describe any sort of process. There is nothing to be done in addition to understanding a sentence in order to know whether its literal import is a thing or not, so that if it is a thing, all parties to the dispute know this, and if it is not a thing, all parties to the dispute know this. An anecdote is to the point in this connexion. On one occasion when Bertrand Russell was present I ventured to say that two things could not occupy the same place at once. Russell's immediate rejoinder was: 'That is not true. A colour and a shape can be in the same place at once.' The next day I related the intellectual skirmish to several learned colleagues. Their unhesitating reply was that colours and shapes are not things. It is evident that no sort of examination of colours and shapes could resolve the disagreement over whether they are or are not things. However unnatural it may strike one, the conclusion that forces itself on us is that the difference of opinion is not over whether a shape is a thing. And it is the the same with the disagreement over whether what an indicative sentence says, the proposition it expresses, is an object.

There is a further possible construction to be considered: the dispute might be construed as being verbal in nature. Many intellectuals have voiced the suspicion that philosophical questions and theories are in some way verbal, and some philosophers have given a kind of recognition to this suspicion in a technique they have developed, linguistic analysis. Looked on as verbal, about the conventional use of terminology, the dispute regarding the existence of propositions is to be interpretaed as a dispute, when conducted in the English language, about the use of the *word* 'proposition'. A philosopher who holds that there are no propositions is to be taken as maintaining, in the non-verbal form of speech, that the word 'proposition' has no use in the language; and a philosopher who holds that there are propositions is to be understood as implying that the word 'proposition' does have a use in the language. This may now seem to have brought us nearer to the true nature of the dispute; but it requires little reflection to see that the paradox we have been seeking to avoid reappears. For it goes without saying that everyone knows perfectly well that the word 'proposition' does have a use in the language: no philosopher engaged in the dispute would think of saying that Turnbull's use of 'proposition' is improper, or, to use Hume's expression, 'wrong apply'd'.

It can be seen that no matter which way we turn and no matter what we identify as the subject under debate among philosophers, the paradox is not avoided so long as we retain the idea that the dispute is one about fact and that the claim and counterclaim have truth-values. That is, so long as the question 'Are there such things as propositions?' is construed as a request for factual information, either linguistic or non-linguistic, we are confronted by the paradox of people advancing different answers and arguing about which is true and which false while in possession of the answer. If, now, we can bring ourselves to give up the notion that the question is a request for factual information, i.e. that it is the kind of question that has true and false answers, and that the dispute is about fact of one kind or another, we avoid the paradox and also reach a promising vantage point. Plainly, we then have to reconsider the words of the philosophers and try to understand them anew, in a metaphor, remove old spectacles and try out new ones. The two sentences, 'There are propositions' and 'There are no propositions', have to be understood in terms of their relevance to each other; and if the second is not to be construed as denying that there are propositions, the first is not to be construed as declaring the existence of propositions.

The first sentence conceals its metaphysics behind the language in everyday use, and an understanding of it can best be reached by first considering the second sentence, which appears to be in conflict with the language in everyday use. To put it briefly, the sentence 'There are no propositions', not construed as expressing a factual claim about propositions nor yet as making an obviously false claim about ordinary terminology, is open to the interpretation that it is a statement embodying a terminological decision, the decision to cast out of the language the word 'proposition'. On this interpretation, the philosophical sentence is related in a special way to the verbal sentence, 'The word "proposition" has no use'. If the terminological decision it introduces were accepted and put into general practice, the verbal sentence would then say what is true. But as things are, the verbal sentence says what is false, whereas the philosophical sentence which introduces the terminological decision expresses what is neither true nor false. So to speak, the content of the philosophical sentence is a verbal innovation; but its form, its linguistic dress, is taken from the mode of speech in which statements of fact are made. It is in the form of words used to make a true or false claim about the existence and nature of things, and this creates the idea that the existence of propositions is being denied. Wittgenstein is one place describes the philosopher as someone who objects to a language convention under the impression that he is putting forward a factual claim. The philosopher, he said 'objects to using this word ["pain"] in the particular way in which it is commonly used. On the other hand, he is not aware that he is objecting to a convention. He sees a way of dividing the country different from the one used on the ordinary map. He feels tempted, say, to use the name "Devonshire" not for the county with its conventional boundary, but for a region differently bounded. He could express this by saying: "Isn't it absurd to make *this* a county, to draw the boundaries *here*?" But what he says is: "The *real* Devonshire is this."[1] Compare 'There really are no propositions!'

The question which now arises is why a philosopher rebels against the conventional use of the word 'proposition', what determines his reading out the word (with bell, book, and candle) from the language. For the word does its assigned work well enough, and for that matter the philosopher does not carry the decision he makes in his 'philosophic moment' into his non-philosophical talk. This question has answers at different levels of our mind; but superficially the philosophical decision to exorcize the word must link up with the counter-sentence. 'There are propositions', or 'There are such things as propositions'. This sentence cannot be

[1] *The Blue Book*, p. 57.

viewed as declaring the fact that the word 'proposition' has a use in the language; i.e. the philosophical sentence which expresses a position entering into the debate cannot be understood as expressing a fact which everyone knows and which is not at issue in the debate. Like its companion sentence it has to be understood as giving concealed expression to a linguistic decision, at least part of which is the decision to retain the word 'proposition' in the language. This construction would explain what makes it possible for the dispute to be carried on in the presence of all the facts. But the decision to retain the word is not the whole decision. This can readily be gathered from the curious fact that some philosophers have held the 'view' that indicative sentences are *names*. Thus Professor Alonzo Church has said that '(declarative) *sentences*, in particular, are taken as a kind of names, the denotation being the *truth-value* of the sentence, *truth* or *falsehood*, and the sense being the *proposition* which the sentence expresses'.[1] These philosophers are as aware as anyone of the grammatical fact that an indicative sentence does not count as a part of speech and is not classified as a noun. Attributing an odd mistake to them succeeds only in presenting us with a situation which flouts the intelligence.

The assumption that is forced upon us is that some philosophers have decided to classify indicative sentences with nouns, and this assumption throws light on the dispute we are considering. A philosopher who says, 'There are propositions', or better, says, 'There are such entities as propositions', has decided not only to retain the noun 'proposition', but has also decided to classify the word with a special group of nouns, nouns which are general names of *things*. Thus, one philosopher, who has rejected the view expressed by the words 'There are such entities as propositions', characterized it, typically in the form of speech employed in talk of things, as 'the metaphysical doctrine that propositions are real entities'.[2] And another philosopher, who came out for a 'reduced ontology',[3] urged that 'meanings themselves, as obscure intermediate entities, may well be abandoned'.[4] Wittgenstein has observed that we tend to look for a substance whenever we find a

---

[1] 'The Need for Abstract Entities in Semantic Analysis', *Amer. Acad. of Arts and Sciences Proceedings*, Vol. 80–1, p. 101.

[2] A. J. Ayer, *Language, Truth and Logic*, second edition, p. 88.

[3] W. V. Quine, 'Semantics and Abstract Objects', *Amer. Acad. of Arts and Sciences Proceedings*, Vol. 80–1, p. 96.

[4] *Ibid.*, p. 91.

substantive; and though it is not altogether acceptable as it stands, his formula is suggestive. In philosophy it is by no means rare to find a noun which is not the general name of a thing, e.g. the word 'nothing', being turned into a noun which is such a name, this, to be sure, only by an artificial stretching of categories, not by actually turning it into a general name of a thing. This would seem to be what has happened in the case of the term 'proposition'. The word is a noun which, like the nouns 'today' and 'existence', is not used in the language to name things, and what the philosopher of the Reality of the Proposition has done is to stretch the word 'thing' or 'entity' or 'object' so that it applies to what is referred to by the phrase 'literal meaning of an indicative sentence'. In this way he artificially assimilates the term 'proposition' into the class of object-naming substantives, and this leads some philosophers to the further artificial assimilation of indicative sentences into the category of proper names. In the grammar book of some philosophers an indicative sentence is the proper name of its literal meaning.[1] A philosopher who is opposed to these reclassifications, which according to his lights conceal important differences between the use of 'proposition' and substantives that denote objects and between nouns and indicative sentences, will eliminate them by exorcizing the offending word 'proposition' from the language.

All this manœuvring with grammar and terminology when carried on in the mode of speech in which things and occurrences are described creates the lively illusion that the existence of an elusive, occult entity is being debated. This illusion is apparently so important to philosophers, to those who are hostile to propositions as well as to those who embrace them, as to prevent their penetrating it and seeing the manœuvrings for the linguistic gossamer that they are. Wittgenstein's observation that we may be 'irresistibly attracted or repelled by a notation'[2] is undoubtedly true. But in itself the shifting of terminology and classifications this way and that can hardly be a fascinating enough game to account for the philosopher's preoccupation with it. Nor can the illusion, created by the non-verbal form in which philosophers

---

[1] Thus Quine has said, 'Statements have frequently been treated as names of propositions, these latter being construed as entities of a sort better described as *meanings* of statements'. *Op. cit.*, p. 90.

[2] *The Blue Book*, p. 57.

present their re-editings of language, account for the continued absorbed interest of the philosopher. Something else must be involved to account both for the illusion having the strength of a delusion and for the philosopher's interest being held captive for so long. Behind the 'entity' which is being debated must hide ideas which are very much alive in the unconscious of philosophers. The linguistic reclassification and also the exorcism of the term 'proposition', which are done at the preconscious level of our thinking and which bring into existence an intellectual illusion at the conscious level of our thinking, must express important material in the deeper strata of the mind. In connection with what he calls a 'pure transcendental idea' Kant makes an observation which might be applied to the illusions engendered by the controversy about propositions: 'Even the wisest of men cannot free himself from them. After long effort he perhaps succeeds in guarding himself against actual error; but he will never be able to free himself from the illusion, which unceasingly mocks and torments him.'[1] We may well think that he cannot free himself from the illusion because of a need for it. In lectures Wittgenstein gave in 1934-35 he described a philosophical problem as 'the product of an obsession—a linguistic obsession that is not recognized'.[2] And in his *Philosophical Investigations* he says, 'The philosopher's treatment of a question [undoubtedly referring to his own procedure] is like the treatment of an illness.'[3] His remarks would seem to have their source in a perception into the nature of philosophy and its deeper roots in the mind.

The unconscious purport of the sentence, 'There are such entities as propositions', and of its denial, 'There are no propositions', is a matter of speculation, speculation which need not, however, be devoid of plausibility. About metaphysics, the part of philosophy which investigates supersensible realities, those lying beyond the range of possible sense experience, Freud has the following to say: 'I believe in fact that a great part of the mythological view of the world, which reaches far into the most modern religions, is *nothing other than psychological processes projected into the outer world*. The obscure apprehending of the psychical factors and relationships of the unconscious is mirrored—it is hard to put it otherwise; one has to use here the analogy with

[1] *The Critique of Pure Reason*, trans. by Norman Kemp Smith, pp. 327-8.
[2] From notes taken by Alice Ambrose.   [3] P. 91.

paranoia—in the construction of *a supersensible reality*, which science has to retranslate into the *psychology of the unconscious*. One could venture in this manner to resolve the myths of Paradise, the Fall of Man, of God, of Good and Evil, of Immortality and so on, thus transforming *Metaphysics* into *Metapsychology*.'[1] As is well known, following the suggestion made here, enlightening analytical studies have been written which have interpreted the myths of Paradise, the Fall, God, and so on in terms of the psychology of the unconscious. It would not be surprising if it turned out that behind the metaphysical talk of the supersensible —behind the illusion that it makes pronouncements about a kind of reality—were to be found the familiar primitive myths of Paradise and the Fall, etc. And these myths have can their soporific effect on the critical powers of so many intellectuals only because of the ideas which hide behind them. The Platonic 'theory' of universals, which is only the verbal imitation of a theory about entities,[2] harks back to the religious Orphic-Pythagorean conception of the Isles of the Blessed. For many thinkers philosophy, and particularly metaphysical philosophy, is a highly intellectualized substitute for religion; and it may well be that behind the façade of philosophical talk about the supersensible a philosopher experiences a highly attenuated form of the state of 'passionate sympathetic contemplation'[3] in which he 'is identified with the suffering God, dies in his death, and arises again in his birth'.[4] In any event, no more is needed than to be attentive to the choice of language which philosophers use in the expression of their theories and to take into account some of their adjacent comments to see that the religious myths of Paradise (in which there is no place for a harsh super-ego), the Fall, God, immortality are very much alive in their minds. When, in the *Phaedrus*, Plato poetically speaks of the realm of universals as 'the heaven above the heavens . . . [where] abides . . . the colourless, formless, intangible essence, visible only to the mind, the pilot of the soul',[5] his words are only

---

[1] Quoted in Ernest Jones' *The Life and Work of Sigmund Freud*, Vol. III, pp. 352–3.

[2] Created by the unannounced, academic reclassification of general words with proper names. See 'The Existence of Universals' in *The Structure of Metaphysics*.

[3] F. M. Cornford's interpretation of the Greek word for 'theory', *From Religion to Philosophy*.

[4] *Ibid.*　　　　[5] Sec. 247, Jowett translation.

a picturesque way of calling attention to the differences between the proper names of ordinary language and the artificially re-classified proper names in the Platonic grammar book. Only in appearance do his words describe a reality, but unquestionably they provoke in us thoughts of Paradise, whether conscious or not. And God, immortality, and even the Fall, can be discerned in the verbal theatre of the Platonic Forms, God and immortality quite clearly, the Fall perhaps less clearly. The latter emerges in Socrates' 'favourite doctrine', the reminiscence theory that knowledge is the remembering of universals which the soul knew in its prior residence above the physical heaven, to use St. Paul's description, 'the invisible kingdom of God'. The question which leaps to mind is what happened to make the soul leave the supersensible realm of the forms to inhabit a physical body, which is its prison and from which it wishes to esacpe. One of the things Socrates is represented as saying in the *Phaedrus* makes it plain enough that the departure was an Expulsion: '. . . intelligence of universals . . . is the recollection of those things which our soul once saw while following God'.[1] The soul is a fallen angel whose wings have 'wasted and fallen away'[2] because they were 'fed upon evil and foulness and the opposite of good'.[2] Psychoanalysis has been able to extract the secret of the nature of the 'evil and foulness', the original sin, that brought about the Fall of man.

For many philosophers, for those who deny the existence of the supersensible as well as for those who construct systems of super-sensible realities, metaphysics is a linguistic sanctuary which provides them with possibilities for resolving their conflicts about religion.[3] It is also a linguistic battlefield. On it are waged shadow wars over terminology and grammar; and behind these wars others can be seen in which religion is the bone of con-tention. Contests about religion and its renunciation that once could not be carried on without violent physical eruptions could, on the whole, be carried on with relative security under the cover of philosophical positions and counterpositions—Platonism, Aristotelianism, Nominalism, Conceptualism, and so on. Some philosophers still prefer this concealed mode of religious warfare,

---

[1] Sec. 249.   [2] *Ibid.*, sec. 247.

[3] Hegel is worth quoting in this connection: 'The objects of philosophy, it is true, are upon the whole the same as those of religion. In both the object is Truth.' *The Logic of Hegel* (Oxford University Press, 1892), p. 3, trans. by William Wallace.

for a variety of reasons, one perhaps being that philosophy in their eyes confers on it an intellectual dignity which it does not have by itself. The following words which introduce a contemporary attempt at a nominalistic reformulation of languages, make plain one determinant which underlies the rejection of the metaphysical view that there are abstract entities. Professors Goodman and Quine write: '1. *Renunciation of abstract entities.* We do not believe in abstract entities. No one supposes that abstract entities—classes, relations, properties, etc.—exist in space-time; but we mean more than this. We renounce them altogether.'[1]

To come back to the view that there are such entities as propositions, which, as will be recalled, represents the decision to look on the word 'proposition' *as if* it is the general name of a kind of object. The 'entity' that is named by the word is said to be *abstract* —which is an oblique way of saying that 'proposition' is an abstract noun that is not used to denote objects.[2] Unlike things that we see and feel, it is intangible to the senses and can be apprehended only in thought. Philosophers who are or who become hostile to the view and support their rejection by declaring that 'proposition' is a word which 'can be construed as syncategorematic: significant in context but naming nothing'[1] are evidently impressed by the difference between the actual use of the term 'proposition' and terms which are names of 'real entities'. That is a difference which they do not wish to see 'hushed up',[3] and they therefore resist the philosophical classification which does this. But their rejection goes deeper than opposition to an idle enlargement of a grammatical category. A philosopher who takes the stand that propositions are abstract entities is giving covert expression to a religious belief, a belief which his sophistication may not permit him to have consciously; and a philosopher who opposes this stand has decided to take the path of heresy. One observation may be quoted here: 'The theory of meaning, even with the elimination of the mysteri-

[1] 'Steps Towards a Constructive Nominalism', *The Journal of Symbolic Logic*, Vol. 12 (1947), p. 105.
[2] The following comment from Wittgenstein is of particular interest in this connexion: ' "The symbol '*a*' stands for an ideal object" is evidently supposed to assert something about the meaning, and so about the use, of "*a*". And it means of course that this use is in a certain respect similar to that of a sign that has an object, and that it does not stand for any object.' *Remarks on the Foundations of Mathematics* (Oxford: Basil Blackwell, 1956), p. 136.
[3] Wittgenstein's expression.

ous meant entities, strikes me as in a comparable state to theology —but with the difference that its notions are blithely used in the supposedly most scientific and hard-headed brands of philosophy.'[1]

There are, quite certainly, other determinants than the one mentioned which enter into the acceptance and rejection of the metaphysical view about propositions. That is to say, there are further ideas which the sentence 'Propositions are abstract entities' is unconsciously made to denote. Two of them are easily guessed and may be mentioned briefly. These concern death and dirt. These two ideas are probably closely linked in the unconscious, for the dead body soon becomes foul dirt in the process of mingling its substance with nature. The scandal created by the odours which came from the holy Father Zossimov's body may have had as one of its determinants the unconscious equation, dead body = faeces. Be this as it may, in the *Parmenides*, in which various Platonic theories about the nature of the abstract entities denoted by general words are examined, Socrates embraces the view that there are 'absolute ideas of the just and the beautiful and the good, and of all that class'.[2] But he resists the notion that there could be 'absolute ideas' corresponding to such things as 'hair, mud, dirt, or anything else which is vile and paltry'.[3] It is clear that the 'heaven above the heavens' is a world free from dirt; it houses non-material entities which are the objects of 'pure' thought. Midas changed dirt into gold which he could not eat; Plato sought to escape from dirt by creating a world which could not be seen or touched, a world (brought about by the magic of philosophical grammar) where reside the impalpable essences.

According to Kant the three great problems of metaphysics revolve around the notions of God, freedom, and immortality, and one of these, which is connected with the idea of death, would seem to play a predominant role in the psychology of philosophers. For in the *Phaedo* Socrates tells us that true philosophers are 'always occupied in the practice of dying, wherefore . . . to them least of all men is death terrible'.[4] Philosophy itself seems to have been a kind of halfway house to death for Socrates, and so it may may be for philosophers in general. Ernest Jones has called death 'the King of Terrors', and Freud thought it important to try to come to terms with it. How philosophers have been able to divest

---

[1] W. V. Quine, 'Semantics and Abstract Objects', *op. cit.*, p. 92.
[2] Sec. 130.   [3] *Ibid.*   [4] Sec. 67.

death of its dread is thus of special interest. If one only looks, one can easily find their solutions buried in many theories, each the presentation of a piece of altered language. An easily recognized instance is the academic extirpation from language of the word 'time', presented in the form of a statement of fact, i.e. the 'theory' that time is unreal. The metaphysical view that there are abstract entities which exist timelessly can be seen to be an important and poetically appealing attempt by linguistic means to come to terms with the emotional problem posed by the ultimate fate from which 'His Majesty, the Ego'[1] can find no real escape. The poetry and metaphors with which Plato surrounds his theories about the nature of the temporal world and the world of the everlasting essences make plain the psychological mechanism used to come to terms with death: the mechanism of reversal. By means of the device of turning a thing into its opposite a philosopher is able to rob death of its terror. In the *Republic*, the world is described as a cave where only the shadows of people are to be seen. This description is reminiscent of the Homeric account of Ulysses' visit to the mythological underworld of the Greeks, and the Platonic description may well have been written under the influence of the Homeric description. In any case, the presence of the mechanism of reversal is unmistakable. This world, the world of colours and odours and sounds, the world of sense experience, is changed into its opposite, into the shadowy world of death; and the final nothingness, wherein is 'the colourless, formless, intangible essence', is psychologically transformed into the ultimately desirable. This world is rejected, and 'the undiscovered country from whose bourne no traveller returns'[2] is transfigured into Paradise. The transformations are of course inner transformations and these are effected with the help of linguistic creations which are presented in the ontological form of speech. So to speak, an *abstract* entity is nothing, which has been verbally transmuted into *something*.

The philosophical view that there are abstract entities, and the special view that propositions are abstract entities, may be characterized as a contrived linguistic structure, intended as a medium for inner contemplation. It is constituted by the introduction, in the fact-stating idiom, of a hidden language change, which at one level of our mind presents us with an intellectual

[1] Freud's expression. [2] *Hamlet*.

G

mirage and at other levels of our mind works to express needed phantasies. To the uppermost level the words 'Propositions are abstract entities' present the delusive appearance of making a factual claim about the existence of things of a special kind, comparable to the claim that there are such creatures as leprechauns. For deeper levels of the mind, the words say that there are objects which cannot soil and also that there are refined and wondrous objects which we shall be privileged to perceive. But the 'objects' are nothing more than inner states projected into the outer world, the externalization of emotions. It is interesting to note that some philosophers have, in a way, begun to realize the linguistic character of the activity that is philosophy. Thus one philosopher has described himself as 'playing a report-writing game for a revised universe'. The 'revised universe' is revised language and the game of report-writing is a way of giving expression to unconscious contents of the psyche—which makes the game one that a philosopher cannot easily give up.

It is permissible to guess that Freud had an intuitive perception into the game-aspect of what philosophers do with words, the nature of their 'convolutions', which made him decide to avoid contact with philosophy. But is was a perception which he never attempted to clarify or pursue. Instead of arousing curiosity about a subject which has attracted very great thinkers over an enormous period of time, his perception seems to have provoked only rejection. But what is rejected without improved understanding has a way of not being left behind. Thus, Freud attempted to bolster his claim regarding the existence of an unconscious part of the mind by unwittingly producing one of the standard philosophical theories about our knowledge of other minds. Any philosopher will recognize the so-called 'argument from analogy' in Freud's words. In his *Autobiographical Study* he argued that giving recognition to the unconscious was 'only treating one's own mental life as one had always treated other people's. One did not hesitate to ascribe mental processes to other people, although one had no immediate consciousness of them and could only infer them from their words and actions. But what held good for other people must be applicable to oneself.'[1]

[1] P. 56.

5

PHILOSOPHY AND ILLUSION

'Once I had been able to tear aside an illusion that had previously dimmed my vision, once I had 'seen through' something, the insight thus gained was never lost.' Ernest Jones, *Free Associations, Memoirs of a Psychoanalyst*, p. 63.
'. . . concealed lighting can make things look very different from what they are. Why not pull the curtains and open the windows? The light will be better, the air will be fresher, and we shall be freer.' John Wisdom, Foreword, p. xii, *The Structure of Metaphysics*.

Ernest Jones has remarked on the 'astonishing contrast between the diversity of philosophical opinions and the widespread agreement in scientific work . . .'[1], and said, in part explanation of this state of affairs, that philosophical questions 'have more important subjective origins than had hitherto been discernible'.[1] There can no longer be any serious doubt that philosophical questions and theories have unconscious determinants, that they have meanings which are hidden from the philosophers themselves and are not available to their conscious reasoning processes. This goes some way toward explaining the astonishing absence of assured results in philosophy. But it cannot be the whole explanation. It does not naturally occur to anyone to question the appearance of a kind of scientific work going on in philosophy, a kind of work in which, for example, hypotheses are constructed to explain various phenomena and evidence is brought forward in support of the hypotheses. But it may be that an important part of the explanation of the contrast between philosophy and science is to be arrived at only through the question as to whether philosophy is a kind of science and whether it actually is about the phenomena it professes to investigate. In fact there exist reasons for thinking that philosophy has the substance of a verbally contrived intellectual mirage and that it is a subject which only in outward appearance seeks to discover truths about things. Psychoanalysis has a special interest in the illusions of

[1] *Free Associations* (New York: Basic Books, 1959), pp. 60-1.

mankind, and what it can learn from philosophers is the linguistic mechanics by which striking and durable illusions are produced. What philosophers have to learn from psychoanalysis are the reasons why the illusions have such overriding importance for them.

Freud explained an illusion as a belief which has its origin primarily in a wish and maintains its hold on the mind through the strength of the wish rather than by virtue of evidence. When a wish is very strong the belief that it is or will be satisfied by the world springs to life and takes the form of a conviction, and any reason, however transparent and feeble, will serve to protect the belief from intellectual criticism. The wish may not, of course, be conscious, and it could, and in many cases does, introduce subjective distortions into reality by the mechanisms of transference and projection. Fantasy and illusion are the mental equivalents of a sanctuary, a refuge from a reality we feel we cannot face and so must deny.[1] In fantasy and illusion we *make* the world accommodate itself to our wishes, but we do this at a price. We resort, in our waking life, to the mechanisms entering into the formation of dreams, and in doing this we place ourselves under the domination of a condition which weakens our sense of reality, which blocks our intelligence and impoverishes our powers of reasoning. Thomas Sturge Moore described the poet Yeats' talk as 'dream soaked', and to the degree to which our perceptions of reality are soaked with our illusions our ability to test reality is weakened. Spinoza said that a passion, i.e. an obsession, is turned into an emotion, a feeling which has lost its compelling strength and no longer dominates us, when we are able to form a distinct idea of it.[2] The implication is that understanding ourselves makes us freer.

The progress of civilization can in good part be described as the series of breakthroughs which have shattered the comforting illusions of mankind and brought in their wake emotional upheavals requiring great readjustments. The three most dramatic breakthroughs, recounted by Freud, were those that destroyed the beliefs that the earth is the centre of the universe, that man

[1] Margaret Anderson said, 'My greatest enemy is reality—I have fought it successfully for thirty years'.

[2] *The Ethics*, Pt. V, On the Power of the Understanding, or of Human Freedom, Prop. III: 'An emotion, which is a passion, ceases to be a passion, as soon as we form a clear and distinct idea thereof.'

was God's special creation, and that consciousness characterizes all of our mental processes. Coming to terms with the ideas that our physical home is not the hub of existence, that we evolved from lower forms of life, and that we are strangers to the greater part of our own minds means giving up some of our infantile narcissism and facing up to fact. And this in turn can, and frequently does, lead to an increasing interest in our surroundings and our prizing understanding for its own sake as well as for its practical consequences.

The passing away of general illusions (an old expression for some of these is 'innate ideas') which have their roots in wishes deep in our minds is a continuing process. As it turns out, there is an accumulation of evidence tending to show that philosophy, reasoned, technical philosophy, such as that found, for example, in Kant's *Critique of Pure Reason* and F. H. Bradley's *Appearance and Reality*, is an illusion which has imprisoned the intelligence not only of ordinary intellectuals but of the greatest thinkers. There already is considerable evidence for the claim that in occupying ourselves with such questions as whether there are abstract entities or whether beauty is an objective quality of things, we have been doing one thing, on which we place small or no value, while believing ourselves to be doing another thing, on which we place great value. It is possible that the greatest philosophers, from Plato through Descartes, Kant, Hume, and Russell, to the contemporary linguistic analysts, have succeeded only in contributing chimeras to a chimerical subject, a subject which presents itself in the guise of a fundamental investigation of the world. Wittgenstein said that a philosophical problem arises when language goes on holiday[1] and it is not unlikely that a philosophical theory is only the spurious imitation of a theory, that it is merely a piece of re-edited terminology intended, not for practical adoption, but only for inner contemplation. The reality of technical philosophy, its substance, is, according to this iconoclastic hypothesis, concealed, artificially retailored language, the superimposition of different will-o'-the-wisp uses on the familiar language of common discourse. The illusion of philosophy is that its pronouncements state theories about the nature of things and that its arguments are pieces of evidence for or against the claimed truth-values of the theories. What is beginning to come through,

[1] *Philosophical Investigations*, p. 19.

in consequence of certain eccentric features of philosophy im-
pressing themselves on us with increasing force, is that we have
been the intellectual dupe of a linguistic deception of our own
contrivance. The ancient Greek painter Parrhasius fooled a bird
with his realistic painting of cherries; Xeuxis fooled Parrhasius
with a realistic painting of curtains; and the philosopher deceives
himself as well as his audience with his realistic imitation of a
theory. It is natural to think of philosophy as standing somewhere
between religion and the empirical sciences. Religion is concerned
with the supernatural in relation to the natural, and its tenets rest
on faith; whereas science is concerned with the natural, and its
propositions are founded on experiment and observation. Philosophy is thought of as overlapping in subject-matter with both
and relying on reason. No one but a metaphysical philosopher
would be rash enough to say that science is an illusion.[1] As is
well known, Freud declared religious beliefs to be illusions,
sealed off from our scientific curiosity by a complex of psychical
needs. And now some philosophical analysts have, in a non-
quixotic spirit, put forward the unappealing thesis that philosophy
consists of statements which, instead of being the pronouncements
about phenomena they appear to be, introduce academically
refurbished language. To illustrate, these philosophers maintain
that instead of making a true or false claim about the world, the
sentence 'I alone am real' introduces a theatrically contracted use
of the word 'real'. It is interesting to note in this connexion that
in the Smith College courses of study bulletin philosophy has
been grouped with religion and theatre under the general course
requirements. One may wonder whether this grouping represents
an intuitive perception into the character of philosophy. For the
construction a small group of philosophical analysts places on
philosophy represents it as a kind of linguistically staged theatre.
This, for example, is how it represents the long argued Humeian
view that what we take to be productive causation is nothing more
than constant conjunction. This view, instead of being interpreted
as stating what connexions in fact hold between classes of events,
is taken to constitute a banishment of the word 'cause' from our
vocabulary, a banishment which is not carried out in our use of
language for recording and conveying information.

It will be instructive to take a look at the metamorphosis of our

[1] F. H. Bradley characterized science as self-contradictory.

conception of philosophy, the changes in our idea of what it is about and what it is capable of achieving. Plato gives us the exalted picture of the philosopher as the cosmic seer, 'the spectator of all time and all existence'. Spinoza gives us the picture of the philosopher as the deductive geometer of reality who classifies fundamental propositions into axioms and theorems covering all of its aspects and demonstrates the latter propositions from the former. He conceives himself to be giving a comprehensive and detailed accounting of what there is and how things hang together. Leibniz, by implication, delineates the philosopher as the mental penetrator into concepts, who by wholly analytical procedures is able to extract from them the answers to the ultimate questions about reality. F. H. Bradley gives us the lofty image of the philosopher as the profound thinker who speculates on 'ultimate truth' and determines what is real and what is appearance by the power of thought. These philosophers, and many others in the metaphysical tradition, seem to have laboured under the notion that by thinking alone it is possible to unlock the secrets of the world, determine its composition, and map the interrelations of its parts. The underlying idea is that philosophy is the highest science, 'the Divine Science' according to Aquinas, which leads us 'beyond the region of ordinary fact',[1] without requiring recourse to the procedures of the natural sciences.

The empiricist philosophers give us a more modest, perhaps more down to earth picture of the philosopher at work. Instead of describing him as the *a priori* contemplator of concepts they represent him as being primarily an analyst of experience, concerned to determine the sources of our ideas and the nature and limits of our knowledge of things. The empiricist tradition is complex and overlaps at a number of points with rationalism, and to try to define it would be a considerable undertaking. It seems, on the whole, to differ from rationalism in placing part of its reliance on sense-experience. Some of its professed findings appear to be the results of empirical investigations—so much so that a recent anthology of the British empiricist philosophers was published under the title, *The British Empirical Philosophers*.[2] The adjective 'empirical' in the title suggests that the British

---

[1] Bradley's phrase.
[2] Edited by A. J. Ayer and Raymond Wrinch (London: Routledge & Kegan Paul, Ltd., 1952).

empiricists' views were arrived at empirically—something which, to use G. E. Moore's famous expletive, is 'a howler'—if one looks at what philosophers *do*, as against what *scientists* do. But the illusion that philosophy uses observation is there. Thus, according to Hume, what universally appear to be instances of a change being brought about in a thing by the action on it of another thing turn out on careful observation to be instances of independent, concurrent happenings. If, to use Hume's phrase, 'I turn my eyes to two objects' which appear to stand in a causal relation to each other, e.g. a stationary billiard ball which to all appearances is made to move by another billiard ball colliding with it, the reality which comes to light is the concurrent but independent behaviour of the two balls. What we see on looking closely at the billiard balls in action is like seeing at the same time a shooting star and a tree falling. Consider for a moment a different case. In connexion with the view that our perception of things is indirect, G. E. Moore remarked that some philosophers have doubted that 'there are any such things as sense-data';[1] and to remove their scepticism he invites them to look at the back of their hands, whereupon they will discover that they can 'pick out' certain objects which are sense-data. And A. J. Ayer has argued that 'all that our senses reveal to us are sense-data',[2] the ostensible implication being that this claim, like Moore's conclusion, is arrived at by some sort of empirical process of examining the elements in our perception of things. But it is easily seen that it is no more possible to pick out a sense-datum, when *all* that our senses reveal to us are sense-data, than it is possible to pick out a green thing in Emerald City.

Rationalism and empiricism are the two classical masks which philosophy has presented to thinkers, and they have been taken to be rival procedures with a common goal, namely, knowledge of reality. Our idea of philosophy began to change after G. E. Moore introduced his method of translation into the concrete. This method amounted to restating an abstractly formulated view in concrete, specific terms, which placed it in its proper, realistic setting. Thus, the general view that the existence of any relation implies an infinite regress of relations and hence that relations are

---

[1] 'A Defence of Common Sense', *Contemporary British Philosophy*, II (London: George Allen & Unwin Ltd., 1925), pp. 217–18.
[2] *Philosophical Essays*, p. 141.

unreal, when translated into the concrete, becomes the statement that there are no relational facts, that, concretely, nothing is to the left or right of anything, that no one is anyone's parent, etc. Such restatements of theories seemed to many philosophers to prick metaphysical bubbles, expose the theories as bizarre speculations which flout plainest fact. But what could not in time fail to impress itself in some way or other is the paradox involved in supposing that anyone, whose sense of reality in the normal pursuit of life was unimpaired, could actually hold, and continue to hold, views which are in such violent and obvious collision with fact. When it dawned on thinkers that whatever a philosophical theory was about it could not be about what Moore's translation into the concrete suggested, philosophy began to appear in a new light. This appearance acquired sharper outlines when the method of translation into the concrete was joined to Moore's increasing concern to examine the correct use in ordinary language of the words occuring in the expression of theories. The attention of philosophers began to shift more and more to language. In a metaphor, many philosophers began to look at their subject through linguistic spectacles, which is to say that something of the linguistic character of philosophy was beginning to show through its theadbare, if still colourful, traditional ontological dress. Thus, logical positivists—Carnap, Ayer, and others, set forth a twofold claim, (1) that the statements of metaphysics are not false but are, instead, pieces of literal nonsense, and (2) that the proper task of philosophy is the analysis (and perhaps the 'logical' reform) of language. The idea behind analytical lexicography is that it will lead eventually to 'a true and comprehensive science of language'[1] which will realize Leibniz' ideal of a *characteristica universalis*. And the crude idea behind a *philosophical* Science of Language is that it will enable us to determine the truth-values of propositions about the world. One recently expressed claim for the philosophical investigation of language is, superficially, more modest than this. Professor J. L. Austin has said: 'When we examine what we should say when, what words we should use in what situations, we are looking again not *merely* at words (or "meanings", whatever they may be) but also at the realities we use the words to talk about: we are using a sharpened awareness of words to sharpen our perception of, though not as

[1] J. L. Austin, *Philosophical Papers* (Oxford University Press, 1961), p. 180.

the final arbiter of, the phenomena.'[1] We sharpen our perception of things by looking more carefully at the *things*, not at words; and the idea that shows through is the old Leibnizian idea. According to Leibniz, 'If we had it [i.e. an ideal language] we should be able to reason in metaphysics and morals in much the same way as in geometry and analysis'. In his own quaint words, 'If controversies were to arise there would be no more need of disputation between two philosophers than between two accountants. For it would suffice to take their pencils in their hands, to sit down to their slates, and to say to each other (with a friend as witness, if they liked): Let us calculate.' The idea, which is as old as philosophy[2] and is still current, is that it is possible to draw inferences about the world from the structure of language. The notion, which is shared with rationalism, is that the analysis of the meanings of words will yield knowledge of the nature of the objects denoted by the words. It is likely that this notion links up with vestiges of magical thinking still in the depths of our minds.

Wittgenstein's work made the linguistic morphology of philosophy show through more distinctly than ever before. Many general remarks he made about philosophy, usually in arresting and imaginative language, and a good deal of his actual work, changed our idea of what it is and what it can do. And it also began to change our opinion of its value. To go back for a moment to Moore, in lectures he gave in London in 1910–11 he stated: 'It seems to me that the most important and interesting thing that philosophers have tried to do is no less than this; namely: To give a general description of the *whole* of the Universe. . . .'[3] In the same lectures he declared that philosophy is not concerned with 'mere questions of words'. At that time it seems to have been a gratuitous thing to say, unless it served to fend off a growing suspicion within himself. Several years later he was led to remark: 'It seems to me very curious that language . . . should have grown up just as if it were expressly designed to mislead philosophers. . . .'[4] Wittgenstein, in many of the things he said, represented the philosopher as being in some way or other concerned with 'mere questions of words'. The picture he gives us is that of a person

---

[1] *Philosophical Papers*, p. 130.   [2] See Plato's *Cratylus*.
[3] *Some Main Problems of Philosophy* (London: George Allen & Unwin Ltd., 1953), p. 1.
[4] *Philosophical Studies*, p. 217.

whose intelligence has fallen under the bewitchment of language, someone who has got lost in its labyrinthian turnings and mistakes forms of expression for theories. The philosopher is, to use Wittgenstein's famous metaphor, a fly held captive in a fly bottle. The idea he gives us of the nature of philosophical problems is that they have their source in a confusion, the 'confusion that considers a philosophical problem as though it concerned a fact of the world instead of a matter of expression'.[1] In plain, unequivocal words he states: 'Philosophical problems are, of course, not empirical problems; they are solved, rather, by looking into the workings of our language. . . .'[2] But a philosophical problem which is 'solved' by looking into the workings of language is *dissolved* by getting straight about usage. Much of Moore's work suggests that some philosophical views have their source in muddles of language. Wittgenstein's idea, or at least one of his ideas, is that all philosophical problems are the results of linguistic tangles and can be removed by our commanding 'a clear view of the use of our words'.[3] The philosopher thinks that philosophy will enable him to command a clear view of the universe; and Wittgenstein tells him that commanding a clear view of our use of words will show him that he has been suffering from a delusion induced by his misapprehension of the workings of language.

On Wittgenstein's account, or rather on one of his accounts, philosophers mistake an expression, because of its form, for a theory, and misconceive their objection to the expression to be an objection to a theory. And what will put them straight is correcting their mistaken idea about the actual use of the expression. To illustrate with an imaginary example, if someone were to insist that it is impossible to be *in* a mood, because a mood is not a kind of *thing*, like a house, the way to remove his mistaken notion that he was objecting to a factual proposition would be to make him see how the expression 'in a mood' works in our language, how its use differs from that of an expression like 'in a chamber'. To revert to Wittgenstein's metaphor again, language is the philosopher's fly bottle, from which he can be set free only by being set right about the actual use of expressions. This kind of procedure

---

[1] From notes taken by M. Masterman and A. Ambrose in the intervals between dictation of *The Blue Book*.
[2] *Philosophical Investigations*, p. 47.
[3] *Ibid.*, p. 49.

is part of the programme which some philosophers labelled 'Therapeutic Positivism'.

To some of us philosophy presented itself somewhat differently. It seemed that philosophers, despite their constant debating, their critiques, and defences, did not wish to be freed from their captivity in the fly bottle. Professor John Wisdom wrote: '. . . in philosophy the atmosphere reminds me of a house the inmates of which are forever debating whether, when, and how they could, or should, go out, but never in fact do go out. Professor Lazerowitz would be sure to ask them whether they really *want* to go out. What an insufferable question!'[1] It seems clear that, whatever the nature of his fly bottle may be, the philosopher has no wish to leave it. Indeed, he gives every indication of thinking it a most desirable dwelling. A well-known American philosopher has even declared, with apparent satisfaction, that each philosopher has his own, private fly bottle. One is reminded of Mrs Ladd-Franklin's letter to Bertrand Russell, in which she wrote that she was a solipsist and wondered why more people were not solipsists. A kind of abode she found desirable she was amiable enough to recommend to others. It is plain that the Platonist is content in his fly bottle and has no wish to be removed from it, nor does the nominalist from his; neither do the idealists, realists, sceptics, etc. etc., wish to be ousted from theirs. However much they may appear to try to free other philosophers from their fly bottles, they give every sign of wishing to remain unmolested in their own: a removal is an eviction, rather than a liberation.

An important recent view, which has one of its sources in Wittgenstein, implies that philosophical theories are really linguistic statements about accepted usage, which are formulated in language used to express propositions about the world. On this view a false philosophical theory misdescribes usage and a philosophical problem is a problem as to what actual usage is. But considerations similar to those which show that a philosophical problem is not about a fact of the world also show that it is not about a fact of the language in which the problem is stated. The things which particularly demanded explanation were what might be called the *central enigmas of philosophy*, not only of metaphysics but of every part of philosophy, formal logic, for the most part, being an exception. These enigmas are the endlessness of philo-

[1] Foreword to *The Structure of Metaphysics*.

sophical disagreements, which after hundreds of years still hold no promise of final resolution, and the total absence of any established result, however minor. The explanation that forced itself on us was not that a philosopher misconstrues language, but that under the influence of likenesses and unlikenesses in the functioning of terminology he unconsciously *changes* language. The emendations he effects are presented in a form of speech which produces the vivid, if delusive, impression that he is announcing a theory about a feature of reality. On this account, we can understand why recourse to an examination of non-linguistic fact would not be relevant to the solution of a philosophical problem. The problem is not about matter of fact. This explains why, for example, the questions as to whether motion is real and whether abstract entities exist could be argued endlessly, with no one's experience being different from anyone else's. And we can also understand why recourse to an examination of linguistic usage, and why getting a clear view of the workings of our language, does not succeed in settling a disagreement between philosophers. On the present account, actual usage is no more in question than matter of non-linguistic fact. That is why calling attention to the use of the word 'motion' to describe states of things does not resolve the dispute over the 'reality' of motion. The picture that comes into focus of the nature of philosophical activity is that of a kind of verbal theatre, the actors in which are artfully trumped up expressions and the backdrop of which is ordinary, unaltered language. The reality behind the intriguing intellectual illusion that the statements of philosophy reveal cosmic truths is artificially stretched or contracted or rejected terminology.

Now, one thing which conspicuously stood in need of explanation is the philosopher's attachment to his position, an attachment which is charged with emotion. The explanation of this was found with the help of psychoanalytic concepts. The general explanation is that in addition to the intellectual illusions the philosopher engineers with his manipulation of terminology his utterances give expression to unconscious fantasies. As is well known, an unconscious fantasy, like a dream, functions as the substitutive gratification of a wish, and cannot easily be given up. And it seems hardly a speculation to think that it is the need for his fantasy which makes a philosopher dupe to his own verbal legerdemain; it is this need which holds him captive in his fly bottle.

To sum up, a philosophical theory may be described as a structure in depth, whose major part lies below the surface of his conscious awareness where it is safe from the prying eye of scientific curiosity. One part of the structure is a statement containing an ordinary term which has undergone a non-workaday alteration, that is, an expression which is not recognized as a piece of academically retailored language. Another part is a conscious but false impression, created by the statement: this is that the statement makes a claim about a phenomenon. And still another component of the structure is a fantasy, or cluster of fantasies, which the statement expresses for the unconscious region of the mind.

By means of an appropriately altered piece of language the philosopher creates an illusion for the conscious part of the mind, the illusion of discovering a truth about ultimate reality, and at the same time he effects an inner consolation for himself. Ch. I, verse 1 of the Gospel according to St John reads, 'In the beginning was the Word'; and it can indeed be said that the Word has lost none of its ancient, magical power. The philosopher, the Titan of the Word, knows how to bemuse his own intellect, as well as ours, by means of the magic which is hidden in language. Philosophy, we may say, is the bewitchment of the mind by the art of hidden gerrymandering with terminology.

To illustrate the view in a concrete way, consider Hume's celebrated 'discovery' that causation is nothing more than the constant conjunction of independent occurrences. This claimed finding is represented as being the result of an empirical examination of an omnipresent phenomenon everyone takes for granted. In language that is appropriate to a scientific investigation, he invites us to 'turn our eyes' to occurrences which, to all appearances, are instances of causation and to look with proper care, whereupon we shall satisfy ourselves that we have been taking a mirage for the real thing. It turns out, however, that the mirage is produced by words and not by the world. This can be seen from the following consideration.

In general, anyone who says, 'x is not really ϕ; it only appears to be', implies that he knows what it would be like for x really to be ϕ. Read literally, his words imply that he can say what it is that x lacks, which if possessed by x would make it ϕ. And in saying that x only appears to have ϕ he implies that the appearance pictures x as having what it in fact lacks. Further, he implies that he can *identify* what the appearance pictures that is not to be found in the reality. If he is unable to do this, then whatever it is that he wishes to convey by his words, he is not telling us that x only appears to our senses to be ϕ. He is using an ordinary form of speech to say something else than what his words naturally suggest. And, indeed, it turns out that a philosopher is not using language in the ordinary way when he declares, for example, 'water is not heated by fire; it only appears to be. If we use our eyes with care we shall see that all that really happens is that water heats *of itself*, independently of the presence of fire.' For if we question him, we find that he cannot describe a circumstance which, if it obtained, would make him grant that fire is the cause of the water heating, that it heats water in reality and not only in appearance. He cannot, in general, say what is required to make an occurrence one in which a causal transaction takes place, and therefore cannot say what the feature is whose absence makes him deny that causation occurs. This means that he cannot *identify* anything *in the appearance* of a causal transaction which pictures a possible reality. Externally, the philosopher's talk is the talk of appearance and reality, but the fact is that he only pantomimes such talk. His use of language, whether mistaken or contrived, is not to describe a phenomenon.

Once it is seen that the philosopher is not using his words to express an experiential proposition, viz. the words, 'Nothing is the productive cause of anything else; causation is no more than the constant conjunction of independent occurrences', it is natural to think he is using them to make a statement about causal terminology. Construed as verbal in import, they are to the following effect: The phrase 'x is the cause of y' appears to mean 'y is brought about by x', but in fact the phrase is used in the language to mean 'y regularly occurs with x'. The causal sceptic seems to be making a threefold claim:

(1) 'x is cause of y' does not mean 'the occurrence of y depends on the occurrence of x';
(2) 'Dependent occurrence' has no descriptive use in the language;
(3) 'x is cause of y' means 'y regularly occurs with x'.

Taking the sceptic to be stating the accepted meanings of terminology, he strikes us as somehow having got a wrong notion about the use of causal language. He appears to have the queer idea that 'causation' *means* 'constant fortuitous conjunction'. But his use of language for the everyday purpose of communication makes it evident that he knows better, that he is aware of the linguistic fact that 'x is cause of y' does not mean 'y regularly but accidentally occurs with x'. It is unplausible to suppose him to be labouring under a mere verbal misapprehension, a misapprehension which does not intrude itself into his normal use of language and from which he cannot be moved by our calling his special attention to it. If we look closely at his putative threefold claim, a peculiarity emerges which suggests the conclusion that he is not misdescribing language, but rather is in some way changing it. It is easy to see that the expression 'independent occurrences' has a use in ordinary speech only because 'dependent occurrences' is an expression which describes actual or conceivable states of affairs. If 'dependent occurrences' were deprived of its use, without some sort of linguistic reparation being made, the expression 'independent occurrences' would lose its use: it would no longer have its descriptive function in the language. To think that 'dependent' has no application to occurrences commits one to thinking that the descriptive force of 'independent occurrences' is identical with that of 'occurrences'. For if 'dependent' did not apply to occurrences, 'independent' would not serve to distinguish between kinds of occurrences and would not have its present place in the language. In Emerald City where the only colour is green there would be no word for green; for the word 'green' has a use only when it serves to distinguish amongst colours, and it does this kind of work only if provision is made in the language for its use in expressions of the form 'this is not green'.

It is unnecessary to go into further reasons for thinking that the causal sceptic is not making a mistake about the use of language. The unavoidable alternative is that he has unwittingly re-edited language. To put the matter shortly, what has happened is that the word 'independent' (Hume's term is 'loose and separate') has been artificially stretched, by fiat, so as to apply to all occurrences, dependent as well as independent. Parenthetically, it is to be remarked that the everyday term remains unchanged and retains even for the philosopher its ordinary use in our language. No philosopher is a reformer of language. He introduces us to the stretched use of the word only in order to create the illusion that he is presenting a theory about the way the world works. This seems to be the correct conclusion to draw from the fact that he is *not* making a mistake about language and that the use he makes of language does give rise to the idea that he is pronouncing a view about the way things happen. Undoubtedly there is more to the view than has been brought out here, more than just a piece of academically changed language and an illusion that is bound up with it. It is a creation of the mind and must, we are compelled to think, serve a psychical need. Like a dream, a painting, and a poem it undoubtedly caters to an unconscious wish. We may permit ourselves a guess at one of the fantasies linked with causal scepticism. When I was a student one of my philosophy professors declared in a classroom lecture that if he were the lawyer for the defence in a murder trial he would bring forward Hume's arguments against the proposition that one thing can by an action produce a change in another thing. No one, of course, except a professor in a 'philosophic moment', would dream of using Hume's arguments in a court of law, but in dreams things work differently. In a dream, or in unconscious fantasy, Hume's arguments may well play the role of a defence against an inner accusation.

Let us consider another philosophical position, one which belongs to the rationalist rather than the empiricist tradition: the position, namely, that relations are unreal, or to express it in the words of its most famous advocate, 'our experience, where relational, is not true'.[1] The claim that whatever involves relations is unreal leads to the mystical conclusion that the world of space and time is an 'impossible illusion'[2] and that ultimate reality is an undifferentiated something which cannot adequately be grasped in thought. In Bradley's words, '. . . a relational way of thought—any one that moves by the machinery of terms and relations—must give appearance, and not truth. . . . Our intellect, then, has been condemned to confusion and bankruptcy, and the reality has been left outside uncomprehended.'[3] Briefly put, the argument for this view, whose profound appeal can be explained only by supposing that it connects up with material in the depths of the mind, goes as follows. Where there is a plurality of terms, i.e. a

---

[1] F. H. Bradley, *Appearance and Reality* (London: George Allen & Unwin Ltd., 1920), p. 34.
[2] *Ibid.*, p. 30.   [3] *Ibid.*, pp. 33–4.

H

number of things or a thing and its properties or a collection of properties, there are relations between them. Now a relation is *something*, not nothing, and is, therefore, itself a term. Hence a relation, R, between terms is a term which must be related by a new relation, R', to its terms, etc. without possible end. Thus, a plurality of terms implies relations between the terms, which nevertheless cannot relate them. For a relation to hold, an infinite regress of relations would have to be consummated; and this implies a final relation, i.e. a relation that is a term but is not itself related to its terms. This is self-contradictory; therefore, whatever involves relations is unreal.

Different philosophers have reacted differently to this view, and one important philosopher even rejected it with the air of dismissing a mistake too gross and transparent to deserve serious consideration. Bradley and his followers were, of course, not stupid, nor incapable of recognizing a mistake once it was pointed out to them. Indeed, Bradley was a subtle and original metaphysical thinker; and anyone who rejects his argument as grossly mistaken has on his hands the task of explaining why the mistake is not, from the beginning, plain to those who accept the argument, and why they cannot be made to see that the 'mistake' *is* a mistake. If he does not feel the need to seek for an explanation, or is satisfied with one that is overeasy or frivolous, it only means that he is playing the same kind of game as his opponent, a language game in which a holiday use of an expression is in contest. As in the causation example, the putative mistake is not transparent to the philosopher who makes it, because it is *not* a mistake. It is a non-pragmatic re-editing of terminology. And it is rejected as a mistake by the critic (who does nothing more scientific than resist a verbal innovation) because with the language of truth and falsity he, like his adversary, helps conceal the nature of the philosophical controversy.

The philosophical sentence 'Relational wholes are self-contradictory and exist only as delusive appearances', unlike the nonphilosophical sentence 'The sun does not really revolve around the earth, it only appears to do so', is not used to state a factual claim about what exists and what does not exist. Wittgenstein said that 'we could not *say* of an "unlogical" world how it would look';[1] and it requires no complicated reasoning to see

---

[1] *Tractatus Logico-Philosophicus*, 3.031.

that there could not be the sensible appearance of a self-contradictory state of affairs. If there could be, we should be able to say how an 'unlogical' world would look: *it would look like its appearance*. But there cannot be a self-contradictory appearance any more than there can be a self-contradictory reality. This is particularly easy to see in the present case: if being relational is self-contradictory, then the appearance of a relational whole will itself involve differentiation and relations and be self-contradictory. It will be prevented from existing by what prevents the corresponding reality from existing. But the philosopher who says 'Relational states of affairs are self-contradictory and exist only in appearance' does not deny, nor does he wish to deny, the existence of the 'appearances'. His words are not intended to go against any fact.

Neither is it correct to take the metaphysician of the non-relational One as stating, in an oblique idiom, a proposition about the intelligible use of relation-terminology. Contrary to the construction so-called philosophers of ordinary language might place on his declaration, the import of his words cannot with any plausibility be interpreted as declaring that such terms as 'between', 'younger than', and 'to the left of' have no use in the language and that such expressions as 'Saturn is between the earth and Jupiter' and 'Heidegger is younger than Bertrand Russell' are devoid of descriptive sense. For he uses relation-words correctly in his own talk and responds with understanding to their use by others. There is no doubt that if he were asked whether the sentence 'Heidegger is younger than Russell' makes descriptive sense, he would react with surprise that such a question should be put to him and would say that of course it does. This shows that his philosophical utterance is not to be construed as making a factual claim about the actual use of terminology.

If we look with care at the argument for the statement that relations imply infinite regresses and hence are unreal, we can, I think, dispel enough of the vebal fog to see what the view comes to. We shall be able to see how a contradiction is *imported* into terminology that is free from contradiction, and how the delusive impression is created that a proposition is being advanced which denies the reality of ubiquitous features of the world. The gist of the argument is that the existence of two or more terms implies a relation between them, in Bradley's words, 'if there is any difference, then that implies a relation between them';[1] but a relation is *something* and hence is itself a term which must be related to its terms. Thus an infinite regress is generated. It should be noticed that the ordinary use of the word 'relation' does not dictate the application of the word 'related' to whatever the phrase 'different from or other than' applies to; it is intelligible English to say, in some cases, that *x* and *y* bear no relation to each other. The statement that difference implies a relation has to be understood as introducing an artificially stretched use of the term 'related', a use in which it applies to whatever the term 'different from' applies to. The central point of the argument, however, is that relations, since they are not nothing, count as terms, or to put it less ambiguously, count as *things* or *objects*. The metaphysical claim that relations are objects, like the more familiar Platonic theory that properties of things are themselves kinds of things, abstract entities, requires extended explanation.[2] Without going into this here, it will be realized that the rules for the use of 'object' do not stipulate the application of 'object' to whatever 'relation' denotes: e.g. the sentence 'Betweenness is an object' does not exhibit a correct use of the word 'object'. The philosophical assertion that relations are things, instead of being based on a mistaken idea as to the actual use of 'thing' or 'object', has to be construed as introducing an academically stretched use of the word, a use in which it applies to what is denoted by relation-terms. To argue that relations are not *nothing* is a way of pointing out a similarity between relation-terms and *substantives*, which is, that relation-words can be changed into abstract nouns, 'between' into 'betweenness', etc.; and this similarity is used to justify reclassifying relation-terms with substantives. The philosophical statement, 'Relation-expressions are substantives', when formulated in the non-verbal mode of speech, becomes 'Relations are things (or objects)'.

It can now be seen how the regress of relations derives from a stretched use of 'relation' and a stretched use of 'thing': the expression 'stand to each other in a relation' is made, by fiat, to apply to whatever the expression 'different things' applies to, and the word 'thing', or 'term', is made, by fiat, substitutable for 'relation' and relation-expressions. In this way a contradictory

---

[1] *Appearance and Reality*, p. 29.
[2] See 'The Existence of Universals' in *The Structure of Metaphysics*.

regress is manufactured. The ordinary use of 'relation' and 'term' involves no regress of relations which require relations in order to relate. The *altered* use of these terms does involve such a contradictory regress; and there is no doubt that the alterations in terminology were made (unconsciously, in the way in which dreams are made) for the purpose of manufacturing the contradiction. The contradiction, in turn, is used to justify a further retailoring of terminology: the word 'appearance' is stretched so that it applies, in a purely formal and empty way, to phenomena to which 'relational' applies. The philosophical sentence 'Whatever involves relations is unreal and exists only as appearance' gives rise to the idea that it is used to declare the insubstantiality of states of affairs everyone takes for granted, but in fact it presents an academically contracted application of 'real' and a stretched use of 'appearance'. An *ersatz* contradiction is made to justify a non-workaday re-editing of 'real' and 'appearance'.

The metaphysical game that is being played with the words 'relation', 'thing', 'appearance', 'real' consists of concealed manœuvring with terminology which, because of the form of speech in which the game is played, creates the vivid illusion that a remarkable claim about phenomena is being argued for. And it is hard to think that the game is played solely for the intellectual effect it produces and that it does not link up with deeper material in the mind. It seems, indeed, reasonable to think that the game with terminology functions for the philosopher in a special way. The overtones of the view and the atmosphere surrounding it make it likely that with his renovated terminology the philosopher expresses his emotional rejection of the world. The sentence, 'Relational states of affairs are unreal', may well have the underlying meaning: the world for me is unimportant and I wish to detach myself from it. When talk about the unreality of relations is joined with mystifying talk about 'unbroken, simple feeling', it is permissible to guess that the words, 'the relational is mere appearance, only the non-relational, i.e. "unbroken, simple feeling", is real' express the echo of a wish to return to an early state in our pre-history. This state, described so poetically by mystics and metaphysicians, has been explained in the following passage in *The Need to Believe, The Psychology of Religion*:[1]

[1] Mortimer Ostow and Ben-Ami Scharfstein (New York: International Universities Press, Inc., 1954), p. 122.

'The state that is attained by a mystic is a state of euphoria or ecstasy in which the outer world seems to vanish and the self to stretch out, lose its boundaries, and engulf everything. This is simultaneously a projection of the self into the whole environment and an introjection of the whole environment into the self. It is a return to what some psychoanalysts call the "oceanic reunion", the world of the fed, satisfied baby on the delicious edge of sleep. All one's pleasure impulses are withdrawn from external objects and located inside oneself. And the variegated responses of the mind are narrowed and merged until they approximate the semiconscious, slumbrous, undifferentiated pleasure of the baby immersed in the uniform ocean of his feeling.'

6

EMPIRICISM AND RATIONALISM

The two major traditions in philosophy, empiricism and rationalism, are, in Hans Reichenbach's words, 'as old as the history of philosophy', but their rival claims have not yet been adjudicated in a manner acceptable to all knowledgeable philosophers, nor is there any prospect of this being effected by any of the procedures available to philosophers. About the history of philosophy itself, Reichenbach has raised a serious and troubling question: he said, '. . . this story of ever renewed attempts—what is it good for? Why should we teach it if there is no outcome, no recognized truth?'[1] In connection with this question he gave expression to a complaint which a good many scientists and thoughtful laymen have made and which deserves more than the casual notice it has received from philosophers: 'The sciences have developed a general body of knowledge, carried by universal recognition, and he who teaches a science does so with the proud feeling of introducing his students into a realm of well-established truth. . . . Imagine a scientist who were to teach electronics in the form of a report on the views of different physicists, never telling his students what *are* the laws governing electronics. . . . Why must the philosopher forego a generally accepted philosophy?'[2] The contrast between the progress of the sciences and the poverty of philosophy is so striking as to cry out for an explanation, an explanation which will tell us why the philosopher can never reach what he constantly strives for, why, to use Kant's phrase, his 'Sisyphian stone' can never be brought securely to rest at the top. In this essay the primary purpose will be to throw light on the question as to why philosophers have had to forego a generally accepted resolution of the controversy between empiricism and rationalism, that is, what it is in the very nature of the controversy that makes permanent irresolution possible.

It is pertinent to remark at this point that the possibility does

[1] 'Rationalism and Empiricism: An Enquiry into the Roots of Philosophical Error,' *The Philosophical Review*, Vol. LVII, p. 330.
[2] *Ibid.*, p. 331.

not naturally occur to anyone that, unlike physics which is able to report what the laws governing electronics *are*, philosophy has no truths to report *because of what it is*. It does not naturally occur to anyone that philosophy has throughout its history conveyed neither truths nor falsehoods because its statements are not of the true or false kind. Reichenbach's dissatisfaction with the long standing condition of philosophy did not seem to have suggested this possibility to him: it did not deter him from stating what the 'error' in the fundamental thesis of rationalism is, namely, 'the error of identifying knowledge with mathematical knowledge'.[1] And it goes without saying that those who have noticed nothing strange or disconcerting about the condition of philosophy will identify with assurance mistakes in views opposing their own. According to W. H. B. Joseph empiricists 'wrongly suppose that we cannot by thinking discover the nature of anything that we have not perceived'.[2] Bertrand Russell, on the other hand, has said that 'Nothing can be known to *exist* except by the help of experience'[3] and that in going against this point of view rationalists make a basic mistake. These and other critiques and counter-critiques have been, as they continue to be, perfectly well known by all sides to the dispute; but, as Reichenbach implies, they have not had the effect of settling issues.

There is a considerable variety of forms of both rationalism and empiricism; but one fundamental divergence between the two traditions is, to put it roughly, centred on the role of the senses in the investigation of reality. The empiricist tradition would seem on the whole to be an elaboration of the proposition that sense-observation is necessary to determine what exists and that the senses are generally reliable and internally correctible, i.e. correctible by the continued use of the senses. Empedocles has summed up this point of view admirably in one of his Fragments: 'But come, examine by every means each thing how it is clear, neither putting greater faith in anything seen than in what is heard, nor in a thundering sound than in the clear assertion of the tongue, nor keep from trusting any of the other members in which there lies a means to knowledge, but know each thing in the way it is

---

[1] 'Rationalism and Empiricism: An Enquiry into the Roots of Philosophical Error', *The Philosophical Review*, Vol. LVII, p. 335.

[2] *An Introduction to Logic* (Oxford University Press, 1916), p. 193.

[3] *The Problems of Philosophy*, 17th Impression (Oxford University Press, 1943), p. 116.

clear.' Empiricism, which seems to be the position adopted by common sense as well as by the natural sciences, has to be understood as being in part a defence of the senses as a 'means to knowledge' against the threat or the challenge posed by rationalism. Thus, for example, A. J. Ayer has called attention to the possibility of empiricism being 'obliged to give way to rationalism' and has expressed the need of 'taking away the support on which rationalism rests'.[1] As against empiricism, which, on the surface certainly, expresses its confidence in the senses, the rationalist tradition is characterized by what may be called a 'philosophical distrust' of the senses; and in the extreme case of philosophers like Parmenides and F. H. Bradley, sense-observation is rejected altogether as a possible means of acquiring knowledge of reality. Other rationalists, like Descartes and Leibniz, who did not adopt the extreme position, thought it necessary to try to discover, *by reason*, a guarantee of the reliability of the senses. In the one case, the claim is advanced that reflection on concepts, philosophical analysis, shows the senses to be capable only of acquainting us with delusions; in the other case the use of the senses is thought to stand in need of justification by some sort of *a priori* demonstration, one into which no sense-evidence enters and which will show that the testimony of the senses may be counted as evidence.

The disagreement between rationalists and empiricists about the senses is, to all appearances, a disagreement as to what the facts are with regard to sight, touch, taste, etc. According to one well-known rationalistic claim, looking, listening, and tasting are to be dismissed altogether, not because they are not sufficiently reliable but because their use only makes us dupe to illusions: 'Heed not the blind eye, the resounding ear, nor yet the tongue, but bring to this great debate the test of reason.'[2] This position may be put in the following way: It seems to everyone that by looking, listening, touching, etc., we are made aware of the existence of things and of what their properties are, but the 'test of reason' shows that what looking and touching represent to us as being the case is actually no more than phantasmagoria. The senses are exposed by argument as revealing to us what is self-contradictory: what the senses disclose is 'self-contradictory appearance', to use one of Bradley's phrases, which therefore cannot be real. Reasoning on concepts is declared to be the appropriate method for determining the

---

[1] *Language, Truth and Logic*, second edition, p. 73.   [2] Parmenides.

existence and behaviour of things. This view led Ayer to say that if rationalism is a correct doctrine, 'we shall have to accept it as a mysterious inexplicable fact that our thought has this power to reveal to us authoritatively the nature of objects which we have never observed'.[1]

The other rationalistic position regarding sense-perception seems equally to make a claim with regard to the facts of sense-perception, but a less radical one. According to it, we cannot, by looking, tasting, feeling, etc. get to know whether we are actually seeing, feeling, or tasting things or only seeming to see, feel, or taste them, and thus cannot by sense-perception determine whether there are things. An independent proof that 'corporeal things exist'[2] is used by some philosophers as a guarantee that there is a real world of things which correspond to our perceptions and that it is not the case that the senses, by their very nature, delude us. This argument is usually linked with the view that the testimony of the senses can make the existence of a thing increasingly probable but can never make it certain. Mathematics, where a kind of certainty is reached that is unobtainable in the perception of things, is considered the model of knowledge. It is Reichenbach's opinion that the correct way for empiricism to meet the challenge of 'the fundamental thesis of rationalism, according to which genuine knowledge has to be as reliable as mathematical knowledge'[3] is to allow that in sense-perception we can never attain certainty but to deny that it cannot give us 'genuine knowledge'. It is interesting to note in this connection that Plato held that we can have opinion only regarding things in the physical world, and some modern philosophers fancy that by calling opinion 'genuine knowledge' they provide empiricism with a solid foundation. It is difficult to resist the thought that for some people a modest flower can be made to smell the sweeter by calling it a rose.

G. E. Moore did not settle for this sort of compromise nor did he accept this way of meeting rationalism's challenge. He maintained that in certain circumstances it would be absurd for a person to express himself in a way which implied that it was not certain, or not absolutely certain, that an indicated state of affairs exists. He wrote: '. . . I should have been guilty of absurdity if, under the circumstances, I had *not* spoken positively about these things, if I

[1] *Op. cit.*, p. 73.   [2] Descartes, *Meditation* VI.   [3] *Op. cit.*, p. 335.

had spoken about them at all. Suppose that now, instead of saying "I am inside a building", I were to say "I *think* I am inside a building, but perhaps I'm not: it's not *certain* that I am", or instead of saying "I have got some clothes on", I were to say "I think I've got some clothes on, but it's just possible that I haven't". Would it not sound rather ridiculous for me now, under these circumstances, to say "I *think* I've got some clothes on" or even to say "I not only think I have, I know that it is very likely indeed that I have, but I can't be quite sure"?"[1]

It cannot fail to be noticed that Moore's words throw the view advocated by Reichenbach into an unexpected light. It is natural to think of the view as being about the *nature* of knowledge, or about the nature of genuine knowledge, but Moore's words represent it as being in some way about language, about the proper use of terminology. The absurdity, if it is an absurdity, to which he refers is linguistic, an absurdity which results from a misuse of the words 'probable' and 'certain'. Russell on one occasion related an exchange that took place between him and Reichenbach which helps bring out this point. They were in Los Angeles watching a solar eclipse taking place and discussing the view that a matter of fact can be known with more or less probability but not with certainty. Russell wished to see whether he could, in a practical situation outside the classroom, move Reichenbach from his position; and while the moon approached the sun Russell repeatedly asked the question, 'Is it certain now that there will be an eclipse?' The answer each time was, 'No, it is not certain; it is only probable, but more probable than it was a moment ago'. When the eclipse finally occurred Russell asked, with the encouraging tone of voice used in teaching children, 'Isn't it certain *now* that there is an eclipse?' The answer was, 'No, not certain, but now it is *very* probable that there is an eclipse'. A mathematician present could not refrain from a whispered comment to me: 'I don't care what he calls it; I call it certain.' Moore would have said that Reichenbach was mistaken about the use certain terms have in the language. What emerges from this variety of opinions is that there are at least three constructions that can be placed on the view that our knowledge of things has a probability which always falls short of certainty. One is that it is about the nature and limits of our knowledge of things; another is that it is a false description of the

[1] *Philosophical Papers*, pp. 227–8.

proper use of 'probable' and 'certain'; and still another is that it presents an arbitrarily changed use of 'probable' and 'certain', a stretched use of the first and a contracted use of the second. It seems strange that a familiar philosophical position should be open to such different interpretations, that, so to speak, it should be capable of presenting such different faces to people. It becomes a mystery as to what philosophers are debating, whether the truth-value of a theory about our knowledge, the correct use of terminology, or arbitrarily introduced alterations in the use of words. Even apart from this, if we step back and look at the empiricist-rationalist controversy from some distance, we may quite well become mystified by philosophers who 'reject' sense-observation and also by those who think that the senses need some sort of external justification. And if we think on it for a moment, we may also find ourselves at a loss as to what to make of a philosopher who says that we *can*, and frequently *do*, have knowledge with certainty of the existence of things.

Reichenbach speaks of empiricists being 'committed to the challenge of rationalism', as if there is only one. But in fact there are at least two challenges, one of which, perhaps, is dismissed by most philosophers as too obviously false to count as a serious challenge. Nevertheless it cannot be neglected, for in philosophy what is obviously false to some is undeniably true to others. It might, conceivably, even turn out that the two challenges, which look very different from each other, are underneath actually the same; and it is certainly pertinent to investigate this possibility. In agreement with Heraclitus, we may say that in philosophy it is not impossible for opposites to be one and the same.

What may be called the moderate challenge to empiricism, as against the extreme position that our senses can only delude us, is a view which consists of two propositions: one, the proposition that the use of the senses in the investigation of reality stands in need of justification by an *a priori* argument, and two, the proposition that sense-observation can increase the probability of a statement about a thing but can never render the statement certain. It will be important to determine how each of these propositions is related to the extreme rationalistic view, and then to try to see what the extreme view comes to. To express this in a more concrete way, the object will be first to determine how the sentences 'The proposition that looking and feeling inform us of the existence of things is a proposition which requires justification by reason' and 'Looking and feeling can at most make the existence of a thing probable' stand to the sentence 'Looking and feeling can only delude us'. And it will, of course, be important to try to see what it comes to to say that looking and feeling can only reveal false appearances to us and that only by thought can the 'truth of reality' be discovered.

The notion that the use of the senses to obtain knowledge of the existence of things, whether certain or only probable, requires some sort of nonexperimental justification seems utterly different from the notion that the senses acquaint us with mere appearance, that we never by their use perceive what really exists. And the suggestion that (by one line of reasoning) the first notion can be shown to reduce to, or at least to imply, the second notion carries with it a highly paradoxical air. But in philosophy it is not a novel thing to discover a new paradox in a familiar view; the surprising thing is that more paradoxes have not been brought out into the light of day.[1] The notion that sense-observation stands in need of justification implies the possibility that what the ordinary man as well as the scientist takes for granted is just a superstition. But, against the suggestion that this notion implies the Parmenidean dismissal of the senses, the notion seems also to imply the possibility that it is not a superstition, that scientists and ordinary people are correct in thinking that by looking, smelling, feeling, and the like, we can satisfy ourselves that we are seeing a house, feeling a piece of cloth, or tasting an apple. It turns out, however, that what the notion actually implies does not correspond to what it is natural to suppose it implies.

It is clear that a philosopher who takes the position that the use of the senses requires a kind of justification which is not to be found in sense-experience itself, i.e. an *a priori* justification, implies that no amount of looking, no matter how carefully done and no matter how carefully checked by the use of other senses, can ever justify our saying that we are actually *seeing* an apple, as against its only appearing to us that we are seeing it. He implies that there is, *in principle*, no way of determining by sense-experience that we are seeing a thing, and not only seeming to see one, feeling a thing, and not only seeming to feel it, etc. For if the philosopher thought that experience itself is capable of justifying his stating that he

[1] See 1, 'Paradoxes'.

does actually see a thing, he would not think that a claim to be seeing a thing stood in need of nonexperiential justification. The philosopher, in taking this position, implies that we do not know what it would be like to see a thing, as against its only seeming to us that we are seeing one. He thus can be said to hold that it is impossible to *see* things, or more generally, to perceive them. For he implies that a perception-expression like 'sees an apple' does not describe what can be imagined or conceived, any more than does the expression 'tastes the size of an apple'. To put it differently, a philosopher who argues that we cannot, in any *conceivable* circumstance, by continued looking (along with feeling, tasting, etc.) determine that we are *seeing* an apple holds by implication that it is inconceivable, or impossible, that we should see things, and also, of course, that we should feel, smell, and taste them. For the proposition that it is possible, theoretically, for us to see things, and not just seem to see them, entails the conceivability of determining that we are seeing them, and not only seeming to see them. We are thus led back to the view that the senses do not reveal reality to us.

Few, if any, philosophers have been satisfied by Moore's proof of external objects, a proof, it will be remembered, which consists of his holding up his hand for all to see and, with an appropriate gesture, pronouncing the words, 'Here is a hand'. It must be granted that a curious air surrounds Moore's proof, but one thing his form of proof implies is that our senses are capable of revealing the existence of external objects to us and that by our senses, and nothing else, we can get to know that apples, and chairs, and hands exist. But anyone who maintains, as Descartes did, that sense-experience does not contain in itself the possibility of providing justification for a claim to be perceiving a physical thing implies that the nature of the senses is such as to preclude perceiving things. Zeno's argument against motion implies that, in presenting us with the appearance of bodies being in motion, sight is by its nature delusive, in at least one respect. And the Lockean distinction between primary and secondary qualities implies that in representing things as having colour and odour our senses deceive us. A philosopher who maintains that observation needs some sort of general justification indicates that it is the *nature* of the senses to reveal no more than 'mere appearance'. We constantly believe ourselves to be seeing and feeling physical things; but it follows from his position that we are deluded: we fancy that we see and feel apples and teacups, but just the same it only seems to us that we see and feel them. In Descartes' words, we have 'a very strong inclination to believe that those ideas are conveyed to [us] by corporeal things'; but, on the view that the use of the senses requires justification not forthcoming from sense-experience itself, this belief turns out to be a myth. The Cartesian type of justification, which is based on an *a priori* argument professing to demonstrate the existence of corporeal causes of our sense-contents, will not do the job assigned to it. One consideration, apart from other perhaps more important considerations, shows this.

In an ordinary, nonphilosophical case in which a physical cause is assigned to an occurrence, it is in principle, in conception if not practically, possible to discover the cause by an investigation which employs sense-observation. If, for example, we attribute a physical cause to an image on a screen and wish to learn how it is brought about, we can, after locating the projector which produces it, examine the machine and see its various parts and how they fit together. We see the projector in the way in which we see the image on the screen. In a nonphilosophical case in which something is said to be brought into existence by a corporeal cause, we know what it would be like to perceive the cause—even when it is beyond our physical powers to get to it. In the usual way of speaking, it is perfectly intelligible to say that we see or feel the corporeal cause of a sensory event, for instance, the chair in the next room which made an unpleasant, banging sound when it fell over. Thus, Moore has pointed out that '. . . we do, in ordinary life, constantly talk of *seeing* such things [doors and fingers], and that, when we do so, we are neither using language incorrectly, nor making any mistake about the facts—supposing something to occur which never does in fact occur'.[1] In ordinary language, to say that we are 'perceiving, by sight or touch' or that we see the physical object which is the cause of a perceived occurrence is not to express what is in principle inconceivable.

The philosophical case in which a physical thing is said to be the cause of a sense-content is utterly different from the nonphilosophical case. Unlike the common notion that the physical cause of an observed effect is itself theoretically subject to being perceived, the idea which is implied by the Cartesian form of argument is

[1] *Philosophical Studies*, p. 226.

that the physical causes of observed effects are not themselves subject to being perceived; they do not fall within the purview of the senses. The corporeal things which 'convey' ideas or sense-contents to us are not themselves possible sense-contents, either to man or to God. They are the cause of whatever enters into perception, the cause of objects of sight, touch, taste, but cannot themselves enter into perception and become objects of sight, touch, and taste. On the Cartesian type of view, it is impossible to see corporeal things. And not only are our eyes blind to the world of things, God, if he is capable of perception, must also be blind to things. The senses are, by their very nature, such that physical reality is intangible to them.[1] It is a curious consequence of Descartes' position that God could not perceive his own creation. It is also curious that despite his devout conviction that God could not be a deceiver, Descartes' position implies that he is a deceiver: for built into us is a natural and 'very strong inclination' to believe that we do see and touch and smell things. Perhaps in the deeper recesses of his mind Descartes never gave up the possibility of a demon against which he sought reassurance by argument. By way of an aside, it may be observed that the unconscious does not relinquish its wishes nor lose its fears; and it would seem that the Abraham and Isaac story represents a fantasy that is capable of remarkable and subtle variations, as Descartes' philosophical notion of being threatened by a demon and saved by God would seem to show. Be this as it may, it would appear that the position of Descartes comes down to the stand Parmenides took against the senses: according to both philosophers we are deceived in thinking that we actually perceive things.

The outcome of the Reichenbach way of meeting the challenge of rationalism, on one line of reasoning, also turns out to be the Parmenidean position. According to Reichenbach, as well as many other philosophers, the correct and effective way to defend empiricism is to oppose 'the prejudice that mathematics is the prototype of all knowledge'.[2] The way to a 'consistent empiricism' is to 'interpret empirical knowledge in its own right',[2] and to do this, according to him, consists in holding that statements referring to physical objects or to physical occurrences can be rendered

---

[1] Or we may say that it is the nature of physical things that makes them intangible to the senses. It does not matter which we say.

[2] *Op. cit.*, p. 338.

probable to any degree we please, short of certainty. Empiricism can defend itself successfully against rationalism by maintaining that there is no 'absolutely reliable knowledge'[1] of things and that statements referring to physical reality are and must remain hypotheses.[2] The plain and immediate implication of this philosophical empiricist position is that it is possible to determine with a high degree of probability that we are perceiving a thing—tasting an orange or seeing a sheet of writing paper or feeling the top of a desk—but we can never make certain that we are actually perceiving a thing: it can never be more than a probable hypothesis that we are tasting an orange or seeing a sheet of writing paper. We can never, no matter how careful and protracted our observations are, obtain 'absolutely reliable knowledge' that we are seeing a sheet of paper and not merely seeming to see one, or feeling the top of a desk and its not merely seeming to us that we are feeling it. There always remains the possibility, which cannot be eliminated, that we do not see and feel things.

It will be recalled that two different linguistic interpretations of what this view comes to were mentioned earlier: Moore's interpretation which represents it as a misdescription of the use in the language of the words 'probable' and 'certain', and the further interpretation according to which the view introduces an altered use of these words. The natural way of looking at the view is to take it to be about the nature of our knowledge of things, and having nothing to do with usage, although it is evident that this way of looking at the view and the interpretation which represents it as being about the correct use of terminology are in some way bound up with each other. But considered ontologically, i.e. as about the nature and limits of our perceptual knowledge of things, the view implies that it is theoretically out of the question to get to know with complete certainty that we are seeing or feeling a material thing. It is possible to make the probability of a statement to the effect that I am seeing a sheet of paper amount 'almost to certainty', or make it 'nearly a certainty', but it is impossible to bring the probability up to certainty and change the status of the statement from that of a hypothesis to that of an established fact.

Philosophers who have adopted this view, whether to meet the challenge of rationalism or for some other reason, seem to have

[1] Reichenbach's phrase.   [2] A. J. Ayer's characterization.

I

failed to notice a point which is by no means inconspicuous or elusive. If, as is maintained, it is in principle impossible to render a statement certain, it is also in principle impossible to make it amount almost to certainty or to bring it as near certainty as we please. It is just as impossible to approach what cannot conceivably be reached as it is to come nearer to being in two different places simultaneously by constantly accelerating the motion from one place to the other and back again, etc. To speak of approaching what is not even theoretically conceivable is to speak of what is itself theoretically inconceivable. There is no hypothetical approaching or getting nearer where there is no conceivable arriving; and if we do not know what it would be like to attain a putative goal, we do not know what it would be like *to get nearer* to attaining the goal. Hence, if it were possible to make the probability of a proposition approach certainty, it would be possible, in theory at least, to make the proposition certain. It follows that the view that propositions referring to material things cannot be made absolutely certain implies that such propositions cannot be made probable to any degree whatever, however small.

The consequence is that it is out of the question to determine in any way whatever, either in fantasy or in fact, that we are perceiving a physical object rather than its only seeming to us that we are perceiving one. The implication, in other words, is that we do not know what it would be like, that we have no idea of what it would be, to determine in any way that we are reading a book or tasting a lump of sugar. The conclusion to be drawn from this is that it is impossible to perceive things, and thus that we do not perceive them. For if we could conceive ourselves to be seeing and tasting things, we could conceive ourselves coming to a decision on the basis of evidence that we are seeing and tasting things. If we knew what it was like to see and taste a lump of sugar, we would know what it is like to determine in some way or other that we were actually seeing and tasting it. And if the one is impossible, so is the other. Strange as it may appear, the view which, in Reichbach's opinion, is the correct empiricist answer to the rationalistic claim that genuine knowledge is to be obtained only in an *a priori* discipline, implies the extreme position of Parmenides. The senses, it turns out, are incapable of revealing physical reality to us: the eye is blind to books and tables, the ear deaf to the sounds made by things, etc. The world eludes perception, and by creating in us the impression that we see, feel, and hear things our senses make us their dupe.

In view of the fact that the extreme rationalistic position with respect to the senses lies buried in a widely held empiricist theory it is understandable why empiricists have not attempted to refute it in the standard way, by an argument. On the surface, the impression created is that the extreme position is not considered to be a serious challenge, apparently because it is thought to be so bizarre and obviously false. Empiricists have, of course, declared that sense-experience is required for obtaining information about things and have stated that rationalists were mistaken in believing that sense-experience is to be dispensed with in the pursuit of knowledge. But to pronounce a belief false is not the same as to produce an argument against it. Moreover, thinking the belief obviously false carries with it the need to explain how anyone could adopt it and continue to hold it. But empiricism, which now appears to be the Siamese twin of extreme rationalism, begins to be an equally mystifying view. We may wonder whether philosophical empiricism could survive the elimination of rationalism.

The extreme form of the fundamental rationalist tenet is, in Ayer's words, the view that 'thought is the only source of knowledge',[1] and this is coupled with the view that the senses are a source of deception only. Plato gave poetic expression to this twofold position in the *Phaedrus*, when Socrates is made to say: 'If we are ever to know anything absolutely, we must be free from the body and must behold the actual realities with the eye of the soul alone.' These two views, one about the senses and the other about the power of thought, though they are bound up with each other, have to be considered separately. And the question which needs to be investigated is whether they are the kind of views they appear to be, views as to what the senses and thought are capable of revealing to us about 'actual realities'. The claim that our senses are incapable of disclosing reality to us looks like the non-philosophical proposition that with the eye alone, unaided by a microscope, we cannot see bacteria. In some ways philosophers treat their claim as if it were on a footing with the nonphilosophical proposition.

It is hard to resist the idea that the sentence, 'Our senses can only present us with illusion, they are incapable of revealing

[1] *Op. cit.*, p. 73.

actual things to us', states a factual proposition about the limitations of the senses.[1] But to be convinced that it states no such proposition it is only necessary to attend to certain features attaching to the sentence. For one thing, it is to be noticed that a philosopher who asserts that we can neither see nor feel fountain pens and sheets of writing paper, or asserts that we do not *really* see or feel them, finds himself ruled out from being able to describe what it would be to see or feel them. A person who says that no one can see anything with closed eyes or that no one even with open eyes is able to see a mosquito at a distance of a mile, can say what it would be like to see an object with closed eyes and what it would be like to see a mosquito from a distance of a mile. He can imagine, and describe to others, what he says cannot be seen. It is the same with regard to a person who says, truly, that unlike the princess in the fairy tale, no one really can feel a pea underneath thirty mattresses. He can describe in words, or by other means, what he asserts cannot be. But the Parmenidean philosopher who announces that no one really sees or feels physical things is not in a comparable case: instead he is in the peculiar position of not being able to say what it would be like to perceive a physical thing, what it would be to see a sheet of writing paper or to feel a pen. He rules himself out from describing what would have to be present in a perception which would make it an instance of seeing or feeling a thing. He gives the impression of going against what everyone takes for fact and of declaring a common notion to be a superstition; but it is easily realized that the actual situation does not correspond to this impression. For since the philosopher is unable to say what a case of actually seeing a thing would be like, he is not to be construed as denying that what is normally taken to be a case of perceiving a thing is really a case of perceiving a thing. Despite the form of language he employs, he is not to be understood as making a factual statement about the limitations of the senses. His philosophical complaint does not

---

[1] *Vide* Descartes, who was 'almost deceived by the terms of ordinary language': '. . . I should conclude that I knew the wax by means of vision and not simply by the intuition of the mind; unless by chance I remember that, when looking from a window and saying I see men who pass in the street, I really do not see them, but infer that what I see is men, just as I say that I see wax. And yet what do I see from the window but hats and coats which may cover automatic machines? Yet I judge these to be men. And similarly solely by the faculty of judgment which rests in my mind, I comprehend that which I believed I saw with my eyes.' *Meditation* II.

refer to an inadequacy of sight or touch or taste, whatever else it may come to.

It is to be noticed, for another thing, that the reason given in support of his statement is that objects of the kind appropriate to our senses are *self-contradictory*, or, more accurately, that the concepts whose instances would be appropriate objects of sight and the other senses imply contradictions. The formula, which is contrary to the formula adopted by many mystics, is that whatever is self-contradictory is unreal and can exist only as 'mere appearance'. Thus the implied reason for holding that our senses are incapable of disclosing reality to us is that objects of sense do not exist. We cannot see mountains, books, chairs, and the like, because there are not any to be seen. Wittgenstein observed that you can look for a thief who does not exist, but you cannot hang a thief who does not exist. And the Parmenidean view might be summed up in the formula, you can think you see what does not exist but you cannot see what does not exist. In short, the Parmenidean investigator of the world is by implication holding that there is no perceiving trees and books, because, as his argument purports to show, books and trees do not exist. It only seems to us that we actually see and feel books and trees; but this is because we are taken in by tricks our senses constantly play on us. The eye is blind because there is nothing for it to see. What the view seems to come to is that concrete objects, which, if they existed, would be proper objects of perception, do not exist and thus that our senses acquaint us only with illusion. The things that really exist, the abstract entities which are grasped in thought, are intangible to the senses. Thus we may say that the eye is doubly blind: it cannot see what does not exist and it cannot see what does exist.

As before, it may be seen that the words 'The senses fail to disclose reality to us', when considered in conjunction with the kind of argument backing their claim, are not to be interpreted as expressing a factual proposition about the senses. In an ordinary circumstance in which, for example, we look into an empty drawer and say we see nothing, we can perfectly well imagine something in it which we are seeing. But there is no imagining ourselves seeing a self-contradictory thing in the drawer. It is *logically* impossible, not impossible as a matter of fact, for what is self-contradictory to exist; and it is logically impossible to perceive the self-contradictory. We fail to perceive a round billiard ball that is nevertheless a cube, not because such a billiard ball does not as a matter of fact exist, but because it is logically impossible for one to exist. The self-contradictory does not fail to exist as a matter of fact: for if it failed to exist as a matter of fact, then the self-contradictory *might* exist. The rationalistic contention of Parmenides, Bradley, and others that our senses do not reveal reality to us because sensible phenomena are self-contradictory and hence are unreal is no more a factual declaration about our senses than is the statement that we cannot see a two-dimensional globe.[1] It is easily seen that the further claim that we cannot perceive abstract entities, that we can neither smell, touch, nor see them, also is not a factual claim about the shortcomings of our senses: it is instead to the effect that is it logically impossible to perceive by the senses 'abstract entities' like triangularity and horseness.

The nature of logical impossibility, and its difference from a factual impossibility like that of disintegrating the moon by a sneeze, has been misrepresented in different ways by philosophers. One misrepresentation, which apparently has great appeal and is invariably in the background of philosophical thinking, pictures logical impossibility as an inflexible factual impossibility, an impossibility which we can never hope to change or circumvent. But it can be seen that the difference between the impossibility of disintegrating the moon by sneezing and the impossibility of a person running a mile in one second, staggering as it is, is altogether unlike the difference between the impossibility of drawing a five-sided circle and the impossibility of disintegrating the moon by sneezing. We can imagine or conceive the moon being disintegrated by a sneeze and a runner doing the mile in a second, but there is no imagining or conceiving someone drawing a five-sided circle. And this is not because our powers of imagination or conception are not up to imagining or conceiving what is described by the words[2] 'draws a five-sided circle' but because these words describe nothing to be imagined or conceived. They have no descriptive function in the language. It is noticing this feature of sentences which denote logical impossibilities, namely, that their

[1] This is why it does not matter whether, on the extreme rationalistic position, we say that it is the nature of sight which prevents us from seeing things or that it is the nature of things that prevents us from seeing them.

[2] Or by an expression that translates into them.

descriptive parts do not have a descriptive use, that has led many philosophers to the conventionalist 'view' that necessary propositions are really verbal. Without going into the ins and outs of the various philosophical theories about logical necessity and logical impossibility,[1] two features of sentences expressing logically necessary propositions which emerge distinctly may be noted. These are that their form, the mode of speech in which they are formulated, is non-verbal, and that their import is verbal, about usage. What we *convey* by pronouncing a sentence expressing a logical necessity or impossibility is a fact of usage in the language in which the sentence is framed; but what is conveyed is not, because of its idiom, *expressed* by the sentence. Thus the sentence, 'It is logically impossible to draw a five-sided circle', does not describe what cannot be done. Neither does it assert that 'draws a five-sided circle' lacks use in the language; but what in an oblique way it calls attention to is the fact that the phrase has no use.

Taken as expressing a logically necessary proposition, the sentence 'We do not really see or feel things', or the sentence 'It is impossible to see or feel things', conveys the putative verbal fact that such phrases as 'sees a table' and 'feels a pen' have no descriptive use. And the sentence 'Physical-thing concepts are self-contradictory and cannot have instances' conveys the putative verbal fact that words which are commonly taken to denote things, such words as 'table' and 'pen', have, in language, no application to anything, actual or imagined. It does not, of course, need to be remarked that, unlike the sentence 'No one can draw a five-sided circle', which does convey the fact that a certain expression lacks use, the sentences 'No one can see tables and pens' and 'Physical-thing concepts are self-contradictory and can have no instances' do not convey *facts* to the effect that a great part of the vocabulary of our language lacks use. It is certainly not a fact that the general names of physical things have been given no application, and it is equally not a fact that perception-expressions like 'sees a tree', 'tastes an apple', and 'feels a piece of ice' have no descriptive use. The Parmenidean rationalist who urges on us the view that the eye is blind and that things are self-contradictory knows, of course, that words like 'tree' and 'table' and that phrases

[1] See 'Logical Necessity' in *The Structure of Metaphysics* and pages 37–56 in *Studies in Metaphilosophy*.

like 'feels a piece of ice' and 'sees a tree' have a use and also what their use is. And he no more dispenses with them than does anyone else. Despite his remarkable view, it would be the height of absurdity to say that he does not know that thing-words and perception-terminology have a use and that he actually thinks they have none.

There is only one conclusion to come to: this is that the view is no more with regard to facts of proper usage than it is with regard to facts about things. Wittgenstein has observed that a philosopher rejects an expression under the illusion that he is rejecting a theory. One might call this 'the illusion of philosophy'. In announcing his 'view' the philosopher rejects a part of language, or it would be better to say, changes it, under the impression that he is announcing a theory. A consideration of the conclusion he draws and also of the conclusion he fails to draw from his professed contradictions, i.e. the *use* he makes of them, bears out the idea that in some way language is being unconsciously reconstructed by the philosopher.

It has to be realized that the philosopher's 'contradictions' differ in a remarkable way from the contradictions we are familiar with in mathematics and elsewhere—this quite apart from the fact that the contradictions he lays bare in everyday terminology when doing philosophy do not intrude themselves into his everyday talk. A nonphilosophical contradiction, like the contradiction in the concept of a five-sided circle or in the concept of a thing that is shorter than something which exactly equals it in length, implies only that the concept cannot, logically, have instances but also that the concept cannot, logically, have apparent instances. There can no more be a self-contradictory appearance than there can be a self-contradictory reality; there can no more be the sensible appearance of a five-sided circle than there can be a five-sided circle. By maintaining that physical things cannot, in principle, exist, because their existence would imply a contradiction, and thus that it is logically impossible to perceive things, while at the same time allowing that physical things exist in sensible appearance, the philosopher informs us that his contradictions and logical impossibilities are not standard contradictions and logical impossibilities. He informs us that his contradictions do not have the kind of work that the more usual kind have. Their job, in the game the philosopher plays with language, is to provide justification for the terminological moves he makes.[1] The 'contradictions' he discovers in the concept of things and the 'logical impossibility' he discovers in the concept of the perception of things lend an air of science to the game he plays with thing- and perception-terminology. He uses his contradictions to preclude existence-sentences employing names of physical objects and also sentences employing perception-terms, i.e. sentences like 'There is a tree in front of the house' and 'I see the book I have been looking for'; but he does not use the contradictions to rule out sentences like 'There is the appearance of there being a tree in front of a house' and 'It seems to me that I see the book I have been looking for'. It is plain that the Parmenidean rejection of the senses comes down to casting out part of ordinary perception talk. The rejection eliminates a certain part of terminology while retaining the language of appearance, i.e. the terminology of 'seems to perceive', but stretches its use, in a semantically idle way,[2] to cover all those cases to which such expressions as 'sees a tree' and 'feels a smooth surface' normally apply. Doing this generates the remarkable illusion that the philosopher is advocating a disquieting theory about what our senses reveal to us. If we relate the linguistically contrived illusion to processes in the unconscious, which hardly seems unreasonable, we come to the conclusion that the philosophical shifting of language is done for the purpose of *creating* the illusion of a theory, for whatever underlying satisfaction doing this may give. A person whose mind is not bewitched by the illusion may very well object to the philosophical game played with language in words which parallel an earlier objection to Reichenbach's view: 'I don't care how the Parmenidean rationalist talks about what we call "seeing a tree", I call it "seeing a tree", and not just seeming to see one.' And when Moore said that ordinary talk in which we speak of seeing such things as doors and fingers is not incorrect,[3] he is not to be construed as merely pointing out something the rationalist already knows but rather as resisting a game with terminology he has no wish to play.

The second rationalistic thesis, which is joined to the proposi-

[1] For a discussion of how philosophical contradictions are created, see 'The Metaphysical Concept of Space' in *Studies in Metaphilosophy*.

[2] Wittgenstein has compared the philosophical use of language with an engine that is idling, not working. In one way it is not idle. Its work is to create an intellectual illusion.

[3] *Philosophical Studies*, p. 225.

tion that our senses cannot yield knowledge of reality, is that knowledge of reality may be obtained through thought. It is with this thesis that Plato's grandiose and moving description of the philosopher as the spectator of all time and all existence is associated. Picasso's friend Dora, who had 'religious tendencies, semi-philosophical in nature at first and then veering more and more toward Buddhism', is reported to have said: 'I have the revelation of the inner voice . . . I see things as they really are, past, present, and future.'[1] One may wonder whether behind Plato's lofty and poetic language does not lie Dora's narcissistic delusion that she had omnipotence of thought, and whether indeed the expression of this delusion in one or other subtle form is not an important part of the hidden motivation for the doing of philosophy. Certainly the air that surrounds rationalism carries with it suggestions of the occult and the supernatural; the picture of the philosopher it tends to bring up in us is that of a cosmic clairvoyant who sees all simply by the power of his mind. Thus Ayer was led to say that to give way to rationalism would require us to accept it as a 'mysterious inexplicable fact' that thought has the power to reveal to us things we have never observed.

The unconscious image the rationalistic philosopher has of himself may very well be that of a clairvoyant, but his expressed philosophical theory is, of course, something else. This is that by reasoning on concepts knowledge of the existence and nature of things may be obtained. The results of pieces of correct reasoning on concepts are *a priori* true propositions, propositions which explicate necessary connexions among concepts or which state logical impossibilities. And the point of an *a priori* proposition, to repeat briefly what has already been said, is a verbal point about the functioning of an expression, although, it has to be remarked immediately, the proposition is nevertheless not itself verbal. To put it differently, a sentence which in fact expresses an *a priori* true proposition conveys a matter of verbal usage to anyone who understands it, although the sentence is prevented from expressing this by the mode of speech in which it is formulated. Thus, a person who understands the sentence ' "C has 7 elements" entails that C has 2 more elements than 5', which in the English language expresses a necessary proposition, has his attention called to the

---

[1] Françoise Gilot and Carlton Lake, *Life With Picasso*, p. 89.

fact that the phrase 'has 2 more elements than 5' has a use which makes it correct to apply it to whatever the phrase 'has 7 elements' correctly applies to. We may say that the sentence reminds him or makes him aware of the fact which is expressed by the sentence 'The rules in the language for the use of "has 2 more than 5 elements" make it applicable to whatever "has 7 elements" correctly applies'. What a philosopher is made aware of, and all that he is made aware of, by knowing a truth of reason is a fact about terminology; and however interesting and important such a fact may strike one, being made aware of it can hardly count as being made aware of a fact about things. The 'reality' the philosopher speaks of has to be manufactured. To put the matter more precisely, the belief that a reality is being referred to, which arises in consequence of reasoning on concepts, can only be brought about by linguistic means. In a metaphor, language is the philosopher's Aladdin's lamp. To describe in a general way how the philosopher engineers such notions as unknowable substratum, the Absolute, supersensible universals,[1] etc., we may say he produces them by the same linguistic mechanisms he uses to disparage the senses and to make familiar phenomena dissipate into mere appearance. His sentences describe neither fact nor actual usage; rather they embody terminological alterations which are introduced in such a way as to create, against the backdrop of ordinary language, the intellectual illusion that recondite realities are being described. His statements share certain features with statements expressing necessary propositions: they are secure against upset by recourse to usage, although not for the same reason. Their purport is not to indicate conventional usage, hence recourse to usage is irrelevant to their acceptance or rejection. It becomes clear why a philosopher who has no wish to give up his position can never be compelled to do so by a counter-argument.

It cannot be seriously doubted that behind the intellectual fantasy that a theory is being expressed by his utterance there lie deeper fantasies of which the philosopher has no conscious awareness but which are of the greatest importance to him. One fantasy buried in the view of Parmenides, the Oedipus of Metaphysics, can be discerned behind his condemnation of the senses, behind his talk of 'the blind eye', etc. Without going into the

[1] For detailed studies see *The Structure of Metaphysics* and *Studies in Metaphilosophy*.

detail of the content and form[1] of his poem, it may be remarked that the Two Ways represent a conflict between a refined form of asceticism and the 'enticement of the senses'. The pleasures of the senses are sacrificed, certainly symbolically, and to some degree in fact. The senses are 'quarantined', to use the expression of one scholar, and an attenuated activity, thought, is made to substitute for them. This, and deeper material, is hidden in the advice not to make an instrument of the blind eye, and also by Socrates' famous words: 'I decided to take refuge from the confusion of the senses in argument, and by means of argument, to determine the truth of reality.' With his words the Parmenidean rationalist, at one level of the mind, gives the impression of stating a theory about the poverty of the senses and the power of thought, while all he is doing is rearranging terminology. At a deeper level, his words serve to express unconscious thoughts. We may indeed say that the essence of a philosophical theory, what repels us or holds us in bondage to it, is its unconscious content, the inner drama to which it permits us to give expression.

To come back briefly to Reichenbach's answer to the rationalistic contention that only *a priori* knowledge is genuine, it is easily seen what manœuvres with terminology his view employs. His view consists of the introduction of a contracted use of 'certain', a stretched use of 'probable', together with the retention of the usual use of 'knowledge'. But these terminological innovations are introduced in the ontological form of speech and hence, against the background of ordinary, undoctored language, give the delusive but lively impression that a circumspect scientific theory is being propounded. We may guess at some of the unconscious content of the theory if we remember that embedded in the position is the view of Parmenides. And a possible, if iconoclastic, answer to Reichenbach's question as to why a philosopher 'must forego a generally accepted philosophy' is now at hand. This is that philosophical sentences do not, apart from their unconscious purport, express theories; they only embody non-workaday, autocratic redrawings of terminological boundaries. And such linguistic shifts lend themselves naturally to unending debate.

---

[1] There is, for instance, an interesting similarity between the form of the poem, symbolized by the Pythagorean Y, and the juncture of the roads where Oedipus came into conflict with his father.

7

TIME AND TEMPORAL TERMINOLOGY

'The poets have lamented the power of Time to sweep away every object of their love.' Bertrand Russell, *A History of Western Philosophy*.

The concept of time has given rise to a number of philosophical theories which are remarkable for the way in which they differ from each other. According to one theory, time is not real and exists only as a self-contradictory appearance. According to another theory, time is a component of our perceptual apparatus and is a 'form of inner intuition'. According to a third theory, time is a self-subsistent phenomenon which is held by some philosophers to be capable of existing empty of occurrences and by other philosophers not. And there are still other theories. The differences between these claims are so startling as to incline one to suppose that philosophers are talking about altogether different things, that they are using the word 'time' in different senses, rather than that they are using the word in the same sense and are advancing different theories about the nature of what is denoted by it. But it would be unrealistic to suppose this: for that would imply that the many philosophers who have engaged in debates about time have constantly been misunderstanding each other and talking at cross purposes, rather than arguing against each other's positions. But the many years in which controversies about time have been going on makes ridiculous the notion that philosophers have been blind to each other's use of terminology, especially as the arguments a philosopher gives in support of his position as well as against other positions could not fail to indicate what his terminology referred to. Thus St Augustine, who posed the question, 'What is time?', observed that, despite the fact that philosophers have for so long been at loggerheads about it, '. . . we certainly understand it when we talk about it; we even understand it when we hear another person speaking about it'. In view of this it becomes a problem as to how to understand

rightly the question, 'What is time?', for which such remarkably
diverse answers could be proposed. It presents us with the meta-
question as to what sort of information is requested by the
philosophical question—factual, analytical, or verbal, or perhaps
something else. That the question is unusual and may have a
hidden character is suggested by St Augustine's famous complaint,
'What, then, is time? If no one asks me I know; but if I want to
explain it to a questioner, I do not know.' If his complaint is
taken at face value, it would indicate that the question had a
property which played odd tricks on his mind, made him lose
the answer when he was asked for it. But it is not to be supposed
that he found himself unable to teach the use of time-indicating
language to someone who asked to be instructed or, to put it
somewhat differently, that he found himself unable to explain the
meanings of time-indicating expressions, i.e. to explain in the
customary ways the use of such terms in the language as 'now',
'minute', 'an hour ago', 'a long time'. And it would seem clear
that anyone who knew the meaning of the word 'minute', say,
would know what a minute is, and hence would know what time
is and would not be at a loss for an answer to the question. Nevertheless, it is not to be denied that St Augustine found himself in a
quandary.

The question, 'What is time?', may at first glance seem to be
verbal in import; it may seem to be a non-verbal way of asking
for the meaning of the word 'time'. And it would seem that what
it comes down to, concretely, is the question, 'What is the use in
the language of such terms as "minute", "month", "less than an
hour ago", "earlier", "later"?': the question, 'What is time?',
would seem to translate into the non-mystifying question, 'What
is the actual use of time-denoting terminology?'. But on this
construction of the question the *philosophical* problem vanishes
along with the mystification, which would indicate that there is
something wrong with the translation. The first question is a
philosophical question, which produces what Wittgenstein has
described as a mental cramp; the second question poses only the
practical problems encountered in the teaching of language. The
translation seems correct, nevertheless. For the meaning of the
word 'time' is not something distinct from the use it has in the
language, and the use of 'time' is given by the use of temporal
terminology. We do not learn the use of the word 'time' and in

addition to learning this go on to learn its meaning; we learn its meaning by being taught its use—and by nothing else. And we learn the meanings of time-denoting expressions in the same way, by being taught their use. But the meanings of 'time' and of time-denoting expressions are so connected that in learning the use of 'time' we do not learn anything in addition to what we know about the use of words like 'minute', 'later than', 'now', etc.: so to speak, the word 'time' sums up the uses in the language of temporal terminology. Nevertheless something gets lost in the translation of Augustine's question, 'What is time?', into 'What is the use of such time-indicating terms as "minute" and "later"?' The first question, unlike the second, seems to possess a hidden property which makes it capable of producing strange effects. St Augustine describes one effect; and other philosophers have in different connections described equally strange effects of philosophical views and arguments. Moore has remarked, with regard to a large class of views, that philosophers have found it possible to hold them while knowing that they are false. And Norman Malcolm has called attention to the strange power of philosophical reasoning to 'blind one to the obvious'.[1]

No philosophical problem is involved in thinking about time in concrete terms, i.e. in terms of the applications of such expressions as 'minute', 'later than', 'now', but a Pandora's box is opened when we think about time in the abstract, about what time itself is. We then tend to think of it as an object of some sort, as 'a *queer* thing',[2] whose nature is under investigation. In G. E. Moore's words, 'Time, with a big T, seems to be a highly abstract entity',[3] and thinking on this entity brings to light paradoxes which have troubled and intrigued the minds of philosophers from the time of Parmenides to the present.

It would now seem that what St Augustine wished to convey was that when he thought about time in the abstract, 'time with a big T', he found himself beset by a host of difficulties which suggested that time is an elusive thing whose investigation results in paradoxical findings, in some ways comparable to results encountered in modern physics. This would seem to be a reason-

[1] *Knowledge and Certainty* (Englewood Cliffs, N.J.: Prentice-Hall, Inc., 1963), p. 180.
[2] Wittgenstein's phrase, *The Blue Book*, p. 6.
[3] *Philosophical Studies*, p. 209.

able explanation of St Augustine's complaint that he did not know what time is, although the question remains whether there is anything more to knowing what time is than to knowing the use of time-denoting language. There is, to be sure, more to be known about a grain of sand than being able to identify one and knowing what it is called, but it may be that there is nothing more to be known about time than knowing the use of temporal language. It may be that the philosophical question, 'What is time?', is only outwardly like the question, 'What in its inner constitution is a grain of sand?', that their likeness is only in their idiom, and that they are altogether different in respect of what they ask. The aim here will be to improve our understanding of what it is that the philosophical question asks.

One answer that has been given to the question, 'What is time?', is that time is a kind of entity, a moving object of some sort, often pictured as a cosmic river on which things are carried from the future down to the present and into the past. As is well known, Newton distinguished between absolute and relative time, and described the difference between them in the following way: 'Absolute, true, and mathematical time, of itself, and from its own nature, flows equably without regard to anything external, and by another name is called duration; relative, apparent, and common time, is some sensible and external (whether accurate or unequable) measure of duration by means of motion, which is commonly used instead of true time—such as an hour, a day, a month, a year.' Newton's words represent true time, 'Time with a big T', as a kind of medium which flows at a uniform rate, i.e. as a flowing substance.

It is natural to suppose that his words express a view about the nature of time, about what sort of thing it is and how it behaves, and hence to think that they make a factual claim. On this supposition, the question to which Newton's words express a possible answer is an empirical one, to the solution of which some sort of observation or an experiment is relevant. The difficulties about measuring time that St Augustine brings to our attention are obviously connected with the idea that time is some sort of moving object, and they also tend to lend an empirical air to the question, 'What is time?' The following passage helps show this: '. . . we measure periods of time as they are passing by; we do this measuring at the time of sense-perception. So, who can measure the past periods which are already out of existence, or the future ones which do not yet exist. . . . Therefore, while time is passing into the past, it can be perceived and measured; but, when it has passed away, it cannot, for it does not exist.' The difficulty in measuring the part of time that is present to sense-perception is that it flits by too quickly: it 'flies over from the future to the past so quickly that it does not extend over the slightest instant'. The picture of time these words conjure up is of something in rapid motion, something of which only small parts are presented singly to us, like the individual cars of a train which flash by one by one. Thus, Wittgenstein has written: 'Augustine, we might say, thinks of the process of measuring a *length*: say, the distance between two marks on a travelling band which passes us, and of which we can only see a tiny bit (the present) in front of us.'[1] In Wittgenstein's opinion, the difficulties in measuring time are to be resolved by discriminating properly between the meaning the word 'measurement' has when it is applied to a distance on a moving band and the meaning it has when applied to time. This would seem to imply that the puzzles about time are puzzles about the use of temporal terminology, about their 'grammar', to use his expression; and it would thus appear that the philosophical question, 'What is time?', is a verbal question which, underneath, is a request to be freed from confusions engendered by terminology. Something like this may be the case. But it is not to be denied that the question seems to be more than a 'mere question about words', and the conclusion that it is about words will have to be reached by considerations which will in some way show that the question is not a request for factual, non-verbal information, i.e. for information about the nature or behaviour of a substance.

Instead of proceeding directly to St Augustine's question, let us consider first the statement, which naturally suggests itself in answer to it, that time is a kind of thing, however rarefied and ghostly, that is in a constant state of motion. It will be useful to divide this statement into the two component claims it makes, that time is a kind of thing and that time is in some sort of motion, and consider them separately. The statement that time is a thing, a substance or a kind of medium, looks like a factual declaration about time, comparable to the statement that a certain ball is solid rubber. But the difference between the two statements emerges

[1] *The Blue Book*, p. 26.

K

when we think of how the propositions they express would be verified. Looking and feeling are relevant to determining the truth-value of the claim about the ball but are not relevant to determining that of the statement about time. It can be seen that saying that time is a thing is more like saying that a shadow is a thing than it is like saying that the ball is solid rubber. Further looking, feeling, etc. are appropriate procedures for deciding that what is before us is only a shadow, but no amount of inspecting a shadow could in the slightest help determine whether a shadow is a thing. If two people were to disagree about whether what was before them was a shadow or a tree, they could resolve their disagreement by going up and looking, and feeling if necessary. But if, after having determined that what they saw was a shadow, they were to disagree over whether a shadow is a thing, further looking would be of no use. For a person who says that a shadow is a thing does not say this because he perceives in it what the other fails to perceiver nor does a person who says it is not a thing take his position because of what he sees, or thinks he sees. And neither imagines that the other overlooks what he sees, or thinks that he sees what in fact is not there. Looking can be of no use in determining the truth-value of the statement that a shadow is a thing, not because of the presence of some sort of barrier which prevents an adequate examination of shadows, but because it makes no literal sense to speak of verifying by the use of the senses that a shadow is a thing or that it is not a thing. If a shadow is a thing it is so by logical necessity: if it is true to say that a shadow is a thing, then being a shadow *entails* being a thing. And if it is not a thing it is logically impossible for it to be one, just as in the case of a number, if it is even it is so by logical necessity, and if it is not even it is logically impossible for it to be even.

It is the same with regard to time. Observation can play no role whatever in terminating a dispute over whether time is a thing, or a substance, not because of a physical barrier which stands in our way but because of a logical barrier, i.e. the logical character of the statement. If it is true that time is a thing, then being a time *entails* being a thing (or part of a thing); and if it is true that time is not a thing, then being a time *entails* not being a thing. If the statement is true it is necessarily true; and if it is false, it is necessarily false. In other words, *if* it has a truth-value, it has it necessarily, not contingently. Russell has said that 'We cannot point to a time itself, but only to some event occurring at that time. There is therefore no reason in experience to suppose that there are times as opposed to events: the events, ordered by the relations of simultaneity and succession, are all that experience provides.'[1] His saying that experience provides no reason for supposing there are times in addition to occurrences, since all that we encounter are occurrences, makes it look as if he is inferring the nonexistence of something from its not being discoverable in experience. Saying that we cannot point to a time itself suggests that we are prevented in some way from doing something, either because of the presence of an obstacle or because of the non-existence of the required object. But what cannot be done for such reasons could in principle be done: the obstacle could, conceivably, be removed and the thing could, conceivably, exist. What cannot as a matter of fact be can be in principle. But it is easy to see that the impossibility of pointing to a time as opposed to pointing to something going on at the time is not a case of something not existing which could exist. For 'points to a time itself' describes nothing. The 'cannot' in Russell's statement is not the 'cannot' of empirical fact, however much it may at first sight appear to be. It is the 'cannot' of logic. In fact Russell's remark helps us see that whatever the philosophical words, 'Time is a thing', may say, they do not make a factual claim about time. It would seem natural to conclude that the words state a true or false *a priori* proposition, one that is either necessary or impossible.

The idea that time is in some form of motion, that it flows or flies, etc., adds to our picture of time as a substance; but it nevertheless supports the conclusion that the proposition that time is a kind of thing is not empirical, and hence shows the in-appropriateness of the empirical picture to the philosophical words. It brings to our attention the fact that the use of 'substance', in the sense in which water is said to be a substance, is such that the phrase 'at rest or in motion' has tautological application to whatever is denoted by the word. Being a substance entails being either at rest or in motion, whereas being a number, for example, does not entail this: '*a* is a substance but is neither in motion nor at rest' implies a contradiction, whereas '*b* is a number but is

[1] *Our Knowledge of the External World* (New York: W. W. Norton & Co., 1926; London: George Allen & Unwin Ltd.), p. 125.

neither in motion nor at rest', far from implying a contradiction states a necessary truth. If we take time to be a substance we are constrained to think of it as at rest or in motion, and characterizing it as 'equably flowing' would seem to be describing the special behaviour of a certain substance. But characterizing time in this way, regardless of the imagery it carries with it, brings into clear view a contradiction in the statement that time is a kind of thing, which destroys any empirical picture we may associate with the statement. For apart from using language metaphorically, to say that time moves is to imply that it has a rate of motion, in the determination of which time enters: e.g. *time flows* implies *n amount of time flows by in t length of time*. And this implies that time is distinct from itself, for that which flows cannot be the time which enters into its rate of flow. It follows that the notion that time is a flowing substance is self-contradictory. It is the notion of a substance which is identical with time and yet cannot be; it is a substance which cannot be what it is. It is interesting in this connexion to note that Plotinus rejected the notion that time is an accompaniment of motion. His reason was that if it were, then time would be an accompaniment of motion in time and hence that time would itself occur in time.

The alternative notion that time is a stationary substance also implies a contradiction. When Christopher Marlowe's Faustus cries,

> Stand still, you ever moving sphere of heaven
> That time may cease, and midnight never come,

the picture brought to our mind is that of an invisible object whose motion is so linked with the motion of visible bodies that when they are brought to a stop it also comes to a stop and stands still for as long a time as they stand still. But although it implies no contradiction to say that the sun stands still for seven hours, it does imply a contradiction to say that time stands still for seven hours. To suppose that time is a stationary thing is to imply that it is intelligible language to ask the question, 'How long has time remained stationary?'[1] The implication is that to say that time is a

---

[1] Compare Aristotle's question, 'How long has time existed?', which is posed by his proof that time is eternal, and *always* has existed. The implication would seem to be that time exists at all times.

thing which has remained stationary for a period of time is to speak intelligibly, to describe a conceivable state of affairs. But, as in the case of the preceding alternative, that which is a stationary substance cannot be indentical with the time during which the substance remains stationary; and this also implies that time is a substance which cannot be what it is. Thus the notion of time as a thing or a substance is a self-contradiction: being a substance, it must be either at rest or in motion, and since each alternative implies a contradiction, the notion is self-contradictory. The contradiction is not inconspicuous, but as the notion has been embraced by some philosophers it may seem reasonable to surmise that the contradiction has somehow been overlooked. There is, of course, the possibility that the philosophical words, 'Time is a thing which flows', have, at the conscious level of our thinking, been misinterpreted by us and that the contradiction is bound up in a special way with the misinterpretation.

Putting this possibility aside for the moment, however, it is important to notice that philosophers have taken two widely different positions regarding what the presence of a contradiction in a concept, whether recognized or not, implies. According to some philosophers it shows that no reality can correspond to the concept and that what is commonly taken to be a reality corresponding to it is nothing more than delusive appearance. Thus, the arguments which Zeno and F. H. Bradley adduced to show that time is self-contradictory and cannot, therefore, exist, have not been taken by philosophers of one tradition to disprove the existence of the corresponding temporal appearances. According to other philosophers the presence of a contradiction in a concept implies that the terminology which denotes it has no descriptive use in the language in which it occurs, i.e. has no use to convey information about an actual or possible phenomenon. According to this position, if Newton's view about the nature of time were correct and Zeno's arguments did, actually, demonstrate contradictions in temporal terminology, nearly the whole of ordinary language would lack the use we suppose it to have. Such everyday sentences as 'Jones sneezed suddenly' and 'Smith strolled for a half hour yesterday' would have no more literal intelligibility than the sentences 'Smith runs without moving any part of his body' and 'Jones will sneeze one hour ago'. And, accordingly, a philosopher like Zeno or Bradley, or McTaggart, who professes to have discovered a contradiction in the concept *time*, implies that he has shown that temporal language has no use to describe situations, real or imagined—if, to be sure, he thinks the contradiction to be the genuine article. If Zeno claimed, as he seems to have, that the concept of a time-interval is self-contradictory, then he implied, whether wittingly or not, that the names of time-intervals have no use to communicate information: he implies that 'ran a mile in four minutes' makes no more sense than does 'ascended the ladder to its lowest rung'.

We may be at a loss to understand what makes it possible for philosophers to divide on what the presence of a contradiction shows, some maintaining that it shows the nonexistence of phenomena, other that it shows the senselessness of terminology. But it would seem clear enough that expressions which denote self-contradictory concepts, e.g. 'fewer than 3 but more than 7', have no descriptive function in the language in which they are formulable. And it is natural to think that any argument which purports to demonstrate that a term or a form of words in everyday use is self-contradictory must contain an error. In fact, some philosophers counter views which are erected on claimed contradictions in the meanings of expressions in everyday currency with the contention that if an expression has an ordinary use its meaning is not self-contradictory. One philosopher has stated: 'Some [philosophers] have seemed to think that statements describing temporal relations, e.g. "Charles came later than the others, but before the doors were closed", are self-contradictory. Some philosophers think that it is self-contradictory to assert that an empirical statement is known for certain, e.g. "I know for certain that the tank is half-full". The assumption underlying all of these theories is that an ordinary expression *can* be self-contradictory. This assumption seems to me to be false.'[1]

Philosophers who dispose of a paradoxical view by recourse to usage seem to think that their consideration does two things: it shows that the arguments supporting the view are mistaken and it shows, also, that the view is false. It should be noticed that appeal to everyday language does not bring to light the putative mistakes contained in any of the standard arguments against time. It does not, for example, bring out any error in the argument

[1] Norman Malcolm, in *The Philosophy of G. E. Moore*, ed. by P. A. Schilpp, p. 358.

formulated by Aristotle: 'One part of it has been and is not, while the other is going to be and is not yet. Yet time . . . is made up of these. One would naturally suppose that what is made up of things which do not exist could have no share in reality.'[1] But it does, according to these philosophers, show that the argument is a mistaken piece of reasoning—the underlying notion obviously being that the function of a philosophical argument is to demonstrate the truth-value of a proposition. The refutation by recourse to usage is also taken to upset the proposition. The formula behind the argument from ordinary language is that self-contradictory expressions have no descriptive function and that a chain of reasoning purporting to demonstrate a contradiction in the meaning of an expression which has such a function is therefore erroneous. Some philosophers also take an argument from usage to show, in at least some cases, something more than that an expression has an intelligible, non-contradictory meaning; it is taken to show also the existence of what is described by the expression. In connection with temporal terminology it is taken to demonstrate that 'time is intelligible and real'. These words are in what might be called the 'composite idiom': they make a declaration about temporal language, to the effect that it is intelligible, and in addition declare the reality of what temporal language is used to refer to. This additional claim requires special comment. It is obvious, of course, that an expression which has a descriptive use is intelligible language. But in general, from the fact that a form of words is descriptive, or has a use to convey information, it cannot be inferred that there actually are situations to which it applies. For example, from the fact that 'blue swan' has a use it cannot be inferred that there are blue swans. This point was made by Russell when he criticized certain philosophers for arguing that 'There is a linguistically correct use of the words "free will", and therefore there is free will'.[2] The claim that temporal language is an exception to the rule that the existence of an intelligible expression does not imply the existence of a corresponding reality certainly stands in need of justification, to say the least. For even in the case of a word which has only an ostensive definition and is learned by applications to instances,

[1] *Physica*, 218a.
[2] Introduction to *Words and Things* by Ernest Gellner (Victor Gollancz Ltd., 1959), p. 13.

e.g. the colour-word 'yellow', the existence of something described by the word cannot be inferred. The sentence, 'There is
nothing whatever, neither a thing, an appearance of a thing, nor a
mental image, which is yellow' could, logically, express a true
proposition; and it could not do this if it implied the existence of
something answering to 'is yellow' or to 'looks yellow'.

To come back to the linguistic refutation of the view that time is
unreal, a metaphysician who holds the view will resist the charge
that by his claim to have established the self-contradictoriness of
temporal language he implies, not that it has a use to describe
appearance, but that it has no descriptive sense whatever. He will
oppose the contention that on his view 'read for five minutes' no
more describes anything than does 'shorter than itself' or 'yellow
numerosity'. One philosopher has said: 'One of the arguments of
the British idealist, F. H. Bradley, serves as an excellent example
of the way in which the unordinary use of temporal language can
get us into metaphysical trouble',[1] and we can imagine Bradley
making the rejoinder that what some philosophers take to be his
unordinary use of language is quite straightforward language
which describes a feature of ordinary usage, i.e. that his 'unordinary" words correctly describe the ordinary use of time-
indicating terminology. In defence of Bradley, it might be argued
that the assertion, 'Time is self-contradictory and unreal', in an
oblique way states a fact about temporal language and describes
a feature of its use, namely, that it is self-contradictory and that
its legitimate use is confined to describing appearance. It will be
remembered that the traditional answer to the protest of common
sense that our senses unmistakably attest to temporal facts—facts
like people consulting their watches and rivers flowing, invokes
the distinction between appearance and reality; it allows that time
does exist in sensible appearance, but insists that, as the arguments
show, it can have no more reality than a mirage. The arguments
are not in disproof of the existence of the appearances; their force
is only to show that the corresponding reality does not exist.
Parmenides, who was obliged to account for phenomena, has been
defended against the charge of inconsistency by Gomperz in the
following words: '. . . in this there was nothing inconsistent; for
though he rejected sense-perception as illusory, yet it had not

---

[1] Milton D. Hunnex, 'Time, Persons, and Novelty', *Pacific Philosophy
Forum*, Vol. IV, no. 2, p. 11.

therefore vanished from the world.'[1] As Bradley put it, 'Nothing is actually removed from existence by being labelled appearance'.[2]

Nowadays the critique has, superficially at least, shifted away from one which has recourse to 'the evidence of the senses' to one which has recourse to ordinary language. The surprising thing is that philosophers have failed to notice a possible and obvious parallel defence at the linguistic level. For it could be maintained that Bradley's position does not imply that time-denoting terminology has no use in expressions which have a descriptive function in the language. Against the claim that if a form of speech is self-contradictory, it lacks use in the language, it could be argued that the consequent is by no means necessitated by the antecedent. A Bradleian metaphysician could maintain, as indeed he would have to, that establishing a contradiction in terminology which has everyday use shows, not that the terminology does not have its everyday use, but rather, that its use is to describe 'mere appearance', or 'self-contradictory appearance'.[3] With the support of arguments, in which no mistake has ever been shown, he could reject the contention that 'To analyse [temporal relations] as not real is to indicate an incorrect analysis or incorrect use or both'.[4] And with a show of philosophical reason on his side, he could urge that his analysis is correct and brings to light an important feature of the use of words denoting temporal relations. The defence of a Zeno or a Bradley against the attack by philosophers of ordinary language might be phrased in a manner paralleling Gomperz' defence of Parmenides:

'Zeno and Bradley declare that time is self-contradictory without implying that temporal words have vanished from the language, or that they have no function in descriptive expressions. And in this there is nothing inconsistent. For what they show by their arguments is that temporal language does not apply to reality, and not that it applies neither to reality nor to appearance.'

It has been said that 'The philosophies and cultures, such as for example may be found in India, which ascribe illusion to temporality, do so at the price of finding the ordinary world illusory also'.[5] Putting aside the question as to whether a metaphysician

---

[1] Theodor Gomperz, *Greek Thinkers*, Vol. I, p. 180, trans. by Laurie Magnus.
[2] *Appearance and Reality*, p. 15.   [3] Bradley's phrase.
[4] 'Time, Persons, and Novelty', *op. cit.*, p. 10.   [5] *Ibid.*, p. 30.

of the unreality of time would consider the illusoriness of the world a price for, rather than a desired outcome of, his view about time, he could point out that in ascribing 'illusion to temporality' he does not imply that time does not exist as an illusion, and neither does he imply that temporal language does not describe illusion. Just as the illusion of time is not made to vanish from the world, temporal terminology is not made to vanish from the language. This linguistic defence against the attack of philosophers of ordinary language cannot be disregarded; it needs to be examined.

The remarks of one philosopher indirectly suggest a way to assessing the metaphysician's claim that his view about time, instead of failing to square with the fact that temporal language has an intelligible use, brings out an important feature of its use. Elsewhere I have argued that the presence of a contradiction in a concept implies the same thing with regard to the existence of a sensible appearance of a reality answering to the concept as it does with regard to the existence of the reality itself. Put shortly, there no more can be self-contradictory representations, whether sensible appearances or images or pictures, than there can be self-contradictory states of affairs: there no more can appear to be an unoccupied bench on which people are seated than there can be an unoccupied bench on which people are seated. Some philosophers have, if we take their words at face value, denied this, and Professor Brand Blanshard, in defence of their devotion to reason, writes: 'If motion [or time] is impossible logically, then it is impossible that anything should *seem* to move. In denying what their senses revealed, these metaphysicians were thus committing themselves to irredeemable absurdity. I do not think Zeno and Bradley would have been much perturbed. They would no doubt reply that the choice between absurdities confronts us still. It is absurd to deny that we have even the illusion of motion; granted. It is also absurd to say that even in that illusion we are experiencing the ending of an endless series. Forced to choose, these men think it more credible that we should be deluded about sense-experience[1] than that it should really elude the law of contradic-

---

[1] Blanshard does not explain the nature of this delusion, whether it is a false belief that certain expressions describe sense-experience or whether it itself is a sensible delusive appearance of some sort. Each alternative is paradoxical.

tion. They may of course have been mistaken that motion does violate that law. But this is not at the moment the point. They thought they saw clearly that it did, and if one does think this, what other course can one take as a philosopher? It is surely a hard fate that an uncompromising devotion to reason should incur the charge of psychopathology.'[1]

The charge of psychopathology does not, of course, apply to anyone in the predicament described by Blanshard, but that is because he is a *philosopher*.[2] But it is hard not to wonder about the nature of a subject which puts one into this sort of intellectual quandary. The important thing to notice, however, is what is implied by allowing that self-contradictory appearances are ruled out from possible existence equally with self-contradictory things. This is that temporal appearances do not fail to exist, as a matter of empirical fact; their existence is logically impossible. What does not exist, for the reason that its existence would imply the truth of a self-contradictory, i.e. necessarily false, proposition cannot, unlike centaurs, exist even in theory. And this means that a self-contradictory appearance-expression has no application to any theoretical appearance, which is to say that it has no use to describe appearances. Thus an expression which, because it is self-contradictory, fails to have a use to describe a possible reality, fails also to have a use to describe a possible appearance. It seems clear that the outcome of granting that sensible appearances of self-contradictory states of affairs are on a logical footing with the self-contradictory states of affairs is that phrases using temporal terminology have no descriptive sense whatever. In fact, it can be seen that to say that self-contradictory temporal appearances cannot exist is only a nonverbal and more graphic way of saying something about the function in the language of time-indicating expressions.

---

[1] *Metaphysics: Readings and Reappraisals*, ed. by W. E. Kennick and M. Lazerowitz (Englewood Cliffs, N.J.: Prentice-Hall, Inc., 1966), p. 348.

[2] Wittgenstein is reported to have described an imaginary conversation in which a philosopher says to him repeatedly, pointing to a nearby tree, 'I know that that's a tree'. Turning to someone who overhears the conversation Wittgenstein explains, 'He's not mad. We are just philosophizing.' (Last notes, on knowledge and certainty, 1.51.) These words both shock and reassure us, because they show an unappealing similarity and also a reassuring difference between the talk of the nonphilosophical madman and the nonmad philosopher. The philosopher can say in the classroom what the ordinary man cannot say in the street without being thought mad.

A metaphysician may, of course, not make the concession Blanshard makes for him. He may maintain that reason can take us only so far, that the world is not wholly rational, and continue to hold that, though there can be no self-contradictory realities, there can be self-contradictory appearances. A metaphysician who takes this stand has two things to explain. He has, for one thing, to explain what it is in the nature of contradiction which makes possible its doing such different work in the two sorts of cases. For another thing, he has to explain why in some cases the presence of a contradiction rules out the possible existence of an appearance and in other cases not. He has to explain what makes possible the existence of the self-contradictory appearance of there being a blue lake in the distance and makes impossible the existence of the self-contradictory appearance of there being a blue lake which is uniformly orange. He is obliged to help us understand the difference between 'It is impossible for Jones to seem to sneeze while seeming not to, because that is self-contradictory' and 'It is not impossible for Jones to appear to sneeze, though time is self-contradictory'. It may be that the contradiction paraded by the metaphysician is only a contrived imitation of the genuine article and has a different kind of work to do than the work done by an ordinary contradiction. But this cannot be gone into here.[1]

In order to evaluate the view that temporal language is confined to describing appearances it is necessary to get clear on the relation between expressions descriptive of appearances and expressions descriptive of real states of affairs. It is readily seen that an expression of the form 'appearance of there being ϕ' is so related to the corresponding phrase 'there being ϕ' that it describes nothing if the corresponding phrase describes nothing. This is not to say that the existence of something satisfying the first description implies the existence of something satisfying the second; but it is to say that the first will function descriptively in the language only if the second does. Thus, 'appearance of roundness being taller than mauve' describes nothing, because 'roundness which is taller than mauve' describes nothing. And the linguistic fact that such phrases as 'appearance of there being a mauve mountain', 'there seeming to be a mauve mountain',

---

[1] For an extended examination of one philosophical contradiction, see 'The Metaphysical Concept of Space' in *Studies in Metaphilosophy*.

'its looking as if there is a mauve mountain' are descriptive implies that 'there being a mauve mountain' has a descriptive use. Thus, quite generally, the sentence 'There appears to be ϕ' (or 'There exists an appearance of there being ϕ') and 'There is ϕ' are so related in their functioning that if the second sentence describes nothing the existence of which it asserts, the first sentence describes nothing the existence of which it asserts. It follows directly that if 'ϕ' is self-contradictory and does not function descriptively in a sentence of the form 'There is ϕ', it does not function descriptively in a sentence of the form 'There is an appearance of there being ϕ'. Specifically, if temporal language is self-contradictory and has no use in sentences conveying information about realities, it has no use in sentences conveying information about appearances. If Aristotle's consideration did show that time is self-contradictory and can 'have no share in reality', then sentences using temporal terminology would not have the function of asserting or denying the existence of appearances.

We may be perplexed to know what a philosopher is doing who holds, directly or indirectly, that time-indicating language is self-contradictory while recognizing that it does descriptive work in its everyday use. His behaviour with regard to ordinary self-contradictory language is utterly different from what it is with regard to language he believes has been shown, philosophically, to be self-contradictory. He acts as if statements condemned by philosophy as self-contradictory are not self-contradictory. Indeed, if we become attentive to the philosopher's behaviour in relation to the two sorts of contradictory utterances, it begins to take on the aspect of a surrealistic painting in which dream and reality are represented side by side. It would be ridiculous to suppose that the philosopher has the idea that a contradiction in an expression sometimes prevents the expression from being descriptive and sometimes not: that would be like having the idea that in some cases being even makes a number divisible by 2 without remainder and in other cases not. If anything, his behaviour gives the impression that he does not think philosophical contradictions to be contradictions. He seems to think that they are not the real thing, and are not intended to do what a normal contradiction does, i.e. prevent an expression from having application.

We can arrive at some understanding of what the philosopher is doing if we notice that the statement, 'Self-contradictory expressions have no use to convey information', is not empirical. It is of course possible to assign arbitrarily a descriptive meaning to an expression which by the usual conventions is self-contradictory. But with respect to its new, artificial meaning (which cannot be read off from the meanings of the words and their grammar), it will not be self-contradictory. In addition to being a self-contradictory expression, it will then be a non-contradictory linguistic unit—just as in addition to being a numeral, '3' might also be used as a symbol denoting an odour, in which capacity it will not count as a numeral. It will be a symbol which in one of its functions is a numeral and in another is not. And in respect of being self-contradictory, a form of words lacks descriptive sense, not as a matter of fact but by *a priori* necessity. This is paralleled in the English language by the verbal fact that 'descriptive' does not correctly apply to expressions to which 'self-contradictory' applies and that 'self-contradictory' does not apply to what 'descriptive' applies to.

Without making a special study of philosophical contradictions here, what may be learned from this is that they are not contradictions, that what philosophers choose to call 'contradictions' rather than 'curiosities' or 'puzzlers' are *ersatz* contradictions, and are in some way recognized as such. A paste diamond is not a diamond and a philosophical contradiction is not a contradiction, however difficult it may be to get clear on how it is contrived and on how it differs from the actual thing. But being able to lay bare the morphology of a philosophical contradiction is one thing and knowing that it is a puzzling curiosity rather than a contradiction is another thing, and the first is not a prerequisite for the second. Recognition of the fact that language which has been shown philosophically to be contradictory is nonetheless used to refer to situations and occurrences, whether real or imagined, is all that is required to know that *in that use* it is not self-contradictory language. The metaphysician's 'uncompromising devotion to reason', i.e. to his arguments, which enables him to take sides with his contradictions and deny the existence of the appearances becomes understandable, if we take a philosophical contradiction to have a different kind of job from that of a usual contradiction. This is that demonstrating a contradiction in terminology is not to be taken to show the terminology descriptively senseless but, rather, is intended to justify an artificial redescription of its function. For example, the pronouncement of the metaphysician, 'Motion is self-contradictory and therefore mere appearance', becomes understandable, if we take him to use the contradiction he adduces to justify artificially stretching the word 'appearance' beyond its actual use, so that it applies to whatever motion-terminology applies to. Linked with this stretched use of 'appearance' is an artificially contracted use of the term 'real', the application of which is now artificially withheld from whatever motion-expressions apply to. All this, we have to think, is done for the dramatic effect produced; and undoubtedly it connects up with material in the depths of the mind.

Philosophers like Zeno, Augustine, McTaggart, and Bradley have, in appearance at least, discovered a variety of unsuspected contradictions in temporal language, contradictions which are surrounded by an atmosphere of verbal magic. The problem with regard to these contradictions is to know how to *dissolve* them, to use Wittgenstein's expression; and what is required for this is a correct understanding of their nature, which is not to be reached by looking for a mistake in the reasoning leading to the contradictions. No doubt the correct understanding of metaphysical contradictions will remain a vain hope so long as the wish to be under their spell is stronger than the wish to be freed from them. The compromise escape of putting them out of mind is obviously unsatisfactory. Wittgenstein remarked that 'It is easier to bury a problem than to solve it'[1]. But the easier thing is not satisfactory—one cannot help but wonder whether the Gordian knot returned to nag at Alexander's mind. To come back to the matter of understanding metaphysical contradictions, it should be noticed that in addition to these, whose work is to justify redistricting words like 'reality' and 'appearance', there are other sorts of contradictions, with jobs that seem to be different. Some of them are contradictions philosophers find in each other's positions, and the ostensible work of these is to upset the claimed truth of philosophical views. One such contradiction is that discovered in the view that time is something which flows, or in some way moves. Its presence in the view would normally be taken to show that the view is false.

[1] *Philosophical Investigations*, p. 112.

Regardless of what the contradiction shows about the truth-value of the view, however, it helps us see that the view is not empirical. The proposition expressed by the sentence, 'Time is a substance', is not one in the investigation of which observation can play a role; and the contradiction implied by 'Time moves' would make it seem that the sentence, 'Time is a substance', advances a nonempirical claim. Taken as stating an *a priori* proposition, the sentence would, in a nonverbal mode of speech, call our attention to a putative fact of usage in the language in which it is formed, namely that 'substance' applies to whatever 'time' applies to. But the contradiction implied by the propositions expressed by both 'Time is a flowing substance' and 'Time is an immobile substance' shows that it is false to say that as a matter of usage 'substance' applies to what 'time' applies to. The contradiction implied by 'Time is a substance' brings to our attention the fact that 'substance' does not, in point of usage, apply to what 'time' is used to apply to. It shows that to apply 'substance' to a minute or an hour is to go against the ordinary criteria for the use of the word, just as to apply 'cerise' to aches and pains is to go against the conventional rules for the use of 'cerise'. Parenthetically, it is worth remarking that a philosopher who for some reason wished to call attention to a feature of the use of the colour word 'cerise' in relation to pain words might do so in the form of an argument which shows a contradiction in the notion of a cerise pain: pains cannot in principle be seen, cerise things can in principle be seen, therefore the notion of a cerise pain is the self-contradictory notion of something not theoretically visible which can be seen. C. D. Broad, in a different connection, argues a matter of usage in a comparable way. Against the proposition that two people can have, literally, the same belief, he presents the following consideration which can easily be developed into one showing a contradiction: 'My belief cannot literally wander out of my mind and turn up in yours.'[1]

It is hardly necessary to note that a philosopher who holds that time is a substance is not ignorant of the everyday meaning of the word 'substance', the meaning it has in such phrases as 'liquid substance' and 'malleable substance'. The contradiction which appears in the words, 'Time is a substance', is entailed by their common use, which he knows as well as anyone, whether he

---

[1] *Scientific Thought*, p. 230.

remarks the contradiction or not. Understood in their common signification, he knows the impropriety in the words 'Time is a substance' as well as he knows the impropriety in the words 'Time is a liquid'. If anything, his failing to remark the contradiction, which is certainly not inconspicuous or elusive, would indicate that the contradiction is not entailed by his use of the words in the philosophical statement. And the fact that he knows usage indicates that his use is not the common one, even though it is in some way bound up with it. Consider in this connection Russell's remark that we cannot point to a time itself, as against something taking place at that time. Philosophers have an overriding tendency to express themselves in the ontological form of speech, i.e. the form of speech in which things and occurrences are described, when they wish to call attention to matters of usage; and Russell's remark appears to use the ontological idiom to call attention to the fact that 'substance' does not, in its common use, apply to time. The impossibility of pointing to a time itself is logical, which means that Russell was calling attention, indirectly, to a matter of language. This is that the phrase 'points to a time itself' describes no act of pointing to anything. And it fails to describe an act of pointing because the expression 'a time itself' does not have a use to denote a thing. The obvious point involved in this is that 'substance' or 'thing' does not apply to what 'time' is used to refer to, which seems to be one feature of these words that Russell, in the nonverbal form of speech, wished to call to our attention, and this is a point of usage not unknown to philosophers, regardless of their views about time.

The philosophical sentence, 'Time is a substance which flows equably', does not use the word 'substance' in order to convey factual information about a subtle and elusive phenomenon, nor in order to call attention to a supposed matter of linguistic convention. The metaphysician who declares time to be a substance, whether explicitly or by implication, does not, if he expresses himself in English, put forward the verbal claim that the word 'substance' (or 'entity' or 'object') applies to what is denoted by 'time' and by such terms as 'last year', 'tomorrow', and 'minute'. Nor does discovering a contradiction in the sentence show that the metaphysician is advancing a false verbal claim. It is plain, however, that whatever his sentence comes to, the word 'substance' occurring in it is in some way linked with the popular use of the

L

word, but linked in such a way that its occurrence does not make the sentence express an empirical proposition about time. Nor does it make an *a priori* claim the point of which is to call attention to a rule of language, to 'the grammar' of 'substance'. The only plausible conclusion to come to regarding the construction to be placed on the words 'Time is a substance' is that it presents an academically stretched use of 'substance', a use in which it applies to what is referred to by phrases employing the word 'time' without carrying over its old meaning to its new applications.

Wittgenstein has observed that there is a tendency to look for a substance corresponding to a substantive: 'We are up against one of the great sources of philosophical bewilderment: a substantive makes us look for a thing that corresponds to it.'[1] This observation undoubtedly connects up with the fact that some philosophers have held the view that all, or nearly all, words are names. Taken literally, as making a claim about the vocabulary of a language, the view is false. It is not true that all the words in a language like English are names, or even that all the words are classified as nouns under parts of speech; and philosophers who may be inclined to hold the view know this perfectly well. Nor is it true that 'we try to find a substance for a substantive',[2] taking these words literally. Wittgenstein could not have wanted to say or imply that a person who knew the meaning of the substantive 'tomorrow' or 'height' would think of looking for a corresponding object. The expression 'hunts for tomorrow' makes no sense, and if someone were to tell us that he was looking for tomorrow we should think he had a wrong notion about what the expression means, not that he knew what it meant and was made to look for an object by the fact that the word is a substantive. What Wittgenstein perhaps intended to say was that, regardless of what we know about the actual uses of various sorts of nouns, e.g. 'tomorrow', 'button', 'infinity', we are inclined to look on them as object-denoting substantives. There may indeed be a tendency to view substantives in this way, a tendency which may hark back to the very beginnings of language; but it is hard to think that all substantives are actually *believed* to be nouns which denote objects, that 'tomorrow', alike with 'button' and 'moon', is used

---

[1] *The Blue Book*, p. 1.
[2] This is the phrasing in the original, unedited *Blue Book*.

to refer to an object. A number of remarks Wittgenstein has made about the nature of philosophical statements suggest that the thought he intended to convey was that philosophers have a tendency to assimilate, by artificial linguistic fiat, substantives which are not general names of things to those which denote objects, without of course turning them semantically into nouns which denote things. But regardless of whether he intended this, this is what, in one connection or another, a philosopher sometimes does when he presents a theory: a philosophical theory sometimes presents in a linguistically disguised form the reclassification of a group of substantives under an artificially stretched use of 'general name of an object'. The following statement is a particularly interesting example of an elaboration which is woven around a comparable reclassification of general words with special names of particular things, a classification which when introduced in a certain way creates the illusion that a philosopher is talking about a kind of object:

'To those who object to the introduction of abstract entities at all I would say that I believe that there are more important criteria by which a theory should be judged. The extreme demand for a simple prohibition of abstract entities under all circumstances perhaps arises from a desire to maintain the connection between theory and observation. But the preference of (say) *seeing* over *understanding* seems to me capricious. For just as an opaque body may be seen, so a concept may be understood or grasped. And the parallel between the two cases is indeed rather close. In both cases the observation is not direct but through intermediaries—light, lens of eye or optical instrument, and retina in the case of the visible body, linguistic expressions in the case of the concept.'[1]

The view that time is a substance moving at a uniform rate can be seen to be an example of creating a philosophical theory by covertly recategorizing a noun not in fact used as the name of an object with object-denoting nouns. The sentence, 'Time is a substance', neither expresses an experiential proposition nor calls attention to a putative fact of usage; it presents the noun 'time'

[1] Alonzo Church, 'Abstract Entities in Semantic Analysis', *Proc. of Amer. Acad. of Arts and Sciences*, Vol. 80, No. 1 (1951), p. 104.

as belonging to the category of substantives which denote entities. So to speak, it confers the title 'name of a substance' on 'time' without giving it the status that normally goes with the title. An analogous example that comes to mind is that of a Kentucky colonel, who has the title but not the work of a colonel. The illusion of a disclosure about the nature of time, created by the form of the academic reclassification of 'time' and the names of time intervals, casts a spell over the mind which keeps us at a distance from its linguistic structure. Undoubtedly the strength of the spell has springs in the mind other than the gratification derived from the belief that a fundamental scientific investigation is being conducted by thought alone.

The semantically idle[1] redescription of the use of 'time' naturally collects around itself further empty alterations in familiar terminology. Verbs like 'flows', 'moves', 'glides', which are descriptive of timekeeping devices like water clocks and hourglasses are stretched in a way which makes them play, in appearance, the role of words denoting an action in sentences in which 'time' has, in appearance, the role of the name of a substance. Russell's remark that we cannot point to a time itself, and therefore, it might be added, that we cannot point to the passage of a time as we can to the flowing sands in an hourglass, is now to be understood somewhat differently. It is to be interpreted as an indication of his acceptance of the philosophical language game in which there is talk of a time-substance and a time-action and as also marking the difference between the game talk and ordinary substance and action talk. But the language game he played with the terminological innovations, which he joined to Occam's razor, took a somewhat different direction. In his revised notation, 'time' is classified with substantives which name fictions: 'Time' names 'a metaphysical entity', which by Occam's rule can be dispensed with. Moore holds a different view: '. . . Space and Time really *are*— . . . they are *something*; and it is obvious that they are *neither* material objects *nor* acts of consciousness';[2] by contrast to material objects and acts of consciousness, Spade and Time are

---

[1] Wittgenstein remarked in *Philosophical Investigations*, p. 51: 'The confusions which occupy us in philosophy arise when language is like an engine idling, not when it is doing work.' We might add that in philosophy language has a different kind of work, more like that of an actor than like that of a merchant who uses language for practical purposes.

[2] *Some Main Problems of Philosophy*, p. 16.

'*unsubstantial* kinds of things'.[1] What Moore wishes to highlight is a difference between the substantive 'time' and names of substances, e.g. 'water'. And he marks the difference by linking the noun 'time' with the phrase 'unsubstantial thing'. He accepts the philosophical classification of the term with nouns denoting things but marks the difference between it and them by giving it a special classification in the category of thing-words. Russell marks the difference by classifying 'time' with names of metaphysical fictions, and Moore does this by classifying it with names of unsubstantial things. Both Moore and Russell play their games in the style of language which makes it look as if theories about time are under consideration.

St Augustine's question, 'What is time?', in one of its meanings, is to be construed as a request for an academic decision on how to describe the substantive 'time', whether as the name of a substance or not. And his strange complaint can be understood as an expression of unconscious ambivalence about a semantically empty redistricting of the boundaries of certain words. Other and related deployments of the language of time easily give rise to similar complaints.[2] Wittgenstein remarked: 'It is not new facts about time which we want to know. All the facts that concern us lie open before us. But it is the use of the substantive "time" which mystifies us.'[3] The mystification over the substantive 'time' is in part an expression of indecision over a new classification. In part, undoubtedly, it is created by unconscious fantasies which cluster around the word, for the feeling of mystification is like the feeling we frequently have about a dream whose meaning we want to understand but which remains hidden from us. To convince oneself that philosophical theorizing about time has important connections with the unconscious, which charge the theories with

[1] *Some Main Problems of Philosophy*, p. 16. Wittgenstein has called attention to the role that the insubstantial and impalpable play in philosophy: ' . . . when we perceive that a substantive is not used as what in general we should call the name of an object, and when therefore we can't help saying to ourselves that it is the name of an aethereal object. I mean, when we are embarrassed about the grammar of certain words, and when all we know is that they are not used as names for material objects.' (*The Blue Book*, p. 47.)

[2] Wittgenstein's words come to mind in this connection: '. . . there is puzzlement and mental discomfort, not only when our curiosity about certain facts is not satisfied . . . but also when a notation dissatisfies us . . .' (*The Blue Book*, p. 59.)

[3] *The Blue Book*, p. 6.

the greatest interest, one need only attend to metaphors imbedded in talk about time, metaphors which give us glimpses into fears, wishes, and obsessions that are active in us but to which we are strangers.

8

MOORE'S COMMONPLACE BOOK

G. E. Moore was one of the philosophical titans who changed the course of philosophy and our way of doing it. The appearance of his *Commonplace Book* is thus an event of special importance, not only for those philosophers who, in varying degrees, do their work under his influence, but also for those who resist it. Moore kept philosophical notebooks between 1919 and 1953, nine altogether; and Dr Casimir Lewy has published a selection of the entries, in chronological order, under the title Moore gave to his last six notebooks. The reflections recorded in the notebooks, which Moore intended for his private use, are indeed a welcome addition to the things he published during his lifetime: they exemplify the same ideal of clarity and accuracy that his known writings do, and they will undoubtedly add to the effect Moore has already had on the practice of philosophy.

In his memoir of Moore, Professor Braithwaite writes that '. . . after 1925, when "A Defence of Common Sense" caused rumours of his "method of analysis" to spread throughout the English-speaking philosophical world, there was hardly a year in which there were not one or two British or American philosophers, junior and senior, who had contrived, sometimes with great difficulty, to spend a term or a year in Cambridge to sit at Moore's feet.'[1] Moore's 'method of analysis' has of course become an established way of doing philosophy, and it is continuously exemplified in his *Commonplace Book*. There can be no doubt whatever that the effect Moore's analytical method, and particularly that part of it which goes under the name of 'translation into the concrete', has had on philosophy is deep, permanent, and salubrious, and that, despite expected reactions against it, academic philosophy will become less and less available as a sanctuary for intellectuals who work on the premise that depth of thought is incompatible with clarity of thought and who have a predilection for the former. At one important university an attempt has been in process to

[1] 'George Edward Moore 1873–1958', *Proceedings of the British Academy*, Vol. XLVII, p. 300.

revive a way of thinking in philosophy which was popular before Moore's work sobered philosophers, before it brought them down to the earth of Common Sense. But its revival is uneasy, and it is safe to say that the prospects of its having a considerable duration and influence are not excellent—because of what Moore has done for philosophy. What was all right before Moore is not all right after Moore. The two most important things which Moore did for philosophy, to give a general characterisation, were first, to bring philosophical talk into connection with ordinary language, which no philosopher really gives up or even modifies to make it square with his philosophical talk, and second, to show philosophers, by the example of his own work over the years, how to use the technique of analytical elucidation. The first tended to bring to our awareness the splitting mechanism which kept our philosophical talk psychologically sealed off from our everyday use of language. And this awareness enabled us to scrutinise philosophical statements with improved vision. The second, the method of analysis as practised with Moore's enormous skill and in combination with an intellectual integrity which everywhere shows through, enabled us to see, or to begin to see, what the limits of philosophical investigations were, what sort of information it could yield. Socrates gave us the formula: follow the argument wherever it leads. Moore's actual practice gives us the formula, not easy to adhere to: follow the analysis *impersonally* wherever it leads. *The Commonplace Book*, which covers Moore's private reflections for a period of thirty-four years, is a continuous illustration of Moore's method. It will easily be realised that this is a book for thoughtful browsing, not for reading straight through.

Braithwaite states in his memoir that 'Moore rarely directly attacked the question of what it is to give an analysis, and there are only eight pages in his published writings devoted explicitly to this question'.[1] This is substantially correct, and it is interesting that in the *Commonplace Book* also very little is expressly given over to the question as to what the conditions are which govern the correct analysis of a concept. The first entry in Notebook VI reviews some of Moore's discussion in the eight pages referred to in *The Philosophy of G. E. Moore* and contains several interesting and useful observations on the difference between statements

---

[1] 'George Edward Moore 1873–1958', *Proceedings of the British Academy*, Vol. XLVII, p. 301.

which display what might be called a 'decomposition' analysis of a concept and statements whose apodoses are not, either explicitly or implicitly, 'contained in', 'part of', or 'included in' their protases, yet follow logically from them. Thus, although according to the logician's book of rules, the disjunctive statement 'cats mew v dogs bark' formally, or logically, follows from the first disjunct, the statement cannot according to Moore's criteria be properly said to constitute an *analysis* of the disjunct, as it is not contained in or a part of 'cats mew'. A common way of characterising an analytic proposition is to say that it is one the consequent of which is *identical with* some part of the antecedent, so that the joint assertion of the antecedent and the negation of the consequent is self-contradictory. But 'cats mew v dogs bark' is not identical with part (nor the whole) of 'cats mew', although 'cats mew. $\sim$ (cats mew v dogs bark)' is self-contradictory. The criterion of the contradictoriness of the denial is, as Moore by implication maintains, not a condition for analyticity: a proposition may be an instance of a law of formal logic and not be analytic. It is important to point this out, in order to make modern logicians look again at some, at least, of their elementary formulas. The formula '$q. \supset .p$ v q' is not analytic, in that 'p v q' is not an *analysis* of 'q', although 'p v q' is said to *follow from* 'q'. We might be inclined to justify our saying that 'p v q' follows from 'q' by pointing out that '$q: \sim p. \sim q$' is self-contradictory. It could be charged, however, that 'q' has been smuggled into the formula via an inconsistency in which it plays no sort of role. Whatever has happened to create a rift between the criteria of 'Moore-analyticity' and the criterion of the self-contradictoriness of the opposite, the rift needs to be called to the attention of logicians. In the same entry, Moore criticises Professor Hempel who, with other logicians, has put forward the claim that a proposition which is a specification of '$(\exists x)\phi x$' is also a specification of '$(\exists x)\phi x. \sim (\phi x. \sim \phi x)$', that, e.g. 'Something is a cat' is the *same* proposition as 'Something is a cat and it is not the case that it is both a cat and not a cat'. The consequence of this claim that Moore brings out is that 'every tautology is the same as every *other* tautology', which is to say that there is only *one* tautology. But is would seem obvious that 'It is not the case that there is something which is both a beetle and not a beetle' is not the same proposition as 'It is not the case that there is something which is both a granite mountain and not a granite mountain'. In accordance with the conditions Moore has laid down for anything being an analysis, he points out that '$(\exists x)\phi x. \sim (\phi x. \sim \phi x)$' is not *contained* in ($\exists x)\phi x$' and thus is not an analysis of it. A cleavage is shown thereby to exist between logical entailment and Moore-analyticity. The underlying point of this would seem to be, to put the matter quite generally, that '$p. \supset. \sim p \vee p$' and also '$p. \supset. \sim q \vee \sim q$' are logicians' formulas[1] which need further looking at: the negation of the first produces a contradiction between *antecedent* and *part* of the denied consequent (which would indicate that the other part has been smuggled in), while the negation of the second produces no contradiction *between* antecedent and negated consequent.

The *Commonplace Book* contains something under 190 entries, varying in length from two lines to as many as six pages; and as those who got to know Moore would expect, there are no reflections on 'the meaning of life' and related popular topics.[2] With perhaps one exception, Moore throughout addresses himself to technical points, and always with an absence of flamboyance and with meticulous regard for accuracy. The topics touched on or dealt with at substantial length, and in many instances returned to again and again, are varied, including points about time, causality, necessity, language, entailment, propositions and sentences, sense-data, motion, universals, certainty, existence, number. The weight of the subject-matter in roughly the first half of the *Commonplace Book* is theory of perception; the weight of the subject-matter in the latter part is logic and language, although, of course, these subjects are not treated exclusively in one or the other parts of the book. Moore's passionate and abiding desire for truth, or to use a word which carries with it less of an emotional aura than the word 'truth' does, his passionate and constant wish to get at the *facts*, make him come back to and re-examine many times points he had made and analyses he had performed. Moore had a deep respect for philosophy and he approached its problems with the attitude of a scientist. He did not deliver himself with

[1] The first formula results from simple substitution on '$q. \supset .p \vee q$' and the second, in Lewis' notation written '$p. \prec .q \vee \sim q$', is argued for in Lewis and Langford's *Symbolic Logic*, p. 251.

[2] Moore sometimes surprised his friends with the unexpected. Some of us who enjoyed musical sessions with him expected him to have a strong preference for Bach as against such romantics as Schumann and Hugo Wolf, but it was just the other way round.

blithe abandon on a plethora of subjects, an intellectual abandon which in so many shows an underlying disrespect for their subject. In his private notebooks as in the writings Moore published while alive he shows the steadfast concern of the scientist to make sure of his findings; and his limitations are the same as those of a research scientist.

A few comments may be made about two or three of the major topics in the book. As is well known, Moore's published writings played an absolutely central role in the modern development of sense-datum theory, but in none of them, with the exception of his last paper, 'Visual Sense-Data', which appears in the volume *British Philosophy in the Mid-Century* edited by Professor C. A. Mace, did he come to a decision about the question of whether visual sense-data are ever parts of the surfaces of physical things. In his last paper he decides against the view that they are. It therefore comes as a surprise to read in one of his early entries (p.78) 'Double images have convinced me that the sense-datum of which I am speaking when I say "That's a sofa" is *not* identical with any part of the surface of the sofa'. His argument, in this entry, is that when I see the sofa or my finger double (1) 'the two images are two different *things*' and (2) it cannot be 'that one of the two is the surface of my finger, & the other something else, not identical with any physical object.' The conclusion to be drawn from this line of reasoning would seem to be that visual sense-data are *images*, the same in their intrinsic nature as after-images one sees with closed eyes: they are open-eye images, so to speak. The question arises (p. 79) as to 'whether sense-data continue to exist when we don't see them', and this question would seem to have a categorical answer, namely, that they cannot. After-images which we have with closed eyes, like dream images, are the kind of things that do not exist unperceived; and if visual sense-data are *images* they too are the kind of things that do not exist unperceived. A dream does not go on in the absence of a dreamer, nor an image in the absence of a perceiver. Nevertheless to Moore the visual sense-datum of a sofa [the example in the entry changes to that of a visual sense-datum of a jug] is something which when he stops seeing it 'seems only a cessation of [his] seeing it, *not* of the coloured thing [he] saw' (p. 79). So far as I am aware Moore does not resort to the Humean sort of explanation of how we come to have the idea of 'independent and continu'd things', the bogus explanation, that is, of how we form an idea which, according to Hume's own showing, we cannot have.

To restate the matter linguistically, in terms of what it makes sense and does not make sense to say, the terms 'image' (in the sense of mental image) and 'surface of a material thing' have a use which makes the expression 'image which is part of the surface of a material thing' descriptively senseless. They also make senseless, rule out from having any application in the language, such expressions as 'image which exists but which no one has', and such a philosophical form of words as 'independent and continued image'. If, now, the visual appearances that things present are identified with visual sense-data, which in turn are counted as images, then no visual appearance can be identical with part of the surface of a physical thing, and no thing can, logically, be as it looks. For if the surface of a thing could have the visual colour, say, it appears to have, we could picture to ourselves parts of the surface. But what we can picture could, theoretically, be presented to our senses, which is to say that it is a possible appearance, or a possible sense-datum. If, however, a sense-datum is an image, it would make no sense to say that any part of the surface of a material thing is as it looks, as that would imply that part of the surface of a material thing is or could be an image. Furthermore, it would seem clear that if the surface cannot, logically, be as (supposedly) it appears, i.e. cannot have a property ϕ which the putative appearance endows it with, then it cannot present the appearance of having the property. The outcome of the view that sense-data are images would seem to be that it makes no sense to say, e.g., 'The top surface of the button is round and blue', and this implies that it makes no sense to say 'The top surface of the button looks round and blue'. Material things could not present visual appearances.

In several entries other considerations which Moore adduces lead to this result, and also to a further result, of which, perhaps, he was unaware, and which he might have rejected, of course. In one place he writes (p. 225): 'You can say that in "This book is *red*", "I'm having a red after-image", *red* is used in the *same* sense, and that in saying of a book that it "*is* red" and of an after-image that it "*is* red", "is" is being used in a different sense, but "red" in the same: that "is" in the first case = "would look to a

normal eye by good light", and in the second something indefin-
able. "*Is* red", "*was* red", "*will be* red" certainly have different
meanings in the 2 cases, but *one need not say* < ? > that "red" has.'
In another place he writes (p. 147): 'It is quite certain that when
you say of a physical surface that it "looks blue", "blue" is being
used in the same sense as when you say of an after-image (closed
eye) that it *is* blue. Why? (It is a necess. condition of its looking
blue to you, that you should see the colour blue, in the same sense
as when you see an after-image which is blue.) But this being so,
the phrase "it looks blue, but it isn't blue" is deceptive, because it
looks as if you were saying of the very same quality which the
thing looks to have, that it hasn't got it; whereas if I am right
that "*is* blue" in this usage = "would look blue to normal persons
in good daylight at a proper distance", it's really only a play on
words . . . On my view, it throws a curious light on the use of
"looks" of physical things: we only say "looks ϕ" when ϕ is a
property which no physical thing *could* possibly have—which it's
nonsense to attribute to any.'[1] The implication this would seem
to have is that things cannot, logically, *appear* to have properties of
colour and shape. For if it is logically impossible for anything *to be*
blue, then it is logically impossible for anything to look *to be* blue,
and if 'it's nonsense to attribute' ϕ to x (e.g. weight to numerical
oddness) it is nonsense to attribute to x the appearance of its
looking to be ϕ. What a thing looks to be it could, in principle, be,
and what it cannot, in principle, be it cannot sensibly appear to be:
we cannot with sense 'say "looks ϕ" when ϕ is a property which no
physical thing could possibly have—which it's nonsense to
attribute to [it]'.

The result that material things cannot sensibly look to have
colour or shape is strange, as Moore notes. Stranger still, perhaps,
is the further consequence that *nothing* could appear to have
properties of colour and shape (and other sensible properties also,
of course). On the present view sense-data cannot be said to have
the properties material things sensibly *look* to us to have, and it
might be contended that sense-data themselves cannot, therefore,
exist. Putting this aside, however, and looking instead at a common
characterisation of sense-data, namely, that they '. . . always

---

[1] It is interesting that in *Some Main Problems of Philosophy*, p. 38, Moore
had said: 'It seems very probable . . . that *none* of the sizes and shapes seen
were the size or the shape of the real envelope'.

really have the qualities which they sensibly appear to us to have',[1] it can be maintained that sense-data cannot themselves present sensible appearances. In the ordinary use of 'appears' and 'looks' according to which it is intelligible English to say, e.g., '*x* looks (or appears to be) blue but that is not its actual colour', it is literal nonsense to say, 'My sense-datum looks blue, and as closer inspection shows, actually is blue', just as it is not intelligible English to say, 'My after-image looks blue, but perhaps it isn't; I shall have to look again'. When a philosopher makes the statement 'A sense-datum has the properties it sensibly appears to have', he means to say, 'A sense-datum *necessarily* has the properties it sensibly appears to have'. It is clear that in his philosophical use of 'appears', to say with regard to a sense-datum, or an after-image, that it looks blue is to say *the same thing as to say* that it is blue: 'A sense-datum has the colour it appears to have' says the same thing as 'A sense-datum has the colour it has'. In the ordinary, nonphilosophical sense of 'appear' and 'look' it is 'nonsense to attribute' appearances to sense-data: 'in the case of a [closed eyes] after-image there is no sense in saying that it would look red under certain circumstances, but doesn't look red now' (p. 327). If it is logically impossible for a sense-datum to look blue or round, and also logically impossible (on the view that Moore was trying out) for material objects to look blue or round, then the plain consequence is: *nothing* can, logically, look blue or round. Moore undoubtedly would have said about this, as he does say about the consequence he elicits, that its 'strangeness might be used as an argument that it isn't true' (p. 147). Common Sense is his final criterion, and it is interesting to realize that a good many years ago he was impelled to write about a type of view under frequent discussion in recent years: 'Broad says, & Russell commends his opinion, that I can never tell (even with the smallest probability?) that when I judge with certainty that a particular colour is a shade of blue, what I mean by using the words "is a shade of blue" is the same as what anyone else means. This view seems to me to be nonsense. I know not only with great probability but with certainty, that *I* mean by "is a shade of blue" what other people mean by it: though *how* I know this I cannot tell' (p. 18).

Two closely related topics which Moore considers in a number

---

[1] 'A Defence of Common Sense', *Philosophical Papers*, p. 56.

of entries are universals and propositions, with regard to which he consistently takes a Platonic position, i.e. he holds that universals and propositions are a kind of entity. Braithwaite states that he has not been able to detect any positive influence whatever on Moore by Wittgenstein, and certainly Moore's thinking on universals and propositions was not in any way affected by the various things, now so much in vogue, that Wittgenstein said about them. Moore confided to me only a few years ago that in his opinion *all* that Wittgenstein meant by 'rule of grammar' was what he, Moore, meant by 'necessary proposition'. Moore and Wittgenstein respected each other, but neither succeeded in influencing the other. And perhaps this was as it should be, for each had his own things to say.

To return to universals and propositions, in one place, interestingly enough, Moore asks the question 'But what *is* a proposition?', rather than the question (the form of which he made famous) 'What is the analysis of the meaning of the word "proposition"?' One has the impression that he was never satisfied that he knew *what* a proposition was, its breed. With the great clarity which was almost unique with him, he distinguishes in various ways between sentences and propositions, between saying a sentence, understanding a sentence, asserting a proposition, etc. To give one example of a distinction he makes, whose implications it is worthwhile to try to get clear about, he writes (p. 359): 'The words (or sentence) "He said it *was* raining" obviously don't mean the same as the words "He said the words 'It *was* raining' ". A man may quite well have said it was raining without saying those words; & he might quite well have said those words without saying that it was raining.' There are a few places where Moore slips into using the word 'proposition' to mean sentence (p. 260). However, with typical accuracy he distinguishes in a number of enlightening and useful ways between the uses of 'proposition' and 'declarative sentence'. He remarks on the 'illegitimate sense in which people use [the word "true"] when they say that sentences are *true*' (p. 231), and later he says (p. 375): 'Every proposition which is true, except propositions about sentences, *could* have been true, even if there had been no sentences: from the fact that it's true that the sun is shining it doesn't follow that there are any sentences, since if the sun *is* shining, it follows that it's true that it is, & it obviously does not follow that there are any sentences.'

It is not easy to see how philosophers like F. P. Ramsey and A. J. Ayer would, following Moore's carefully drawn distinctions, be able to meet Moore's Platonic claim about propositions, without invoking the so-called Verification Principle. And it hardly needs to be said that Moore knew the Verification Principle and was perfectly familiar with its application to statements about universals and propositions. Moore's version of Ramsey's view about propositions is that '. . . a proposition is a class of sentences, grouped together as having the same meaning' (p. 359). Ayer's statement of the position is the following: '. . . we may define a proposition as a class of sentences which have the same intensional significance for anyone who understands them. Thus, the sentences, "I am ill", "Ich bin krank", "Je suis malade" are all elements of the proposition "I am ill".'[1] Against this view Moore could say (p. 375): 'It is *not true* that if there were no instances of sentences there would be no propositions; since, even if there had never been any sentences, some propositions might have been true & others false. . . .' A curious consequence of the Ramsey view would seem to be that understanding an indicative sentence in one language implies knowing sentences in all languages which translate into it. For understanding 'I am ill' implies knowing the proposition it expresses; and if the proposition is the class of sentences which have the same meaning as or translate into the sentence, then understanding it implies knowing the sentences 'Ich bin krank', 'Je suis malade', and their equivalents in all other languages.

Moore's analyses were always guided by considerations of correct language, and it may not be too far off the mark to say that facts of correct or proper usage were the ultimate facts for him. Indeed, if we stop to reflect on the matter we may wonder what it is a philosopher is doing who goes against usage. Moore, as is well known, represents him as making a 'mere mistake'; and if this is not the final explanation of what the philosopher does, it is a necessary step toward the right explanation. In one entry he observes (p. 258): 'To talk of *deducing* one sentence from another sentence is not English. What these people must mean is deducing *what is expressed by* one sentence from *what is expressed* by another.' To point this out is important, and it is also important to point out, as he does elsewhere, differences in use between the 'if *p*, *q*' of

---

1 *Language, Truth and Logic*, 2nd edition, p. 88.

ordinary language and the logician's '$p \supset q$' (p. 391): 'And it is certain that a person who knew either of these 3 possibilities [$p.q$, $\sim p.q.$, $\sim p. \sim q$] to be the case would be deceiving you if he said "if p, q". If you asked him "How do you know that 'if p, q'?" & he said "because I know $\sim p$", or said "because I know q", we should say that it is *not* a good reason for saying "if p, q"—it doesn't shew that you know "if p, q"; whereas it would be a good reason for $p \supset q$.' Being told this would help students of formal logic and it might also have a moderating effect on logicians.[1]

A final fragment of analysis should be cited which occurs in the last entry of the *Commonplace Book*. The whole entry is something more that a page and bears the title *Free Will*. It contains the following sentences: 'What is a "voluntary movement"? When a bird flies away, that is a voluntary movement; but the bird doesn't "choose" to make it. And in general we don't *choose* our voluntary movements, or *decide* to make them.' This presents a distinction which is enlightening, for it calls attention to similarities and differences between 'Mary blushed furiously', 'Mary slipped but managed to right herself', 'She sat down', 'She wrote a letter', 'She decided to go to the cinema'. It is also, perhaps, a piece of autobiography. Moore, more than anyone I have ever known or know about, could with inner dignity come to terms with what has to be.

---

[1] In one way or another the two so-called paradoxes of material implication, '$q. \supset .p \supset q$' and '$\sim p. \supset .p \supset q$', tend to be represented as exhibiting astonishing properties of 'if p, q' rather than uninteresting properties of disjunction artificially freed from conditions of relevance.

9

AUSTIN'S SENSE AND SENSIBILIA

This book[1] was reconstructed by G. J. Warnock from notes Professor J. L. Austin prepared for a course of lectures he first gave in Oxford in Trinity Term, 1947, under the title 'Problems of Philosophy'. The title was changed to 'Sense and Sensibilia' the following year. Mr Warnock deserves to be commended for a piece of work which must have been as difficult as its result is excellent. It is a considerable feat of sympathetic identification to have achieved the kind of continuity and order of thought as well as the stylistic continuity found in the book from the sketchy lecture notes a practised lecturer like Austin would need. Mr Warnock assures the reader in his Foreword that '. . . in all points of substance (and in *many* points of phraseology) his *argument* was the argument which this book contains', and there can be no doubt whatever that Austin's thoughts have been recorded meticulously and with admirable clarity.

The reconstructed lectures, which are divided into eleven parts, are a detailed, point by point, critique of phenomenalism:[2] the first ten parts are a philosophical attack on the doctrine as presented and developed by A. J. Ayer in his *The Foundations of Empirical Knowledge*, with some references to H. H. Price's *Perception*; the last part directs several criticisms at Warnock's Penguin, *Berkeley*, with much of which Austin declares himself to be in general agreement. In view of the destruction Austin thought he had inflicted on phenomenalist theory it would be interesting to know with what he did agree. A good many philosophers, particularly English philosophers, will undoubtedly have

---

[1] *Sense and Sensibilia*. By J. L. Austin. Reconstructed from the Manuscript Notes by G. J. Warnock (Clarendon Press: Oxford University Press, 1962), p. 144.

[2] Austin wishes it to be understood at the outset that he is not going to come out for realism, which he describes as 'the doctrine that we *do* perceive material things (or objects)' (p. 3). Later he states that '. . . . few philosophers if any are so brazen as to deny that material things are ever perceived in any "sense" at all . . .' (p. 103).

the idea that Austin's critique, which in many places is penetrating, delivers the *coup de grâce* to sense-datum theory; but it
may not be out of place here to observe that a philosophical
theory is an intellectual phoenix which springs anew from its own
ashes. I cannot resist an anecdote. At a party in Oxford some ten
years ago I was facetiously asked whether there were any sense-
data in the States. My reply was that probably there were more
sense-data there than in England, as there were more Americans
than Englishmen. Of course, the idea the philosopher wished to
convey was that no competent philosopher would any longer
seriously believe that there are such things as sense-data, any more
than a competent chemist would believe that there is such a
substance as phlogiston. But in fact there were then (as there are
now) very able philosophers who held, and knew how to defend,
sense-datum theory, amongst them G. E. Moore. And this my
colleague in repartee knew perfectly well. The point of all this is
that in philosophy a view which is dead may, nevertheless, be
very much alive and a mortal wound be less than fatal.

Austin's avowed aim in his *Sense and Sensibilia* lectures, which
he gave a number of times over a period of twelve years, on its
negative side was to rid philosophy of 'such illusions as "the
argument from illusion" ' (p. 4). Doing this consists of 'unpicking,
one by one, a mass of seductive (mainly verbal) fallacies, or
exposing a wide variety of concealed motives—an operation which
leaves us, in a sense, just where we began' (pp. 4-5). It is not easy
to see why exposing fallacies in the 'approved reasons' for holding
theories which, according to Austin, are at least as old as Heraclitus
should leave us where we began, in any sense. The only thing that
comes to mind is that in an oblique way Austin is giving recognition to the mysterious property philosophical propositions have,
namely, of remaining in dispute after being refuted—'which leaves
us just where we began'. This is not to suggest that he ever
entertained a notion other than usual current notions about the
nature of philosophical theories and arguments. One of Wittgenstein's remarks was that what the bedmaker says is all right, what
the philosopher says is all wrong; and there is a hint that this idea
lurked in Austin's mind. He characterises the position under
consideration in his lectures as 'typically *scholastic*', which is to
say that it is the kind of position which results from 'an obsession
with a few particular words, the uses of which are over-simplified,

not really understood or carefully studied or correctly described'
and to 'an obsession with a few (and nearly always the same) half-
studied "facts" ' (p. 3). He remarks parenthetically, 'I say "scholastic", but I might just as well have said "philosophical" ' (p. 3).
A scholastic view (or a typically scholastic view) is, one may
gather, some sort of linguistic-factual muddle, and if not a muddle
then not scholastic. That is to say, there can be no true view which
is scholastic. And if Austin's equating of 'philosophical' with
'scholastic' is to be taken seriously, then the implication is that no
theory can be both true and philosophical. In Berkeleian phraseology, to be a philosophical theory is to be a muddle; and when the
muddle is removed so is the philosophical theory. There are hints
of this elsewhere in Austin's writings, but they are not much more
than hints. Thus at the end of his paper 'Ifs and Cans' he writes:
'Is it not possible that the next century may see the birth, through
the joint labours of philosophers, grammarians, and numerous
other students of language, of a true and comprehensive *science of
language*? Then we shall have rid ourselves of one more part of
philosophy (there will still be plenty left) in the only way we ever
get rid of philosophy, by kicking it upstairs'.[1] The idea that comes
through is that philosophy is a muddle which is to be *got rid of*,
and that this is to be effected through a combination of disciplines.
Interestingly enough, Professor D. J. O'Connor has expressed
the opinion that the way to *save* philosophy, make it respectable,
is for philosophers to improve their understanding and increase
their knowledge of the various disciplines with which the parts
of philosophy are, or appear to be, connected. About Austin, the
most that can be said that he probably harboured the idea that
philosophy was compounded of confusion and misrepresentation,
linguistic and factual, but that he was very ambivalent about it—
'there will still be plenty left'.

On its negative side his critique of phenomenalism, by bringing
to light a number of remarkably persistent, seductive fallacies, was
intended to rid us of the 'constant repetition of assertions that are
not true, and sometimes not even faintly sensible', repetition
which he found boring. On its positive side, a 'technique for
dissolving philosophical worries (*some* kinds of philosophical
worry, not the whole of philosophy)' (p. 5) was to be learned
from it. One thing may be remarked before getting on to Austin's

[1] *Philosophical Papers*, p. 180.

examination of sense-datum theory. He describes the fallacies into which a succession of great philosophers since before Plato have been 'bamboozled' as seductive; and it would be natural to think that the fallacies must be extremely subtle to trap great thinker after great thinker over so vast a period of time. Nevertheless, in the course of discussing specific mistakes he uses such expressions as 'plain nonsense' (p. 10), 'grossly tendentious' (p. 47), 'grotesque exaggerations' (p. 54), 'wantonly wrong' (p. 100) 'wanton misuse' (p. 100), 'completely mad' (p. 30), 'wildly wrong' (p. 49), 'impossible travesty' (p. 121), 'perfectly absurd' (p. 122), 'gross misuse' (p. 115). It is not easy to share the claim that a fallacy is seductive with the charge that it is gross and perfectly absurd. He sometimes even suggests that philosophical mistakes are machinations: one mistake is described as 'little better than a frame-up' (p. 138); in another place he speaks of 'a little quiet undermining [of the plain man's position] already being effected by these turns of phrase' (p. 9); and in still another place he says, '. . . to state the case in this way is simply to soften up the plain man's alleged views for the subsequent treatment' (p. 11).

The general doctrine Austin wishes to examine is stated in the following words: 'We never see or otherwise perceive (or "sense"), or anyhow we never *directly* perceive or sense, material objects (or material things), but only sense-data (or our own ideas, impressions, sensa, sense-perceptions, percepts, etc.)' (p. 2). This doctrine seems so strange to him that he thinks one might want to ask how seriously it is intended and how literally those who have held it wish their words to be taken. But he thinks that this question had better not be gone into, at least immediately. It does seem clear to him, however, that the doctrine has been 'thought *worth stating*' (p. 3). The question raised in Part I he does not return to in any of the succeeding lectures, but in any case the answer is not far to seek. There cannot be a shadow of doubt that philosophers who put forward the view, e.g., G. E. Moore, intended it to be treated seriously and their words understood literally. The strange thing is that Austin should even have felt the need to raise the question or to have remarked that philosophers *have* thought the doctrine worth stating. His ostensible reason for allowing that it 'deserves serious attention' is that 'people find it disturbing' (p. 3). He does not explain the nature or extent of their disturbance, for which, it is to be supposed, his lectures were a therapy.

Some people, far from finding it disturbing, are most intrigued by it. Moore told me that what he enjoyed doing most in philosophy, what he was 'most keen on', was sense-datum theory, and in this he was not alone. As for people who may be disturbed by the theory, it is a well-known fact that there is no philosophical theory which has no opponents. In philosophy we everywhere meet with the aggressive wish to refute. I have dwelt at some length on the way Austin introduced sense-datum theory and the atmosphere with which he surrounds it, because of what this may show about how he understood a philosophical theory and what he took its critical examination to be, independently of things he has said or implied about the nature of philosophy.

Part II begins with a quotation from Ayer's *The Foundations of Empirical Knowledge* where the important philosophical distinction between direct and indirect perception is made and where it is pointed out that some philosophers are of the opinion that what we directly perceive when we perceive a thing like a matchbox is never the thing but 'an object of a different kind', the thing itself being perceived indirectly. This passage, as Austin's comments bring out, represents the plain man as having the naïve, unexamined notion that he does frequently perceive material things directly and that his belief in their existence stands in no need of justification; and it represents sense-datum philosophers as being more circumspect, as being scientific investigators whose findings in fact destroy the plain man's superstitions about the perception of things. Against the plain man they claim and profess to demonstrate that '. . . whenever we "perceive" there is an *intermediate* entity *always* present and *informing* us about something *else*' (p. 11), and of course they fancy themselves to be showing that the plain man is never right when he imagines himself to be perceiving things directly. Two out of a considerable number of comments Austin makes may be noted. He observes that '. . . talk of deception only *makes sense* against a background of general non-deception. (You can't fool all of the people all of the time.) It must be possible to *recognize* a case of deception by checking the odd case against more normal ones' (p. 11). And he also observes that '. . . if we are to be seriously inclined to speak of something as being perceived indirectly, it seems that it has to be the kind of thing which we (sometimes at least) just perceive, or could perceive, or which—like the backs of our own heads—others could perceive. For otherwise we don't want to say that we perceive the thing *at all*, even indirectly' (p. 18). These are important things to note and to develop, if we are to be led to an understanding of how the philosopher's saying that we are deceived about ϕ differs from an ordinary statement that we are deceived about ϕ, and what the philosopher's words come to. Cf. Descartes' '. . . what has especially to be noted is that our apprehension of it [the piece of wax] is not a seeing, nor a touching, nor an imagining, although it may formerly have *seemed* so' (italics mine). And what Austin says about indirect perception holds promise of improving our understanding of the elusive philosophical distinction between direct and indirect perception. Unfortunately for us, Austin develops neither of his remarks.

The lectures move on at a rapid pace, and within the compass of a hundred and forty pages a surprisingly large number of points are touched on in quick succession. Austin was obviously bent on a complete and detailed refutation of phenomenalist (and some related) theories, in various of their ins and outs. Total annihilation appears to have been his aim, and he conducts blitzkrieg after blitzkrieg; and even if his criticisms are not as devastating as he took them to be, they are an interesting and welcome addition to the controversies centring on sense-datum theory. A proper account of the contents of this packed little book together with assessments not only of his criticisms of tenets but also of the correctness of some of his formulations of philosophical views and arguments would require an essay longer than the book itself. Here an account can be given only of a small number of arbitrarily selected views and of a few of Austin's attempts to deal with them. He gives over some of his discussion to an examination of the actual uses of the words 'looks', 'seems', and 'appears' and to 'real' and 'not real', the point being that it is fatal 'to embark on explaining the use of a word without seriously considering more than a tiny fraction of the contexts in which it is actually used' (p. 83), and that going against usage gets philosophers into trouble, mires them in linguistic muddles: words with fixed meanings can't be 'fooled around with *ad lib.*' (p. 62), 'one can't abuse ordinary language without paying for it' (p. 15). To me the relevance of Austin's lexicography to the doctrines under consideration does not emerge with any clarity, and will be neglected here: the talk is usage discrimination talk, but the refutations are the refutations of standard philosophy. Austin does make an important observation about the functioning of 'a real x' and 'a not real x' with respect to each other: '. . . we make a distinction between "a real x" and "not a real x" only if there is a way of telling the difference between what is a real x and what is not' (p. 77). But he does not adequately develop this point nor make subsequent use of it. He drops the matter with the remark that 'A distinction which we are not in fact able to draw is—to put it politely—not worth making' (p. 77), which seems to imply a contradiction.

The main doctrines which Austin subjects to critical examination are the following:

(1) There are such objects as sense-data, i.e. directly perceived non-physical objects which have the properties they appear to have.

(2) We never directly perceive anything but sense-data, i.e. 'all that our senses reveal to us is the presence of sense-data' both in veridical and in non-veridical cases of perception; or to put it another way, what we are directly aware of is never 'part of a material thing'.

(3) The phenomenalist doctrine of two kinds of entities is really a two languages theory, i.e. phenomenalism is a linguistic theory to the effect that physical thing statements have a 'suitably vague translation' into statements about sense-data.

(4) Statements exclusively about an immediate experience are incorrigible.

(5) Physical things are inferred entities, i.e. the truth-values of statements about material things are inferred with more or less probability from statements about immediate experiences: in Ayer's words, '. . . the direct evidence for the existence of physical objects is sense-evidence'.

(6) Expressions used to refer to material things are intrinsically vague, whereas expressions used to refer to sense-data are precise. Austin thinks all of these propositions are false.

As is well known, the so-called argument from illusion, together with a supplementary consideration, is used to back the claim that there are such objects as sense-data. Bishop Butler gives us the formula, 'A thing is what it is and not another thing', and Austin's protest against the argument from illusion may be summed up in the formula: when we see a material thing under other than standard conditions, e.g. a straight stick partly immersed in water, what we see is the thing and *not something else*. What we are seeing '*is a stick partly immersed in water*; and it is particularly extraordinary that this should appear to be called in question—that a question should be raised about *what* we are seeing . . .' (p. 30). To bring out his point more forcefully, he considers a case of his own invention: 'If, to take a rather different case, a church were cunningly camouflaged so that it looked like a barn, how could any serious question be raised about what we see when we look at it? We see, of course, *a church* that now *looks like a barn*. We do *not* see an immaterial barn, an immaterial church, or an immaterial anything else. And what in this case could seriously tempt us to say that we do?' (p. 30). It should be noted that a sense-datum philosopher does not deny that we *see* things under non-standard conditions. He only maintains that we do not perceive them directly; what we perceive directly is how they look.

Having, according to his own lights, disposed of the philosophical claim that there are sense-data, Austin considers the argumentation designed to show (2), that we never are, in perceiving a material thing, directly aware of anything except sense-data. It would seem that having disposed of the claim that there are such objects as sense-data, he would have supposed himself to have refuted at the same time this doctrine as well as the two-languages doctrine and others in the list. Instead, he considers afresh each further claim. Here only a small number of his criticisms can be indicated. The main argument for (2) is that since what we directly perceive in both veridical and non-veridical perception is 'generically the same', or 'qualitatively indistinguishable', in each case we are directly aware only of a sense-datum. This he counters with the contention that things which are generically different may be qualitatively alike: 'For why on earth should it *not* be the case that, in some few instances, perceiving one sort of thing [a physical thing] is exactly like perceiving another [a sense-datum]?' (p. 52). That is, against Berkeley's contention that an idea can only be like another idea, he urges that an idea can be like a material thing.

With regard to (3), the view that sense-datum theory is nothing more than an invented terminology into which talk about material things translates, Austin claims that Ayer does not really believe the theory is linguistic, rather than factual, although it is his 'official doctrine' (p. 105). But taking it as a theory about language, he argues that the view embodies a number of 'serious mistakes'. One mistake consists in supposing that material thing words are introduced by 'looks', 'appears', etc. statements: 'We learn the word "pig", as we learn the vast majority of words for ordinary things, ostensively—by being told, in the presence of the animal, "*That* is a pig"; and thus, though certainly we learn what sort of thing it is to which the word "pig" can and can't be properly applied, we don't go through any kind of intermediate stage of relating the word "pig" to a lot of *statements* about the way things look, or sound, or smell' (p. 121). This is undeniably true, and it would indeed be astonishing if any philosopher actually thought the contrary. I cannot profess to speak for a linguistic phenomenalist and explain how he might agree without giving up his view. It is not, however, hard to imagine him arguing that we learn a word like 'pig' ostensively, by having it correlated for us with a set of appearances, smells, sounds, etc., and *later* learn the special words for the various appearances, smells, etc., i.e. sense-datum words.

This book is persistently polemical, so much so that it is out of the question to try to give an adequate idea of the variety and acuteness of the objections Austin raises against the aggregate of doctrines which fall under the general designation 'phenomenalism'. Undoubtedly many philosophers will be persuaded by its arguments, others not. In either case, reading the book should deepen one's understanding of a philosophical position which is important, if for no other reason than that it has been held and is being held by so many important philosophers. In my opinion it is a matter for regret that Austin did not think it necessary to explain how 'wild' and 'gross' errors could be continuously seductive to highly skilled, practised reasoners. It would be enlightening to have a serious explanation of the philosophical blindness to such a 'plain truth' as that 'there is no longer any question of collecting evidence' for the existence of, say, a pig which 'stands there plainly in view' (p. 115). Nevertheless, various of Austin's analyses will be considered enlightening by all philosophers, regardless of creed.

POSTSCRIPT

Something might be said about the nature of one point of disagreement between Ayer and Austin, for the purpose, primarily, of trying to understand Austin's ambivalent attitude toward the 'mistakes' on which phenomenalist theory is erected. The manner in which phenomenalism was presented by traditional philosophers, including Moore and Russell, created the idea that a theory about physical objects was being elaborated. But according to Ayer, to suppose that phenomenalist theory is about what chairs and shoes really are is to mistake statements about talk about things for statements about things. He, of course, puts forward the view that phenomenalism merely introduces the sense-datum way of speaking as 'a substitute for the physical object language'.[1] Austin rejects the linguistic version of phenomenalism as being Ayer's real view: '. . . it is not really true that he himself believes the questions raised to be questions about language, though this is his official doctrine' (p. 105) and '. . . I should like to point out the highly interesting fact that his way of "proving" that the whole issue is purely verbal actually shows (what I am sure in any case is quite true) that he does not regard it as really verbal at all—his real view is that *in fact* we perceive only sense-data' (pp. 59-60). Putting aside the question as to which is Ayer's real view and which his official view, the question that comes up is whether the words 'we perceive only sense-data' express a factual proposition about what we perceive or whether their import is purely verbal. It would seem that a philosophical utterance is capable of presenting at least three faces, a verbal face, an *a priori* face, and an empirical ontological face. In one of Ayer's statements all three faces are made visible at the same time: 'For, as I have already shown, the term "sense-datum" may be defined in such a way that if anyone is perceiving a physical object it *follows* that he is sensing a sense-datum: and not only that but that all that his senses reveal to him is the presence of sense-data'.[2] The second half of the quotation generates the notion that phenomenalism is an empirical theory about the nature of the sensible manifold, arrived at by induction from what our senses reveal to us. If, so to speak, we draw nearer to the words 'all that anyone's sense reveal to him is the presence of sense-data', despite the empirical atmosphere surrounding them (which tempts one to preface them with Austin's phrase 'in fact'), we can see that they do not express a factual proposition. For a philosopher who utters these words uses them in such a way that there is no describing what else than

[1] 'Phenomenalism', *Philosophical Essays*, p. 143.   [2] *Ibid.*, p. 141.

sense-data, what in addition to them, our senses might, theoretically, reveal to us: the expression 'is revealed by our senses but is not a sense-datum' is literally senseless. Nor is their import 'purely' verbal, despite the factual-linguistic appearance the theory may present, once the mists of their expressing an ontological theory are dissipated. Ayer has said, 'But surely those who have taken, or accepted, the title of phenomenalists have thought that they were doing more than extending their patronage to a word'.[1] And there can be no doubt that there is more to the controversy about sense-datum theory than just hospitality and inhospitality to a word. It is not the case that 'The only question involved is whether you agree with the proposal to use the *word* "sense-datum" '.[2] The mere introduction of a word into the language, whether by verbal or by ostensive definition, could not possibly be such a *cause célèbre*; and of course it has to be remembered that phenomenalist theory preceded by several thousand years the introduction of the term 'sense-datum' into the English language. It is the proposals behind the proposal to use the term, the hidden philosophical alterations in language, that are the real source of the continued disputation. One of the linguistic changes which hides behind the substantive 'sense-datum' is a stretched use of the word 'thing', to cover what such a term as 'sensible appearance' applies to. This is justified by the 'argument', to put it shortly, that sensible appearance, even when delusive, is *something*, not nothing. Another change consists in counting as 'just an appearance' of a thing the appearance it presents under normal conditions, i.e. erasing the ordinary distinction between talk about real properties of a thing and talk about its apparent properties. This is justified by an 'argument' which lodges the complaint of perceptual favouritism or, what really comes to the same thing, by the argument from continuity. These two language alterations, obviously intended for academic, non-commercial consumption, are brought in behind the word to which a phenomenalist extends his patronage. Presented in the guise of a theory and against the background of unaltered, everyday talk about physical things, an arresting intellectual illusion is brought into existence: a sense-datum becomes 'an *intermediate* entity *always* present and *informing* us about something *else*'. Sometimes what is being done with language will come through to some degree and then it will seem

---

[1] 'Phenomenalism', *Philosophical Essays*, p. 141.   [2] *Ibid.*

that the theory is linguistic rather than ontological. Sometimes the appearance of a factual claim about what we 'directly' perceive when we perceive a shoe, and what its nature is as well as how it is related to physical things, etc., will be in the fore, and then it will seem to us that the theory is factual, not linguistic. Sometimes both the verbal face and the empirical, non-verbal face will look out, and this will make a perceptive philosopher say: 'What is the point of introducing the sense-datum vocabulary? The idea is that it helps you to learn something about the nature of physical objects, not indeed in the way that doing science does, but that you come to understand better what is meant by propositions about physical objects, what these propositions amount to, what their "cash value" is, by restating them in terms of sense-data. That is, the fact that you *can* restate them in this way, *if* you can, tells you something important about them.'[1] It is not very difficult to understand now what makes a philosophical 'mistake' both seductive and gross. We are seduced into making a hidden language change by the unconscious need to create an illusion; and if, for whatever reason, we are hostile to the illusion, the linguistic re-editing may show through sufficiently to be represented as a mistaken claim about language, as a misrepresentation of conventional usage.

[1] 'Phenomenalism', *Philosophical Essays*, p. 141.

10

ON PERCEIVING THINGS

We do not ordinarily think that there is a serious question as to whether we ever actually see the moon, smell an orange, or feel the steering wheel of the car we are driving; but as is well known, what is not thought open to doubt in ordinary life, or for that matter in the sciences, is frequently thought to be a proper subject of doubt and of serious and protracted debate in philosophy. Philosophers who, in an ordinary circumstance would not dream of contesting each others' claims to be seeing or not to be seeing certain things, disagree over whether we *ever* perceive physical things. Some important philosophers have held views, which they have supported with reasoned considerations, according to which the common notation that we perceive things is a myth, while others have opposed such views, and have maintained that we do in some sense perceive things. Thus Moore has said: 'I have, indeed, once met a philosopher who told me I was making a great mistake in thinking that such objects [a particular chair, a particular tree, etc.] are ever seen. But I think this philosopher was certainly wrong, and was thinking that the various correct uses of "see" are limited in a way in which in fact they are not limited.'[1]

The philosopher Moore referred to was by no means an isolated instance. Descartes held that, contrary to what certainly seems to everyone to be the case, we do not perceive things by our senses. He wrote: '. . . I am almost deceived by the terms of ordinary language. For we say that we see the same wax, if it is present, and not that we simply judge that it is the same from its having the same colour and figure. From this I should conclude that I knew the wax by means of vision and not simply by the intuition of the mind; unless by chance I remember that, when looking from a window and saying I see men who pass in the street, I really do not see them, but infer that what I see is men, just as I say that I see wax. And yet what do I see from the window but hats and coats which may cover automatic machines? Yet I judge

[1] 'Visual Sense-Data', *British Philosophy in the Mid-Century* (edited by C. A. Mace), second edition (London: George Allen & Unwin, 1966), p. 205.

these to be men. And similarly solely by the faculty of judgment which rests in my mind, I comprehend that which I believed I saw with my eyes.' He also wrote: '. . . what must particularly be observed is that its perception is neither an act of vision, nor of touch, nor of imagination, and has never been such, although it may formerly have appeared to be so . . .'[1]

Other important philosophers have held the same view, or closely similar views; and all of them imply that in believing ourselves to be perceiving physical bodies we are persistently deluded. Thus John Stuart Mill wrote: 'I affirm, for example, that I hear a man's voice. This would pass, in common language, for a direct perception. All, however, which is *really perception*, is that I hear a sound. That the sound is a voice, and that voice the voice of a man, are *not perceptions* but inferences.'[2] It is useful to notice Mill's transition from the term 'direct perception' to 'really perception', and to connect this with Berkeley's observation that '. . . the senses perceive nothing which they do not perceive *immediately*: for they make no inferences'.[3] H. A. Prichard argued that, contrary to the common view about our perception, it is impossible to see things: 'It need hardly be said that this view, much as we should like to be able to vindicate it, will not stand examination'; the 'consideration of any so-called illusion of sight . . . is enough to destroy [it]'.[4] In the same vein, Bertrand Russell has written: 'It is a fallacy to suppose that a man can see matter. Not even the ablest physicist can perform this feat'.[5] And also: 'What I know without inference when I have the experience called "seeing the sun" is not the sun but a mental event in me . . . I do not "see" the furniture in my room except in a Pickwickian sense. . . . We do not actually see physical objects, any more than we hear electromagnetic waves when we listen to the wireless'.[6]

One idea which is frequently associated with the philosophical view that we do not perceive physical things is that it seems to us that we do. Another idea is that the ordinary use of such phrases as 'sees a table' and 'feels a stone' is improper, that such phrases have no application to sense-experience. It is not clear whether

---

[1] *Meditation*, II.   [2] *A System of Logic*, Bk. IV, Ch. 1, sec. 2, my italics.
[3] *First Dialogue*.
[4] *Knowledge and Perception* (Oxford University Press, 1950), p. 53.
[5] *Human Knowledge* (New York: Simon and Schuster, Inc., 1948; London: George Allen & Unwin), p. 229.
[6] *Ibid.*, p. 311.

philosophers who have this idea mean to hold that such a phrase as 'sees a table' misdescribes what occurs, in the way in which 'the sun is going down' misdescribes what actually happens, or whether they mean to hold that it has no descriptive use whatever, that its function in the language is such that not only nothing actual but nothing conceivable answers to it. Neglecting this for the moment, however, G. E. Moore has, to all appearances, rejected both claims, both the claim that we do not perceive things and the claim that such ordinary expressions as 'sees a table' and 'tastes the cheese' are in their everyday use 'wrongly apply'd', to use Hume's phrase. Moore wrote: '. . . I do not know what conditions must be fulfilled in order that I may be truly said to be *perceiving*, by sight or touch, such things as that that is a door, this is a finger, and not *merely* inferring them. Some people may no doubt think that it is very unphilosophical in me to say that we ever can perceive such things as these. But it seems to me that we do, in ordinary life, constantly talk of *seeing* such things, and that, when we do so, we are neither using language incorrectly, nor making any mistake about the facts—supposing something to occur which never does in fact occur. The truth seems to me to be that we are using the term "perceive" in a way which is both perfectly correct and expresses a kind of thing which constantly does occur, only that some philosophers have not recognized that this is a correct usage of the term and have not been able to define it. I am not, therefore, afraid to say that I do now perceive that that is a door, and that that is a finger.'[1]

It is worth remarking, in connection with the position of philosophical Commonsense, according to which we do perceive physical things, that Moore at one time held that we are aware of their existence in the same way in which we are aware of the existence of our sensations. Against Berkeley who, as he said, 'supposed that the only thing of which I am directly aware is my own sensations and ideas', Moore maintained that he was 'as directly aware of the existence of material things in space as of [his] own sensations'.[2] According to him, at the time he put this position forward, 'The question requiring to be asked about material things is thus not: What reason have we for supposing

[1] 'Some Judgments of Perception', *Philosophical Studies* (Routledge and Kegan Paul, 1922), pp. 226–7.
[2] *Ibid.*, 'The Refutation of Idealism', p. 30.

that anything exists *corresponding* to our sensations? but: What
reason have we for supposing that material things do *not* exist,
since *their* existence has precisely the same evidence as that of our
sensations'.[1] Later he came to the view that the perception of
physical objects is not the same as, or not of the same kind as,
the perception of ideas, without, however, giving up the Common-
sense view that we do see and smell things. According to his later
view our awareness of after-images, pains, and the appearances
things present to us is *direct*, but our awareness of material
things is *indirect*. In opposition to philosophers like Descartes and
Prichard and in apparent agreement with the everyday idea that
we see and smell things and that we do not systematically misapply
perception terminology, Moore held that we do perceive things but
that our perception of them is indirect, as against our awareness
of dream images, which is direct.

Philosophers who have held that we do not 'really see' things, or
that our awareness of them is not 'really perception', give the
impression of thinking themselves to have made the disconcerting
discovery that we are in a condition comparable to someone suffering from continuous and convincing hallucinations. Normally, we
should say that we see a clock but not the works behind its face,
but these philosophers tell us that the face of the clock is as much
hidden from sight as the works. Moore reassures us with the words
that he is 'not afraid to say' that we do really see things. He
encourages us to return to common sense,[2] or at any rate to a
philosophical facsimile of common sense, without, however,
dissipating all of our uneasiness. For the idea that our perception
of things is indirect is haunted by the feeling that the Cartesian-
Prichard view has not been exorcised. It in fact leaves us with the
suspicion that buried in the view that our perception of things is
indirect is the view that we do not perceive things at all.

One of Moore's uncertainties centred on whether a visual sense-
datum of a physical thing could ever be part of its surface, and,
as Professor R. B. Braithwaite has reported[3], it was not until after
forty years of 'sitting on the fence' that he decided against direct

---

[1] *Ibid.*, 'The Refutation of Idealism', p. 30.

[2] One philosopher remarked that he liked reading Moore because it 'kept him
in touch with chairs and tables'.

[3] 'George Edward Moore', *Proc. of the British Academy*, Vol. CLVII, p. 299.
In a discussion with me after the appearance of his paper, 'Visual Sense-Data',
Moore formulated his reason against supposing that a sense-datum could ever

N

realism. In giving up direct realism, i.e. in coming to hold that no part of a physical thing is perceived directly, Moore implied that things made their existence and nature known to us through something other than themselves, namely, sense-data. The position has been clearly expressed in the following words: 'We all believe in a world of physical objects, and profess to have a great deal of detailed knowledge about it. Now this world of physical objects makes its existence and its detailed nature known to us by the sensible appearances which it presents to us. And, on the sensum theory, these appearances are sensa. Sensa are therefore in some way the *ratio cognoscendi* of the physical world, whilst the physical world is in some way the *ratio essendi* of sensa.'[1]

Against the theory that we perceive material things by means of sense-data, i.e. through the sensible appearances they present, J. L. Austin has urged that we *see* the things *themselves*. With regard to the bent stick case he wrote: 'Well, we are told, in this case you are seeing *something*; and what is this something "if it is not part of any material thing"? But this question is, really, completely mad. The straight part of the stick, the bit not under water, is presumably part of a material thing; don't we see that? And what about the bit *under* water?—we can see that too. We can see, come to that, the water itself. In fact what we see is *a stick partly immersed in water*; and it is particularly extraordinary that this should appear to be called in question—that a question should be raised about *what* we are seeing . . .'[2] It is not difficult to imagine the reply a philosopher like Moore would make. It undoubtedly would be that the stick is seen indirectly and its appearance seen directly. And the view that material things are seen indirectly, by means of sense-data, does not, on the surface at least, imply that they are not seen. It does not, in any plain way, imply that in seeing the bent appearance of the stick that is partly

be part of the surface of a physical thing in the following way, to the best of my memory: A physical surface could look different to a person from the way it happens at any given time to be looking to him. A sensible appearance, however, like a mental image, could not possibly look different from the way it actually looks. Hence, if the appearance which any part of the surface of a thing presents were identical with that part of the surface, the physical surface could not present a different appearance from the one it presents. It would look the same under all possible conditions, which is absurd.

[1] C. D. Broad, *Scientific Thought* (London: Kegan Paul, Trench, Trubner & Co., 1923), pp. 266–7.

[2] *Sense and Sensibilia* (Oxford University Press, 1962), p. 30.

immersed in water we do not see the partly immersed stick. Nor is our seeing the stick in any obvious way brought into question by the view. Professor A. J. Ayer has remarked that all that our senses reveal to us are sense-data. Moore would have amended this in the following way: All that our senses *directly* reveal to us are sense-data; indirectly they reveal material things. His corresponding claim about usage would be that the English word 'see' has, in its visual meaning, two senses. He might well have said that some philosophers labour under the mistaken idea that 'see' in its visual meaning has only one sense, that of 'directly see', so that they mistakenly interpret a philosopher who denies that we directly see material things to be implying that we do not see them at all. Moore's position nevertheless leaves us with the feeling that there may be something to the objection raised against it.

It is natural to think of the terms 'directly perceive' and 'indirectly perceive' as referring to two different ways in which things are perceived, and also as referring to two ways in which the same thing might in different circumstances be perceived. They would seem to function like the pairs of opposites 'far' and 'near', 'calm' and 'disturbed', and 'hidden' and 'in plain view': what is far could, conceivably, be near, what is hidden could be revealed, and a person who is calm could become disturbed, and conversely. The terms 'directly perceive' and 'indirectly perceive' appear, in other words, to function with respect to each other in such a way that what is said to be indirectly perceived could, in principle, be said to be directly perceived, and conversely. Austin was apparently under this impression when he wrote: '. . . if we are to be seriously inclined to speak of something as being perceived indirectly, it seems that it has to be the kind of thing which we (sometimes at least) just perceive, or could perceive, or which —like the backs of our own heads—others could perceive. For otherwise we don't want to say that we perceive the thing *at all*, even indirectly'.[1] The picture suggested by the view that mental images and sensible appearances are seen directly and material things indirectly calls to mind the Platonic description of the observer who sees only the shadows thrown on a wall by figures behind him, figures he would see if he could only turn around. Broad's idea that things make their existence and nature known to us by the sensible appearances they present conjures up a

[1] *Sense and Sensibilia*, p. 18.

comparable picture. The general idea would seem to be that there are two classes of objects, material things and sense-data, which are related to each other in certain ways, and that we see things of one class directly but are prevented from seeing things of the other class in the same way and have to remain content with seeing them indirectly. Broad has remarked that 'the hypothesis that physical objects literally have colours and temperatures, though legitimate enough, is not capable of empirical verification, and therefore cannot be asserted with any high probability'.[1] His words suggest that if we were to see material things or parts of their surfaces *directly* we would *know* whether material things had colour and temperature.

On the view that things are seen indirectly and sense-data directly, it is natural to identify seeing a thing indirectly with not actually seeing it and seeing a thing directly with seeing the thing itself. In the usual way of speaking we should say that someone who sees only a man's shadow does not see the man who casts the shadow. Even if he sees the reflection in the mirror of a person committing a theft, what he sees would count in a court of law as being as good as seeing the person committing the theft; but nevertheless it would not count as seeing the person himself. He would be said to see the man, as against seeing his reflection, by looking away from the mirror and at the man himself. And it would seem to be the same with seeing a sense-datum of a material thing and seeing the thing. Seeing a thing indirectly, as against directly seeing a sense-datum, would in the ordinary way of speaking amount to seeing the sense-datum but not the thing. Construed as an empirical view about how we see things and how we see sense-data, the view comes to the claim that we see sense-data but are prevented by them from seeing things, just as we are prevented by a mirage from seeing the desert behind it.

Austin's remarks, in which 'indirectly perceive' is contrasted with 'perceive' and 'just perceive', make clear that it is *natural*, even for a sophisticated philosopher, to identify 'perceive' with 'directly perceive'. The idea which comes through is that the philosopher's use of the expression 'indirectly perceives x' is taken to imply that x itself is not perceived, and correspondingly, his use of 'directly perceives x' to imply that x itself is perceived. An important journalist's use of language in one of his articles

---

[1] *Scientific Thought*, p. 281.

supports the notion that it is natural to identify 'direct perceives x' with 'perceives x'. In writing about an American newspaper man reporting from Hanoi he contended that the authorities' wish to influence his beliefs should not 'have stopped Salisbury from reporting what Hanoi had to say as well as what he could observe directly'.[1] And a philosopher who says that *all* our senses reveal to us are sense-data normally would be taken to imply the *possibility* of our senses revealing something other than sense-data and to be saying that they just do not happen to reveal anything else. If he went on to say that things make their presence known to us by the sense-data our senses reveal, we should take him to be asserting that we do not see things—just as we should say that a person does not see the mechanism of his watch, although the ticking and the motion of the hands inform him it is there.

The philosophical view that physical things are perceived indirectly and sense-data directly looks like an empirical theory about how chairs and sheets of writing paper are perceived; and, furthermore, it seems to come down to the Cartesian-Prichard view that we do not actually perceive things, regardless of how strong the impression to the contrary may be. The view which denies that we ever see physical things flouts common sense, while the view that they are perceived indirectly seems, superficially at least, to be consonant with common sense, and to make explicit distinctions imbedded in the everyday language of perception. It is a strange thing that a philosophical view which on the surface seems to be in some sort of agreement with common sense, under its verbal skin flouts common sense as flagrantly as the view that we do not really see things. We might say that the difference between Moore's view and the Cartesian-Prichard view is only terminological and that the first view is the second camouflaged by more sober sounding language. In philosophy we have become wary of the empirical air which surrounds views, and it may turn out now, as it has invariably turned out in the past, that the empirical air gives it a false character.

What has to be looked into with special care is the distinction between direct and indirect perception. As has already been remarked, the term 'indirectly perceive' would seem at first glance to function with respect to the term 'directly perceive' in the way in which 'hidden from view' functions with respect to 'in view'.

[1] Walter Lippmann, syndicate column *Today and Tomorrow*, Jan. 14, 1967.

Now, it is easily seen that either term of a pair of antithetical terms would lose the function it has in a language if the other term were deleted and no expression existed in the language which functioned like the deleted term. For example, 'odd number' would lose its function if 'even number' was suppressed and, without going into qualifications, 'hidden from view' would lose its use to describe situations if 'in view' and its synonyms were cast out of the language. There is, however, a radical and important difference, remarked by Plato in the last argument of the *Phaedo*, between the way in which antithetical terms work with respect to each other. In the case of some antithetical terms, what is truly described by one could, in principle, be truly described by the other, while in the case of other antithetical terms what is truly described by one term could not in principle be truly described by the other. An object x which is correctly described by the words 'x is hidden from view', e.g. a barn hidden by a hill or a garden concealed by a wall, *could* be truly described by the words 'x is now in view': it makes descriptive sense to say, 'x was hidden for part of the way then came into view' or 'x was hidden from view until the wall surrounding it was torn down'. To put the matter nonverbally, what is concealed *could*, logically, be revealed. Other pairs of antithetical terms work differently: 'odd number' and 'even number' not only require each other, but numbers to which one term applies cannot, even theoretically, fall into the range of application of the other term. As 'odd number' and 'even number' are used, it is self-contradictory to say, '2 is an even number which would under certain conditions become odd', or '2 was an even number which became odd'.

It turns out that despite the idea which some philosophers have of the way 'indirectly perceive' and 'directly perceive' work with respect to each other, the terms have been assigned a function like that of 'odd number' and 'even number', rather than like that of 'hidden' and 'in view'. As is the case with the improper fraction $\frac{9}{7}$, which cannot, in principle, become a proper fraction,[1] an indirectly perceived material thing could not under any theoretical condition be directly perceived, or, to use Ayer's phrase, become an immediate object of perception. A physical thing, or any part

---

[1] This is not, of course, to say that the symbol $\frac{9}{7}$ could not be made to apply to a proper fraction; but to make it apply to a proper fraction would be to change its meaning.

of its surface, which as Moore's distinction suggests is accessible to the senses, is nevertheless logically inaccessible to direct perception. Thus, in one place, Moore said that from something he was very much inclined to hold it followed that 'no sense-datum can be identical with a physical surface, which is the same thing as to say that no physical surface can be directly apprehended: that it is a contradiction to say that any is'.[1] It cannot fail to become evident on reflection that a philosopher who declares that sense-data are the only 'immediate' objects of perception cannot tell us what it would be like for a material thing or a physical surface to be an immediate object of perception. His not being able to do this does not mean that he is temporarily at a loss which he might make good later. It means, according to his view, that *in the nature of the case* physical things cannot be immediate objects of perception. For there just is no saying what, in theory, we might do, in addition to going up to a thing, looking at it with care, feeling it, etc., to make it an immediate object of our awareness. The philosopher cannot describe a procedure, in addition to the usual one of using our eyes, nose, and ears which give us a direct perception of a thing. And he cannot do this, not because of ignorance or insufficient command of language, but because it makes no literal sense to speak of such a procedure.

The view that physical things are seen indirectly, i.e. through the intermediation of sense-data, which themselves are seen directly, turns out not to be an empirical theory about how things are seen. It is not a fact-stating theory, not one which would be understood to imply that we never in fact see chairs, trees, sheets of writing paper, or any other objects that count as material, but in their place always see something else. The words, 'material things are perceived indirectly, sense-data directly', instead of making a declaration about what sort of things are in fact hidden from sight and what sort are given to sight, would seem to state that it is *logically impossible* to see material things: that by necessity things are seen only indirectly, and by necessity sense-data are seen only directly. On the present interpretation of the distinction between direct and indirect perception, Ayer's words, 'All that our senses reveal to us are sense-data', have to be construed as expressing a logical entailment rather than a material implication:

[1] *The Philosophy of G. E. Moore*, The Library of Living Philosophers (edited by P. A. Schilpp), (Open Court Publishing Co., 1942), p. 658.

'If α is revealed to us by our senses, then α is a sense-datum' becomes ' "α is revealed to us by our senses" *entails* that α is a sense-datum'. His pronouncement would seem now to advance an *a priori* claim, namely, that it is logically impossible for α to be revealed to us by our senses and not be a sense-datum.

The Descartes-Prichard view, which in plain language denies that we see chairs, doors, and sheets of writing paper, also turns out not to be the fact-claiming theory it is naturally taken to be. If, so to speak, we draw nearer to the view and examine it with care, we can see how vastly different the *philosopher's* words 'we do not really see things' are from such a sentence as, 'He does not, as he thinks, really see a lion and a unicorn in combat; all he sees are projections on a screen'. For the philosopher is unable to say what it would be like to see a material thing, as against its only seeming to us that we are seeing one. He is unable to say what we would have to do in order to put ourselves in a position for seeing a thing. Neither, for that matter, can he tell us what we might, in fact or in fantasy, do to satisfy ourselves that it only seems to us that we are seeing one. It is entirely plain that anyone who sees as we see, hears as we hear, feels things as we feel them, etc., and nevertheless asserts that physical things are not actually seen has ruled out the possibility of describing a situation given which he would allow that a material thing was being seen. Whatever his philosophical reasons might be, holding the view eliminates the possibility of his describing a case of actually seeing a chair or a mountain, as against a case of merely seeming to see one. This means that his view is not the kind that is theoretically open to falsification. It is natural, therefore, to suppose that the philosopher's words, 'we do not see physical things like chairs and mountains', are used to express an *a priori* proposition, namely, that it is logically impossible to see, or more generally, to perceive such objects.

It should be noticed that this understanding of the position implies the impossibility of its sensibly appearing to us that we see things, equally with the impossibility of seeing them. The concepts *sees a sheet of paper* and *seems to see a sheet of paper* are so related that if it is theoretically impossible to see a sheet of paper, it is also theoretically impossible for it to seem to anyone that he is seeing a sheet of paper. If the first concept cannot have an instance, the second concept cannot have an instance either.

Just as there cannot be the sensible appearance of someone pluck-ing a white lily which is yet uniformly yellow, because there cannot, logically, be anything which is white and everywhere yellow, so there could not, in principle, be an instance of a material thing seeming to be seen if it were logically impossible for one to be seen. When Descartes wrote that our awareness of things is neither by sight nor touch 'and has never been such, although it may formerly have appeared to be so', he undoubtedly fancied himself to have demonstrated the nonexistence of a kind of occurrence and to have exposed as delusive appearance what had been taken as occurrences of things really being seen. It seems reasonable to conjecture that he failed to notice that if in fact he had demon-strated this proposition, he would also have shown that it could not have 'formerly appeared' to people that they had perceived material things by the senses. It also seems reasonable to con-jecture that Descartes would not have been prepared to deny that it has seemed, and continues to seem, to us that we do perceive things. For to deny this is to imply that there are no such *beliefs* as that chairs are sometimes seen and felt and that apples are sometimes tasted. And this would not accord with the picture the philosopher has of himself as a kind of scientist who has succeeded in exposing a deeply rooted superstition which has its source in a universal illusion of the senses.

The first conjecture, however reasonable it may at first seem, nevertheless implies an intellectual oversight that is too strange to be attributed to a long succession of thinkers who are practiced in reasoning and in the detection of contradictions. If indeed it is an oversight it is one which certainly cries out for an explanation, not only because it has gone undetected for so long a time despite the fact that the point involved is elementary, but because of a curious feature attaching to it. This is that calling attention to the consequence does not result in the expected correction. One gains the impression that a philosopher who adopts the view is held captive in a predicament from which he is *unwilling* to free him-self. He cannot bring himself to give up his position; nor can he bring himself to deny the existence of the appearances, since denying their existence would destroy the idea that he was holding a theory about the perception of things.

The view that it is logically impossible for material things to be perceived has an important consequence with regard to the use of language, which if noticed can lead to an improved understanding of the nature of the view and also of the nature of the philosophical predicament. It is clear that the fact that a concept is self-contradictory, e.g., the concept of a white expanse which is everywhere yellow, implies that the concept can have no theoretical exemplification. It is prevented from having instances by its being self-contradictory or by its being logically impossible. This implies that any expression which stands for a self-contradictory concept or which involves one as part of its meaning has no theoretical application, no use to describe a situation or to convey information about the existence or nonexistence of things or occurrences. A form of words which has a self-contradictory meaning has no descriptive function in the language; and thus a philosopher who holds a view according to which it is logically impossible to perceive objects implies that certain expressions have no descriptive use. If, as in the case of Prichard, he states his view in English, he implies that thing-perception expressions such as 'sees a hammer', 'touches an egg', 'tastes honey', 'hears the impact of billiard balls' have no use in the English language to describe occurrences of any sort. He implies this, of course, on the assumption that his view actually is to the effect that it is logically impossible to perceive physical things. And this is an assumption which may turn out to be false.

It is important to notice the difference between asserting that a concept is impossible and saying, in the same language, that the expression denoting it has no use to communicate information about nonlinguistic fact. The problem regarding the nature of logical necessity has been gone into in detail elsewhere,[1] and here only a few unguarded remarks will be made. The difference between saying that a concept is logically impossible and that any expression whose meaning it is has no descriptive use is, to stretch a point, a difference in style of speech. But the difference in style is important. The sentence, 'It is impossible for anything to be yellow while uniformly white', informs us in one mode of speech what is explicitly stated, in a different mode of speech, by the sentence, ' "being yellow and uniformly white" has no descriptive function'. But the difference in their mode of speech is paralleled by a difference in the logical character of the propositions they

---

[1] See, for example, 'Logical Necessity', in *The Structure of Metaphysics*, and 'Methods of Philosophy', sections VIII, IX, X in *Studies in Metaphilosophy*.

express, the one *a priori* and the other empirical. We might say that the difference between what the two sentences say resolves into, or is constituted by, the difference of the idioms in which the sentences are formulated, and that anyone who advances an *a priori* claim is, in an oblique, non-verbal idiom, making a claim about verbal usage in the language in which he expresses his claim. Thus if the words, 'Material things are not perceived by the senses', are used to put forward the proposition that it is logically impossible to see, touch, taste, hear, and smell material things, then in understanding his use of these words we understand him to be stating, in a form of speech in which words are not mentioned, the verbal claim that such everyday expressions as 'sees a table' and 'hears a violin' are descriptively senseless.

Looked on as making a tacit claim about expressions in everyday use, the theory that we do not see things is as obviously false as it is when construed as being about what we in fact see or do not see. As Moore has said, '. . . we do, in ordinary life, constantly talk of *seeing* such things [e.g. doors and inkstands], and . . . when we do so, we are neither using language incorrectly nor making any mistake about the facts . . .'[1] So-called philosophers of ordinary language have thought that recourse to the language in ordinary use was sufficient to refute the philosophical theory that we do not see things. There can, of course, be no serious, non-philosophical question as to how a mistaken idea about the use of terminology is to be corrected: ordinary language is the only court of appeal in which this is to be done. And there can be no real question regarding the correctness of the procedure of the ordinary language philosopher, *if* the philosophical theory is, in some way, about *actual* usage. The refutation is conclusive if philosophers, like someone new to the English language who thinks that the phrase 'sees a door' is nonsensical, have somehow got the idea that it and other phrases in everyday language have no correct use.

The philosophical mistake differs in a remarkable way, however, from an ordinary mistaken idea about verbal usage. It has the curious feature that it can successfully resist correction by recourse to the language in actual use. Instead of relinquishing the mistaken idea a philosopher will raise questions about what constitutes correct usage, or he will appeal to the arguments by

[1] *Philosophical Studies*, p. 226.

which he professes to show that a piece of terminology expresses what is logically impossible. With respect to his 'mistake' the philosopher seems to become a lawyer for the defence. What comes through clearly is that, whatever the nature of his mistake may be, he *protects* it, instead of giving it up. Pointing out to him that he himself talks in the usual ways, in disregard of what he says about the usual ways of talking, has at most the effect of momentarily embarrassing him. He shows a remarkable attachment to his mistaken idea which, if it is the idea we take it to be, he can see as well as anyone else. His behaviour is markedly unlike the behaviour of someone who has a mistake pointed out to him, and indeed, he behaves more like someone who has not made a mistake. The realistic conclusion to draw from all this is that the refutation by recourse to ordinary language is not a refutation of the *philosophical* view, which means, of course, that despite any verbal appearances to the contrary, the philosophical view does not make a factual claim with regard to ordinary language. The view that we cannot perceive things is not a nonverbal way of saying that expressions like 'sees an apple' and 'feels a doorknob' have no descriptive sense in *ordinary language*; and the plausible conclusion to proceed to from this is that the philosopher *makes* these expressions literally senseless in a game he plays with language.

A consideration which supports both the idea that the philosopher does not suffer from a bizarre delusion about a great number of expressions in constant use and also the idea that he is playing a game with familiar terminology is the following. In arguing out of existence the possibility of perceiving things the philosopher does not rule out the possibility of its seeming to us that we perceive things. To put the matter in the verbal idiom, his eliminating from the language such expressions as 'sees a lemon' and 'smells a lily' is not accompanied by the suppression of 'seems to see a lemon' and 'seems to smell a lily'. And this does not square with the notion that he mistakenly thinks the former expressions to be descriptively senseless. For if he did think them senseless, he could not fail to think that the latter expressions also lacked a correct use. Not even the intoxication of metaphysics could induce a state of mind in which someone thought that the phrase 'evenness sits on blue' was not literally intelligible but that the phrase 'the sensible appearance of evenness sitting on blue' made descriptive sense, described an appearance. When a philosopher like Descartes tells us that, though it has seemed to us in the past that we did see and touch physical things, it nevertheless is logically impossible to see and touch them, what he is doing is playing a game with language, a game which for obvious reasons he has to conduct in the ontological idiom. An arresting illusion is created by the words 'it is impossible to perceive things', which would vanish into thin air if the philosopher said, 'In my language game "perceives things" has no descriptive use'.

The view that sense-data are perceived directly and physical things indirectly has a similar explanation, but with an important difference having to do with the invented terms 'direct perception' and 'indirect perception'. It has already been noted that the view that things are not seen hides behind, and we might say is the life of, the view that we see things indirectly. The underlying psychology of both views, i.e. their unconscious content, is undoubtedly the same, for the difference between them turns out to be one of terminology. One is openly shocking, and is taken to be in violent conflict with common sense. The other seems to some philosophers to be consonant with it and is even represented as being an analysis of what we *mean* by saying that we see physical things. But the difference between them is not in what they say, but in how they say it. It has also been noted that the terms 'directly perceive' and 'indirectly perceive' are opposites which function with respect to each other like 'odd number' with respect to 'even number' rather than like 'awake' with respect to 'asleep'. Now, although it is natural to identify the term 'sees directly' with 'sees for oneself' or 'sees with one's own eyes', this is not how the term is used in philosophy. Neither this term (and the more general terms 'perceives directly' and 'apprehends directly') nor its antithesis 'sees indirectly' is taken over from everyday usage. In connection with the introduction of the technical term 'sense-datum' Ayer has remarked that its use is not explained satisfactorily 'by defining sense-data as the objects of "sensing" or "direct apprehension" or "direct awareness" as various philosophers have proposed. For these are technical terms, and there is no familiar usage of them by reference to which their meaning in this context is to be determined'.[1] The failure to realize this clearly has led some philosophers to invent spurious examples of seing things indirectly, e.g. a ship seen through a periscope or a

[1] *Philosophical Essays* (London: The Macmillan Co. Ltd., 1954), p. 126.

person seen in a mirror; and this has created the idea that the philosophical term is linked to ordinary usage. The effect has been to surround an artificial expression with an air of the familiar and to create the misleading impression that possible applications of a term in the language are being described. Seeing a ship through a periscope, the reflection of a person in a mirror, or his silhouette on a screen, are not cases which fall under the philosophical definition of 'indirect perception'. The term 'directly perceive' is also a philosophical invention and does not have the meaning we tend to assign to the journalist's term 'directly observe'.

The literature which has collected around the notions of direct and indirect perception is considerable; but what comes through is that nothing counts as being directly perceived which can 'look other than what it is' and nothing counts as being indirectly perceived which cannot 'look other than what it is'.[1] In his *Third Dialogue* between Hylas and Philonous, Berkeley tells us that it is 'a manifest contradiction' to suppose that a person might be mistaken about what he is directly aware of, or take it to have a property it does not have. The implication of his assertion is that it is impossible to be directly aware of anything which could, theoretically, appear to have a property it does not have. In other words, the implication is that being directly perceived *entails* being such that it cannot look other than what it is. Like a mental image, a sensible appearance which a material thing presents to someone cannot look to him to have a colour or a shape it does not have: it is equally impossible for a yellow mental image to look blue and for the yellow appearance which a white lily presents to someone to look to have a colour other than its actual colour. But it is possible for a red rose or a white lily to look yellow to someone. Thus, it implies no contradiction to say, 'Jones says that the flower he is looking at in the garden is blue, but perhaps he is mistaken about its colour'. But it does imply a contradiction to assert, 'Jones says his mental image is blue, or that there looks to him to be a blue thing, but perhaps he is mistaken'.[2] That is to say, philosophers so use 'direct' that it applies to our perception of what cannot look to have a property it does not have and does

---

[1] H. A. Prichard's phrase, *Knowledge and Perception*, p. 54.

[2] When there is no question of his being mistaken about the name of the colour.

not apply to our perception of what can look to have a property it does not have. Similarly with regard to 'indirect': the term applies to our perception of what can look to have properties it does not have and does not apply to our perception of what cannot look to have properties it does not have. It is clear, thus, that what is indirectly seen cannot, in principle, be directly seen, and that what is directly seen cannot, in principle, be indirectly seen.

One thing which needs to be made explicit immediately about this artificially devised pair of terms is that in the background, and perhaps unconsciously, some sort of identification has been made between the phrase 'sees an object indirectly' and the expression 'does not see the object itself but does see something which indicates its presence'. Reflection on only a small selection of remarks by philosophers suffices to bring home the fact that the meaning of the latter form of words has been made a part of the meaning of 'sees an object indirectly'. Berkeley's statement that '. . . the senses perceive nothing which they do not perceive immediately' throws into sharp relief the implication imbedded in Broad's statement that physical objects make their existence known to us by the sensible appearances they present. Ayer has stated that '. . . the direct evidence for the existence of a physical object is always the occurrence of a sense-datum'[1] and also that '. . . the direct evidence for the existence of physical objects is sensory evidence'.[2] Joined to the statement that 'all that our senses reveal to us are sense-data', the plain implication is that material things are not themselves revealed to us by our senses. In other words, the implication is that what is revealed to us by our senses, i.e. what is directly perceived, counts as indicating or showing the presence of something which is not itself revealed to us by our senses, something which is present but invisible. When Moore finally decided that a visual sense-datum cannot be identical with any part of the surface of a physical object, his decision amounted to holding the view that seeing a physical surface *consists in* directly seeing a sense-datum which is an appearance of it. It amounted to holding that the perception of a sheet of writing paper *consists in* the direct perception of something which is no part of the sheet of paper, and implies that it is impossible for a physical surface to be revealed to us by our senses.

---

[1] *Philosophical Essays*, p. 140.   [2] *Ibid.*, p. 141.

Broad's remark that the hypothesis that physical objects have colours and temperatures is incapable of empirical verification suggests the idea that an obstacle stands in the way of examining physical objects themselves, as against noting the properties of sense-data. But the picture of an obstacle whose circumvention would enable us to check directly a hypothesis which otherwise remains no more than probable is inappropriate to the philosophical position and is produced by a use of language which undoubtedly is designed to bring it into being. For what prevents us from examining a material thing itself is not a physical impossibility but the logical impossibility of directly perceiving it, or of sensing any part of its surface. The expression 'sees a material thing indirectly' is sometimes represented as giving the 'strict' sense of 'see' and sometimes as giving one of the ordinary senses of the word. But the fact is that the expression 'sees a material thing indirectly' has been assigned a meaning which implies that things seen indirectly are not, in any ordinary sense of 'see', seen at all. This is the verbal reality, and it is covered over by the term 'indirectly seen', which it is *natural* to think of as referring to what is *in some way* seen.

The invented expression 'sees something indirectly' has been given a meaning which bars its application to anything which enters into the 'content' of a perception, that is, to anything which counts, philosophically, as an appearance of a thing. The underlying verbal claim would seem to be that the actual use in the language of 'sees x itself' is such that it applies to nothing to which 'sees x indirectly' applies to. Expressed in the nonverbal, entailment idiom, the claim, in part, is that *x is seen indirectly* entails *x is itself unseen.* To revert to the verbal idiom, in the special use assigned to 'sees indirectly' it makes no descriptive sense to say, 'Jones sees the page he is reading but does not see it indirectly'. Hence, according to the view that mental images and appearances are seen directly and physical objects indirectly, the phrase 'sees the page itself and not another thing'[1] has no correct use, does not describe a case of something being seen. Strange as it may seem, the linguistic variant of the Descartes-Prichard view is imbedded in the outwardly more sober philosophical position of Common Sense, where it is thinly covered over by the distinction between direct and indirect perception. The main difference between the

---

[1] With apologies to Bishop Butler.

two ways of holding the view, one behind the philosophical distinction and the other openly, would seem to be a difference in degree of concealment. But in neither case is the view held by inadvertence: neither when arrived at by 'demonstrating' that bodies are not 'really seen',[1] nor when arrived at through the commonsense appeal that we do see things, but that we see them indirectly.

It may not be easy to understand how anyone could bring himself to adopt a position which more or less directly implies that everyday phrases like 'sees a book' and 'feels the table top' have no use to convey information about what people see and feel, and it would seem unnecessary to call attention to the fact that they do have such a use. Wittgenstein has sometimes described himself as 'assembling reminders' with which to bring philosophers back to the verbal realities, but it is hardly to be supposed that philosophers who adopt the position do so in consequence of having been struck with amnesia about usage. There is, of course, no doubt whatever that they adopt it despite their knowledge of actual usage. The picture that comes to mind has the components of some surrealistic paintings—an odd, unrealistic claim about terminology surrounded by the realistic use of the same terminology. Moore's contention that we are not using language incorrectly when we use perception-expressions in the ordinary way has been countered with the charge that it begs the question. And the charge would have substance if the correct use of the expressions were at issue. It has to be granted that the external appearances invite us to think that usage is in question; but the appearances misrepresent the facts. For the notion that perception-phrases have no correct use, that they do not have in the language the descriptive function they are taken to have, has a consequence which is too fantastic to go unseen by anyone who harboured the notion. It implies that people have constantly in their everyday life, over a vast period of time, thought themselves to be in intelligible communication with each other while in fact they were uttering nonsense comparable to 'Jones smells smoothness' and 'Smith hears a colour'. This consequence is unacceptable and if we reject it we have also to reject the interpretation which has the consequence.

The claim that it is impossible to perceive material objects, and

---

[1] Prichard's expression, *op. cit.*, p. 53.

also the related claim that they are perceived indirectly, turns out to be neither about the perception of things nor about the actual function in the language of perception terminology. One further interpretation of the claim, which would otherwise defy our understanding, presents itself. It needs to be said at once that an intellectual discipline, in which the pursuit of truth has been the avowed aim but in which no single proposition remains uncontested, is an oddity whose oddness must be kept at a safe distance from those who find satisfaction in its practice. The fact that philosophy has no secure propositions, when coupled with the remarkable fact that philosophers show no consternation about the condition of their subject, suggests the possibility that philosophers *in some way recognize* that philosophy is not the kind of discipline which yields secure propositions. It strongly suggests that philosophical statements are *by their nature* permanently debatable.

In his controversy with philosophers who reject the notion of an unconscious part of the mind, Freud once remarked that a possible interpretation to be placed on the equation of the mental with the conscious is that it represents a verbal convention, that it is a matter of nomenclature. He went on to observe that if this interpretation is correct, the equation, like any other convention, is 'not open to refutation'.[1] If in the light of Freud's remarks we view the philosophical claim that it is impossible to perceive things, not as putting forward a claim about the actual use of nomenclature, but as introducing a convention with regard to the use of familiar expressions, we can understand why the claim is permanently debatable and why it is not open to refutation. The philosophical position introduces, in the indicative, nonverbal mode of speech, changes in the conventional use of perception-terminology, changes which undoubtedly are introduced for their fantasy value, since they obviously are not intended to modify any of the conventions governing language in actual use. To put the matter briefly, a philosopher who says that we do not perceive things, that we only seem to perceive them, is under cover of the ontological idiom introducing a contracted use of the words 'sees', 'hears', 'touches', etc., a use which confines their occurrence to

---

[1] The Unconscious', *The Standard Edition of the Complete Psychological Works of Sigmund Freud* (London: The Hogarth Press and the Institute of Psycho-analysis, 1953), Vol XIV, pp. 167–8.

phrases like 'seems to see a book' and 'seems to touch the table', etc. On this interpretation of the philosopher's pronouncements, we have an explanation of why he does not feel refuted by anyone who, like Moore, calls attention to the correct use of these expressions. Actual usage does not count against a statement which introduces a re-editing of the usage, whether intended as a practical measure or not. The ordinary language map cannot be used against someone who knows the map and wishes to redraw it.

The view that physical things are perceived indirectly and images and the appearances of things directly has a similar explanation. In one passage Ayer gives us such an explanation, although, as is characteristic of philosophers, he does this in a style of speech which creates the idea that a theory is under discussion rather than that language is being gerrymandered. In the following passage the manœuvring with terminology shows through more perspicuously than it usually does in a piece of philosophical writing:

'If I found that what I now take to be an ash-tray eluded my attempts to touch it,[1] if I had reason to believe that other people could not touch it either, or even see it, then I should at least become hesitant about the truth of my statement that I saw an ash-tray. But whether or not these further claims are justified, the perception on which they are based, the purely visual experience, remains the same. Accordingly, if I am really to be circumspect, to give the fewest possible hostages to fortune, I must not say anything so bold as that I am seeing an ash-tray: I must say only that it now seems to me that I am seeing an ash-tray. The next step is to convert sentences like 'it now seems to me that I am seeing an ash-tray', which allows for the possibility that I am really seeing something else which I mistake for an ash-tray, or not really seeing anything at all, into 'I really am now seeing a seeming ash-tray'. And this seeming ash-tray, which lives only in my present experience, is an example of a sense-datum. Applying the same procedure to all other cases of perception, we thus arrive at the conclusion that only sense-data are given, or in

---

[1] Finding this out is not like finding out that I am prevented by a pane of glass from touching a piece of jewellery in a shop window. It is 'found out' through argument, e.g., the argument that in a delusive perception 'the purely visual experience' is the same as in its veridical counterpart.

other words, that it is always as seeming-object, of whatever sense it may be, that is directly perceived.'[1]

The 'conversion', to which Ayer alludes, of sentences of the form 'it seems to me that I am seeing an ash-tray' into philosophical sentences of the form 'I am now seeing a seeming or a sense-datum) ash-tray' is effected with the help of a stretched use of the word 'thing'.[2] An appearance of a physical object is itself counted as a kind of thing, one which has the properties the physical object appears to have, and, unlike the object, cannot fail to have them. Thus, Broad has written: 'When I look at a penny from the side I am certainly aware of *something*; and it is certainly plausible to hold that this something is elliptical in the same plain sense in which a suitably bent piece of wire, looked at from straight above, is elliptical.'[3] And Moore has written: 'It seems to me quite plain that I cannot "see" in the common sense any physical object whatever without its "looking" *somehow* to me, and, therefore, without my directly seeing some entity which has R to the object I am said to see . . .'[4] What plainly comes through in these words is that the application of the terms 'thing' and 'entity' is being redistricted to cover appearances of things. The sentence, 'An appearance of a thing or of there being a thing is itself *something* (not nothing)', under the guise of stating a fact about the nature of appearances, introduces a re-edited use of 'thing'. In this new way of speaking, the sentence 'It seems to S that he is seeing an ash-tray' turns into the sentence 'S is seeing a sense-datum ash-tray', and the sentence 'S is seeing a physical ash-tray' turns into 'S is seeing a sense-datum ash-tray which has R to the physical ash-tray which he is not seeing'. When Ayer remarked that, in accepting the proposal to use the word 'sense-datum', those who have 'taken, or accepted, the title of phenomenalists have thought that they were doing more than extending their patronage to a word',[5] he was correct, but not in the way he supposed. The invented *noun* 'sense-datum' was introduced to signalize a covert alteration in the use of 'thing' and 'object', an alteration with the help of which a philosophical alteration in the

---

[1] 'Perception', *British Philosophy in the Mid-Century*, pp. 218–19.
[2] And of equivalents like 'object' and 'entity'.
[3] *Scientific Thought*, p. 240.   [4] 'Visual' *Sense-Data*, p. 208.
[5] *Philosophical Essays*, p. 141.

use of perception terminology is introduced. The contracted use of 'sees', for example, is combined with a stretched use of 'thing' in a way which produces the illusion that a theory about what we see and what we do not see is being formulated.

In referring to the step by which the sentence 'it seems to me that I am seeing x' is converted into the sentence 'I am seeing a seeming x', Ayer remarks that 'here by a stroke of the pen we create a whole new world of private objects and, what is more, imprison ourselves inside it.'[1] According to *Genesis*, God created light by pronouncing the words, 'Let there be . . .'; but magical word-powers we may be prepared to grant to Divinity we are certainly not prepared to grant to a philosopher. And we may justifiably become curious about the nature of the 'stroke of the pen', i.e. the manœuvring with language, which gives rise to the philosophical act of creation. The introduction of the pair of terms 'direct perception' and 'indirect perception' is an important part of the manœuvring, which can, of course, take somewhat different forms. Something which Ayer has said throws light on how the language is made to work in the interests of producing an illusion. He wrote: 'Thus it appears that those who would have it said that the only immediate objects of perception are sense-data are making a fairly considerable departure from ordinary usage. They are assimilating all forms of perception to the perception of mental images, achieving the paradoxical result of taking as the standard case of sense-perception something that is ordinarily contrasted with it. To put it fashionably, their thesis is a linguistic recommendation. The interesting question is why it should be made.'[2]

It is clear that in assimilating all forms of perception to the perception of mental images, what philosophers are doing is to confine the application of perception-words, 'sees', 'tastes', etc., to mental images, and that they do this by the fiat of a 'linguistic recommendation'. It is not that in saying that sense-data are the only immediate objects of perception philosophers are 'making a fairly considerable departure from ordinary usage', a departure intended to replace ordinary usage. Rather, with the help of the nonordinary terms 'directly perceive' and 'indirectly perceive', philosophers superimpose their pragmatically idle departures from ordinary perception-language on unaltered perception talk. For the effects they wish to produce they need *both* ordinary

[1] 'Perception', p. 219.   [2] *Ibid.*, p. 217.

language and their departures from it. In the background 'perceives' is equated with 'directly perceives', and 'does not really perceive' is equated with 'perceives indirectly', but the talk of indirect and direct perception creates the illusion of linguistic usage being analysed, not re-edited. Behind the façade erected by the pair of terms, the application of 'sees', 'smells', 'tastes', etc. is artificially restricted to the perception of 'objects' which, like dream-images, cannot appear to have properties they do not have.

The 'interesting question' as to why the thesis which presents the linguistic alterations should be advanced has, in part at least, already been answered. It is to bring into being a magical illusion, the illusion that the thesis describes the creation of a 'whole new realm of private objects' and that it expresses the claim that material things are hidden from our sight. But there is more to it than just a linguististically contrived illusion, which would fade away like the Cheshire cat, without leaving so much as a trace of itself, if it did not receive support from subterranean parts of the mind. We are justified in thinking that there are underlying fantasies to which the philosophical theory that things cannot be perceived gives expression; and the following words permit our guessing at one of them: 'The more I look at objects round me, the more I am unable to resist the conviction that what I see does exist, as truly and as really, as my perception of it. The conviction is overwhelming.'[1] It requires no great amount of psychological penetration to see that these words express a reaction to a tendency which has to be countered by an 'overwhelming' conviction, i.e. by overcompensation.[2] The following words add to our understanding of an unconscious drama which takes place in the minds of many philosophical thinkers: 'I think that there is justification for the withdrawal from 'I am seeing x', where x stands for a physical object or at least for something that is publicly observable, to 'it seems to me that I am seeing x'.[3] We may wonder what occasioned the first withdrawal, but there is no room for doubt that the wish to withdraw is still sufficiently alive to demand its being worked out with the help of a piece of philosophy.

---

[1] G. E. Moore, 'The Nature and Reality of Objects of Perception', *Philosophical Studies*, p. 96.
[2] The mechanism employed is that of counter-cathaxis.
[3] A. J. Ayer, 'Perception', p. 219.

The thought that suggests itself is that the philosophical theories that physical things cannot be seen and that they can be seen only indirectly are bound up with a frightening perception which had to be mastered by the defensive mechanism of denial. For Parmenides the Greek term for not-being apparently acquired 'unspeakable' unconscious content which had to be banished from the mind by philosophically exorcising the term from language. And we may be curious to know what some of the unconscious ideas are with which many philosophers have invested perception nomenclature. The psychological implication of the theories would seem to be that, like the not-being of Parmenides, perception-terminology has acquired frightening subjective meaning. The statements about the perception of things, by generating the illusion of asserting facts about what cannot be seen or about what can be seen only indirectly, would appear to function as reassurance formulas in which the mechanism of denial plays a conspicuous role. The myth of Medusa and Perseus provides a possible clue to one of the unconscious ideas linked with the theories of perception. The paralysing appearance which turned into stone those who looked 'directly' at the Gorgon was disposed of by Perseus with the help of a burnished shield in which he could see her 'indirectly'. The well-known psychoanalytic interpretation of the myth may very well give us the underlying purport of the theories. Regardless of what the specific unconscious fantasy may be, however, the philosophical theory that it is impossible to perceive physical objects, as also the more sophisticated theory that they are perceived only indirectly, is to be viewed as a complex structure the interacting components of which are a covertly gerrymandered part of familiar language, an intellectual illusion engineered by it, and dramatic material in the depths of our minds to which it gives expression.

11

THE PROBLEM OF JUSTIFYING INDUCTION

Philosophy is *als ob* science in the service of the unconscious.

Ernest Jones has described his encounters with philosophy in words which cannot fail to strike a responsive chord in the minds of many people. He has written: 'Time and again I have emerged from a course of reading in philosophy with the conviction that the authors were really avoiding specific problems by converting them into tenuous sophistries that had little real meaning. Then after a while I would feel that this was an unfair judgment on what were obviously great minds, and that it was more likely to be due to my limited powers of intellectual apprehension, which have always been obviously deficient in abstract fields.'[1] The impression these words make on one is that philosophy caused a division in Jones' mind, between the idea that philosophers are great thinkers and the conviction that their intellectual labour has produced nothing better than tenuous sophistries. And it seems that his way of healing the breach was to dismiss his conviction. The judgment he finally came to was that philosophers are 'people who have been impelled to deal with various personal problems in their unconscious by making serious efforts to think consciously; they have intellectualized the emotional conflicts.'[1] He went on to remark that in saying this he was paying philo-sophers a 'high compliment', because so little real thinking is done in this world. It is not difficult to discern the original conviction hiding in the compliment.

It is hard to think that the goal of philosophy is not the same as the goal of science and that its arguments and pieces of analysis are not attempts to establish or confute propositions about various phenomena; but a difference between the two to which Jones refers tends to produce uneasiness about the kind of science philosophy is. And it demands an answer which can only be

[1] *Free Associations*, p. 60.

reached by a re-examination of the subject: the explanation of the difference has to be found *within* philosophy itself. Jones has referred to the 'astonishing contrast between the diversity of philosophical opinions and the widespread agreement in scientific work'.[1] This is a contrast for which philosophers have ready explanations, but other people will be deeply perplexed. Jones' explanation is that in philosophy 'the questions have more important subjective origins than had hitherto been discernible',[1] and this no doubt is part of the explanation. Professor John Wisdom has said that some people have 'exaggerated the degree to which philosophy is an expression of unconscious inclinations, nevertheless it now appears how very powerful unconscious causes are in philosophy'.[2] He has also pointed out that 'the more a question is finally settled by observation and, or, calculation on well established lines, the less scope have unconscious causes'.[3] It may well be that philosophical questions are not the kind of questions that are settled either by observation or calculation. This, if true, would help us understand the strange difference between philosophy and the sciences. And it may be that the unconscious is able to play in philosophy the role suggested by Jones because of the malleability of its theories and arguments, something in its nature which makes possible permanently unresolved disputation and which accounts for the odd lack of concern by philosophers over the complete absence of stable results in their subject. What needs to be looked into are the properties of philosophical statements which will enable us to understand the contrast between science and philosophy. The purpose of this study is to examine a long standing philosophical problem which looks to be scientific, the problem of justifying inductive inference.

In the practice of science as well as in ordinary life the possibility of making predictions with varying degrees of assurance and success is taken for granted and it enters no one's head to think that inductive inference in general stands in need of justification. Statements about the future which are based on inductive evidence are ordinarily considered to be of two kinds. Some of them are made with complete certainty, which is to say that inductive evidence is in some cases taken to have established

---

[1] *Free Associations*, p. 61. [2] In a letter to me, February 1966.
[3] Foreword to *The Structure of Metaphysics*, p. xii.

conclusively propositions about the future. Thus, for example, everyone would think it silly to say, in an ordinary, everyday circumstance, 'It is not certain that tomorrow salt will dissolve in water' or 'Probably water will freeze at 32° Fahrenheit'. It is, of course, easy to imagine salt no longer dissolving in water and water not solidifying in the lowest temperatures. Nevertheless, though we may not be able to identify the mistake, we would think that a person who stated that salt *probably* will dissolve in water tomorrow was labouring under some sort of misapprehension about either fact or language. To put the matter differently, some statements about the future do not count as *predictions*: there is an impropriety in the words, 'I predict that the next teaspoon of salt will dissolve in water'. Other statements about the future that are backed by inductive evidence are of course put forward more or less tentatively, as predictions to which a degree of probability, high or low, attaches. To be sure, we may, and sometimes do, challenge particular inductive inferences as assigning a probability to a prediction in excess of the evidence, but the legitimacy of inductive procedure itself is not, either in the scientific laboratory, in the factory, or in the kitchen, thought to be something which might be brought into question.

In philosophy the matter is otherwise. As is well known, one of the main problems in philosophy concerns the justification of induction. What does not arise as a question in the actual practice of science or in the conduct of everyday life occurs in philosophy as a serious problem which is represented as being of more than just theoretical interest. It is represented by many philosophers as a problem on the solution of which hang matters of the utmost gravity. Thus, Bertrand Russell has written: 'The question we really have to ask is: "When two things have been found to be often associated, and no instance is known of the the one occurring without the other, does the occurrence of one of the two, in a fresh instance, give any good ground for expecting the other?" On our answer to this question must depend the validity of the whole of our expectations as to the future, the whole of the results obtained by induction, and in fact practically all the beliefs on which our daily life is based.'[1] He also wrote: 'The general principles of science, such as the belief in the reign of law, and the belief that every event must have a cause, are as completely

[1] *The Problems of Philosophy*, 17th Impression, p. 101.

dependent upon the inductive principle as are the beliefs of daily life. All such general principles are believed because mankind found innumerable instances of their truth and no instances of their falsehood. But this affords no evidence for their truth in the future, unless the inductive principle is assumed.'[1]

The picture these passages give us of the scientist is that of a person who, for all he knows, is living in a fool's paradise, which may some day dissipate before his eyes. Many philosophers give the impression of thinking that the scientist is in the situation of a gambler who is experiencing a run of luck, and that science rests on nothing more solid than an assumption, one that philosophy alone is capable of investigating but which philosophy so far has not been able to change into a proposition with a known truth-value. It is hard to think that scientists, even those who become enmeshed in the philosophical problem of justifying induction, will accept this idea of the insecurity of science, or, if any accept it, will *feel* that science is insecure. And some philosophers who have thought about the problem also reject this idea. Thus, for example, A. J. Ayer has urged philosophers to '. . . abandon the superstition that natural science cannot be regarded as logically respectable until philosophers have solved the problem of induction'.[2] It may be observed that philosophers who harbour the 'superstition' about the insubstantial foundations of natural science do not, as will be obvious to anyone who troubles to look, give any sign of feeling or thinking that science is not logically respectable or that its structure of results may crumble any moment. We cannot fail to notice the curious bifurcation that exists between their portentous philosophical talk and the rest of their talk and behaviour; and this bifurcation suggests the possibility that the *philosophical* uncertainty about the security of science is not the familiar kind of uncertainty we experience in everyday life. More than this, if we stop to think on the matter we may soon find ourselves wondering whether the problem of justifying induction is the sort of problem it appears to be.

About philosophers who persist in looking for 'power or agency' in conjunctions of events Hume said that '. . . they seem to be in a very lamentable condition, and such as the poets have given us

---

[1] *The Problems of Philosophy*, 17th Impression, p. 107.
[2] *Language, Truth and Logic*, 2nd ed., p. 49.

but a faint notion of in their descriptions of the punishment of Sisyphos and Tantalus. For what can be imagin'd more tormenting than to seek with eagerness, what forever flies us; and seek for it in a place where 'tis impossible it can ever exist?'[1] It may be that these words also describe the plight of philosophers who seek the solution to the problem of justifying induction. It may be that the answer they pursue is a will-o'-the-wisp, not because it is beyond the grasp of mortal minds but because philosophers have, at the conscious level of their thinking, misconstrued the nature of their problem. Wittgenstein epitomized the intellectual condition of the philosopher in the phrase 'the fly in the fly-bottle', and the bottle, we may begin to think, is of a special design. It is an existentialist bottle, one with no real exits. If this should hold in general for technical philosophical problems, it would help us understand the philosophers' protracted imprisonment in their problems, an imprisonment the duration of which has become sufficiently embarrassing to some philosophers to make them fall back on the transparent rationalization of 'the appalling difficulty of philosophical problems'.[2]

In this essay I wish to examine the question concerning the justification of induction, not with the object of discovering the answer, but with the object of arriving at a clear understanding of the nature of the question. Wittgenstein sometimes spoke of philosophical problems as having a *dissolution* rather than a solution; and it may be that dispersing the mists surrounding the problem and arriving at a clear understanding of it is equivalent to solving it. It may be that insight into what the question asks will have the effect of dispelling the problem-appearance which surrounds the question, and thus will remove the compulsion to look for a truth-value answer to a question which has none. Before taking up the problem of justifying induction, however, it will be useful to consider briefly a related problem.

The claim has sometimes been advanced that inductive inference is really deductive inference. Thus, one philosopher has written: 'Inductive arguments are, after all, inferences, and for an inference to be valid the conclusion must follow from the premises. But for this to be so the premises must entail the

---

[1] *A Treatise of Human Nature*, Bok. I, Pt. IV, sec. III.
[2] Sir Roy Harrod, 'Sense and Sensibilia', *Philosophy*, Vol. XXXVIII, p. 241.

conclusion. . . . It is difficult to escape this argument.'[1] Other philosophers have apparently experienced little or no difficulty escaping this argument and have put forward the view that inductive inference is not really inference. One view professes to tell us what inductive inference really is; the other professes to tell us that there is no such thing as inductive inference, that what goes by the name of inductive inference is not inference. These views appear to make incompatible claims about inductive inference, but scrutiny shows that looked on as *factual* claims they vanish into each other. For a philosopher who declares that inductive inference is really deductive inference is saying that all inference is deductive. He tells us there is nothing that counts as an inference which does not also count as a deductive inference. The point of his claim is, perhaps, more clearly brought out by saying that, according to him, there is no inference, actual or conceivable, which is not a deductive inference. And what a philosopher who declares that inductive inference is not really inference wishes to place before us is the proposition that all inference is non-inductive inference. This view comes down to the claim that no conceivable inductive inference is an inference, or that all possible inferences are non-inductive.

Regardless of whether his claim is correct or not, a philosopher who states it is making no sort of statement about the *nature* of inference, about what it is or about what it is not. This can be seen by noticing that according to his implicit claim that all possible inferences are non-inductive the term 'non-inductive' (or its equivalent) used in the expression of his claim does not mark a difference between kinds of inferences: the term does not function in the way in which the term 'formal' functions in the sentence 'All inferences occurring in *Principia Mathematica* are formal inferences'. So far as its descriptive content is concerned, it says no more about inference than does the sentence 'All inferences are inferences'. That is, it is as barren of *information* about inference as the tautology 'If it is raining, then it is raining' is barren of information about the weather. The same consideration applies to the view expressed by the words 'All inferences, including inductive inferences, are deductive'. The term 'deductive' is not used in the philosophical sentence to set off a special

---

[1] A. C. Ewing, *The Fundamental Questions of Philosophy* (London: Routledge & Kegan Paul Ltd., 1953), p. 168.

class of inferences, and so is not used to characterize inferences. The sentence, thus, conveys no information (or misinformation) about the *nature* of inference. Like the words 'All inference is non-inductive', the words 'All inference is deductive' are no more a characterization of the nature of inference than are the words 'All inference is inference'. Strange as it may seem, the two anti-thetical philosophical theories coincide in respect of their informative content.

The more specific claim expressed by the sentence 'Inductive inference is deductive', or to put it in a way which lends to the claim an air of discovery, 'inductive inference is really deductive', can be seen also to have the characterizing force of a tautology. As the argument in support of the claim shows, what is being maintained is that all conceivable inductive inferences are deductive. Construed as making a claim about inference, the underlying implication is that 'inductive' is not used in the expression of the claim to distinguish amongst inferences, nor to refer to a class of inferences some or all of which look to be non-deductive. Contrary to the impression it undoubtedly fosters, the statement does not distinguish between inductive inferences which do not look to be deductive but are, and inductive inferences, actual or possible, which neither are nor look to be deductive. In respect to characterizing inferences, it is as contentless as 'All inductive inference is inference', or as contentless as 'All inference is inference.'

It is puzzling to realize that the views, which create such a vivid impression of being about the nature of inference, are equally devoid of information about inference, deductive or inductive. Like tautologies, which according to Wittgenstein '. . . say nothing',[1] they are all mute with regard to the subject on which they appear to be deliverances. Realizing this has the effect of dispersing some of the fog which prevents us from getting a clear view of the nature of the philosophical theories and of the questions they are designed to answer, and it enables us to move on to a different appearance they sometimes present. Like the Eve of the three personalities, philosophical theories are capable of presenting different faces to different people; and when their ontological mask, i.e. their appearance of being about things or processes, is removed, it is often replaced by a verbal mask. Nowadays

---

[1] *Tractatus Logico-Philosophicus*, 4.461 (trans. by D. Pears and B. F. McGuinness).

philosophers have developed a tendency to adopt without much ado the position that philosophical theories are verbal in character, that they are reports about the uses of expressions in a language. These philosophers by-pass the notion that philosophical questions are requests for factual information about things and that philosophical theories are truth-value propositions about the existence or properties of things, and proceed directly to the notion that the questions are requests for factual information about accepted usage and that the theories report, or misreport, usage. One trouble with this overquick procedure is that the ontological appearance is not dissolved but is, instead, submerged. It is subjected to a kind of intellectual repression, but continues to lead a vigorous life behind the philosophical investigation of language, where it is all the more difficult to get at. It gives rise to the curious idea, which is difficult to cope with because it is for the most part hidden, that knowledge of important things about the world is to be gained from the study of language. Behind the analysis of linguistic usage traditional metaphysical philosophy flourishes, and in fact is the *life* of linguistic analysis.

The view that inductive inference is actually deductive, when construed as amounting to a verbal claim about the accepted use of terminology entering into inference expressions, comes to saying that 'deductive' applies to every inference to which 'inductive' applies. According to the present interpretation, the philosophical view brings to our attention, in the non-verbal mode of speech, the piece of linguistic information (or misinformation) that the term 'inductive inference' denotes a form of deductive inference. Similarly, the views that all inference is deductive and that all inference is non-inductive are to be construed as conveying, respectively, the claims that 'non-deductive inference' has no use, or that the use of 'deductive' indicates its application to whatever the word 'inference' correctly applies to, and that 'inductive inference' has no use, or that 'inductive' applies to nothing to which 'inference' correctly applies. Looked on as being about the nature of inference the views turn out to be empty imitations of theories. They are verbal counterfeits which say nothing whatever about inference. But if taken to be about the correct use of inference-terminology they are just false. It is not the case that 'inductive' is used in the English language to refer to a form of deductive inference. Neither is it the case that 'deductive' applies, in point of usage, to whatever 'inference' applies to, or that 'inductive inference' is a literally meaningless expression. It hardly needs remarking that a philosopher who expresses his view by the words 'Inductive inference is a form of deductive inference' knows perfectly well that 'inductive inference' does not refer to a kind of deductive inference. It is the same with regard to the other views. A philosopher who says, 'It is impossible for any inference not to be deductive', knows that 'non-deductive inference' has a use in the language; he knows perfectly well that in point of usage the application of 'deductive inference' is not coextensive with the application of 'inference'. And a philosopher who says, 'All inference is non-inductive', is not ignorant of usage; he knows as well as anyone that 'inductive inference' does have a use, and also what its use is. He experiences no difficulty in using the phrase to identify inferences.

If we place on the views the constructions which they naturally lend themselves to, i.e. constructions which represent them as being oblique deliverances about the correct use of terminology, we come to a deadlock, with no prospect of understanding what the protracted disagreements are about. It would be reasonable to think that the interpretation was correct if bringing philosophers back to actual language had the effect of resolving their disagreements. But this does not happen. Britain's Chancellor of the Exchequer, Maudling, was reported as quoting his tutor at Oxford to the following effect: 'Philosophy progresses not by finding the answers but by progressively clarifying the questions.' This is a clever rationalization behind which philosophers can cover their chagrin at *never* coming to undisputed answers to philosophical questions. Interestingly enough, in the rationalization itself is to be found the recognition that philosophical questions can have no incontestable answers: reaching incontestable answers is not part of the progress of philosophy. Without elaborating the paradoxical consequences[1] which emerge from construing the theories to be lexicographical reports, it is plain that recourse to facts of usage, which of course are known, will not resolve the disagreement among philosophers who hold the theories. This is why the philosopher's pursuit of a stable, generally

[1] For detailed discussion of these, see *The Structure of Metaphysics*, especially chapters IX and XI, and *Studies in Metaphilosophy*, the first parts of chapters 2 and 3.

accepted answer stirs up the image of a Tantalus who thirsts for knowledge which forever eludes him. When put to it to explain the glaring difference between the condition of philosophy and the steady and secure advances in the sciences, natural and mathematical, he understandably falls back on such rationalizations as that philosophical problems are prodigiously difficult, or that philosophical theories cast a spell over people's minds which blinds them to their mistakes, or that philosophical questions stand in never-ending need of clarification, or that answers are not to be expected since the important task of philosophy is to sharpen the concepts used in *other* disciplines. It can no longer be doubted that the philosopher labours under a misapprehension of the nature of his question and the theories put forward in answer to it, and that he can only liberate himself by getting clear about their nature. Wittgenstein is said to have remarked that the philosopher 'tries the window but it is too high. He tries the chimney but it is too narrow. And if he would only *turn around*, he would see that the door had been open all the time!'[1] What the philosopher needs to do is to resist the conventional notions of what a philosophical question asks and to explore the idea that it is the kind of question that does not have true-or-false answers.

If, to use Wittgenstein's expression, we turn around to the open door, we can understand the philosophical theories about inference. We can see that, underneath their surface appearance, they are introductions of alterations in the use of terminology. The sentence 'All inference is deductive inference' expresses neither a theory about the nature of inference nor a verbal theory about the actual use of 'deductive inference': it introduces a stretched use of the word 'deductive', a use that is academically superimposed on ordinary language. The sentence is not to be taken to declare that the accepted criteria for the use of 'deductive' dictate its application to whatever 'inference' applies to. It is, instead, to be understood as presenting us with an innovation in the use of 'deductive', i.e. a stretched use which represents the non-workaday decision to apply 'deductive' to whatever 'inference' applies to. Similarly, the philosophical sentence, 'No inference is inductive', brings before us the academic, verbal decision to contract to the vanishing point the use of 'inductive', i.e. to deprive it of its text-

---

[1] Norman Malcolm, *Ludwig Wittgenstein: A Memoir* (Oxford University Press, 1958), p. 51.

P

book application to inferences. So to speak, it is made to suffer banishment by linguistic fiat. It is interesting to notice, by way of a brief excursion, what one philosopher has said about the use of the term 'direct' in connection with the philosophical theory of perception: 'We have here, in fact, a typical case of a word, which already has a very special use, being gradually stretched, without caution or definition or any limit, until it becomes, first perhaps obscurely metaphorical, but ultimately meaningless. One can't abuse ordinary language without paying for it.'[1] It seems clear that this philosopher has permitted himself a glimpse into the linguistic workings of philosophy but has come away with the opinion that at least some philosophical retailorings of terminology are *abuses* of ordinary language. The implication is that they are mistakes, to be corrected by an analysis which explicates actual usage. But this is one of the familiar views about the nature of philosophical statements. It has advanced the understanding of philosophy not one whit nor has it brought philosophers any nearer to resolving their differences. It is fair to conclude that a philosopher who characterizes a view as constituted by a stretched (or contracted) use of a word but unites his characterization with the notion that the new use is mistaken has, to use Wittgenstein's metaphor, turned around, and then around again. The reshaping of usage by philosophers, their stretching, contracting, or eliminating the use of words, does not result from mistaken ideas about established usage. They are the free creations of philosophers, whose error lies in their interpretation of the nature of their creations, not in their grasp of usage.

It is not difficult to see that construing the statement, 'All inference is deductive', as introducing a creatively[2] stretched use of 'deductive' and the statement, 'No inference is inductive', as introducing a purposely narrowed application of 'inductive' frees the views from paradoxical consequences. These constructions also dissipate the problem-appearance of the questions, which are not now to be interpreted as requests for information about inference or inference-terminology. They also remove or weaken the temptation in philosophers to 'refute' each other's views and to replace this temptation by the wish to understand them.

The view that inductive inference is really deductive, which

---

[1] J. L. Austin, *Sense and Sensibilia* (1962), p. 15.
[2] Creative in the interests of unconscious fantasy.

strikes many philosophers as being manifestly false, is open to a like interpretation. What has happened in this case is that the actual application of 'inductive' has been retained unaltered but the use of 'deductive' has in a purely idle way been stretched beyond its textbook use so as to apply to inferences to which 'inductive' applies. The way in which the philosopher presents his artificial redrawing of the boundaries of inference-terminology makes it look as if he fancies himself to have made a discovery about the true nature of inductive inference, whereas all he has done is add to the actual use of 'deductive' a sham use of the term. The philosophical, illusion-creating language alterations embodied in the argument for the view that inductive inference is really a form of deductive inference are readily discernible in the following passage, quoted earlier: 'Inductive arguments are, after all, inferences, and for an inference to be valid the conclusion must follow from the premises . . . the premises must entail the conclusion.' In the interest of notational uniformity 'valid' (and with it, 'follow' and 'entail') is stretched so that it applies not only to correct deductive inferences but also to correct inductive inferences. That is, it is made to apply to all correct inferences, so that in this new way of speaking 'valid inductive inference' has a use as well as 'valid deductive inference'. As a next step, the term 'correct deductive inference' is made to apply to whatever 'valid inference' applies to, with the final result being the 'view' that inductive inferences belong to the category of deductive inferences.

To come now to the problem of justifying inductive inference, the fact that philosophers have taken a remarkable variety of positions with regard to it suggests that, like the problem about the nature of inference, it too has only a dissolution. It suggests that the problem has kept philosophers imprisoned through their misapprehension of its nature and that, as in the preceding case, finding the way out is equivalent to breaking the spell of a verbally contrived mirage. In this connection, one thing that needs to be noticed is how utterly different the philosophical problem is from the practical or technical problem of justifying particular inductive conclusions. For example, when a sociologist states that the repeated experience of the consequences suffered from transgressing a certain rule of ownership teaches us that 'the sense of interest has become common to all our fellows, and gives us confidence of the future regularity of their conduct', his proposition may, conceivably, be challenged on the ground that the evidence has not been gathered by trained observers using accredited formulas for random sampling or on the ground that the evidence is insufficient to support it, etc. But circumstances could be described in which people who are practiced in this kind of scientific procedure would withdraw their objections and accept the proposition as well-founded and one on which we can rely. The philosophical problem regarding the justification of induction is in an altogether different case. For this problem remains after all scientific experts have been satisfied that the accepted conditions for gathering and evaluating evidence have been fulfilled and that the evidence does justify the conclusion. This is so not because philosophers are less easily satisfied than scientists are. Their question is not the kind of question to which any sort of examination of the evidence or of strengthening the evidence or of recasting criteria for what is to count as evidence is at all relevant. Rather, it is the question whether what counts in science as evidence for a proposition about the continuation of an observed regularity can, in principle, count as evidence at all.

The problem has usually been formulated in the following way: When two things have in a number of cases and without exception been found to be associated, does a new occurrence of one of the two give any ground whatever for expecting the other? Common sense and science take the principle expressed in this question for granted, namely, that past concomitances, no exception having been observed, *are* grounds for further expectations, the greater the number of observed concomitances the better the grounds. Common sense has been described as having 'natural confidence' in this principle. As is well known, Hume came to the conclusion that this natural confidence was unfounded and, in fact, that the inductive principle has to be given up. In the words of one philosopher, 'The source of Hume's despair was his discovery that reflection destroys our natural confidence in induction, and his only remedy was social intercourse, which distracted his attention from the question of justification and so enabled him to believe and act again.'[1] Hume's investigation of the problem led him to the conclusion that the past can provide us with no

---

[1] W. C. Kneale, *Probability and Induction* (Oxford University Press, 1949), p. 226.

rules for the future, that there is no rational justification for any expectation based on past experience: 'Even after the observation of the frequent or constant conjunction of objects, we have no reason to draw any inference concerning any object beyond those of which we have had experience.'[1] In other words, Hume was of the opinion that the problem of justifying induction had been solved. Inductive inference cannot be justified; no number of observed cases apparently exemplifying a law gives grounds for or lends any probability to the propositon that such cases will continue in the future.

Russell has gone on to develop a number of further positions. At times he implies that induction cannot be justified (or, sometimes, that it has not yet been justified) but that we cannot for practical reasons give it up. Like solipsism which he thinks is theoretically irrefutable but cannot be accepted, the inductive principle cannot be established or justified but must be assumed. Sometimes he says that the inductive principle is to be accepted on the ground of its 'intrinsic evidence'.[2] And he also expressed the opinion that the principle of induction is a logical axiom: '. . . induction is an independent logical principle, incapable of being inferred either from experience or from other logical principles, . . .'[3]

To these views about the problem Ayer has added still a further position. Against such a solution as that offered by Russell and others that induction is a logical principle, he maintains that it is an error to suppose that a logical principle (or a tautology) could be about the world or could make a claim as to matter of fact. Accordingly, the principle that past experience is a trustworthy guide to the future cannot be an *a priori* proposition nor can it be deduced from one. Neither can it be rendered probable, as he thinks Hume has correctly argued, by inductive procedures. Ayer's conclusion, which is different from any of the views put forward by Hume or Russell is ". . . that there is no possible way of solving the problem of induction, as it is ordinarily conceived. And this means that it is a fictitious problem, since all genuine problems are at least theoretically capable of being solved: and the credit of natural science is not impaired by the fact that some philosophers

---

[1] *A Treatise of Human Nature*, Bk. I, Pt. III, sec. 12.
[2] *The Problems of Philosophy*, p. 106.
[3] *A History of Western Philosophy*, p. 674.

continue to be puzzled by it.'[1] In Hume's and in Russell's view the problem is certainly genuine; in Ayer's view it is fictitious. Hume's solution is that the principle of induction is unsound. One of Russell's views is that it is a logical axiom. Ayer's positive view is that the principle has passed the test of success in practice, which is the only test a self-consistent principle requires for its justification, and that there is no real problem regarding its soundness. A curious lapse should, perhaps, be noticed in connection with the considerations which led Ayer to reject as spurious the philosophical question regarding the justification of induction. His argument, for one thing, comes to maintaining that the inductive principle is not analytic, which is to say that the sentence, 'When two things, x and y, have frequently and without exception been observed together there is some probability that a fresh x will be accompanied by a y', does not express an analytic proposition. For another thing, his argument comes to maintaining that the inductive principle is not open to verification in sense-experience, by a series of observations. And this is to say that the sentence does not express an empirical proposition either. The question, thus, cannot be answered by recourse to logic or to empirical procedures and is, according to his well-known criteria for literal intelligibility, a pseudo-question. The curious thing is that he did not, in conformity with the criteria he laid the greatest stress on in his book, draw the conclusion that the sentence expressing the putative inductive proposition in fact expressed no proposition and was literally senseless. Instead he concludes that the proposition is all right but that the question is all wrong.

It is worthwhile mentioning one variant of Ayer's stand that it is senseless to ask whether induction can be justified as a scientific procedure. This variant represents the question as not having been *given* sense, the implication being that the rules of usage of the language in which the question is framed do not prevent its having sense although they do not provide it with a sense. The explanation of why it has been thought to have sense is that the inductive proposition has been confounded with propositions for which it is appropriate to ask for justification. That is, the philosophical question, 'Is the belief in the soundness of induction justified?', which has not been assigned a sense, is thought to have sense because of its outward grammatical similarity to such questions as, 'Is the

[1] *Language, Truth and Logic*, p. 50.

belief in the wish-fulfilment theory of dreams justified?' Thus, with regard to the philosophical question, P. F. Strawson has written: 'No sense has been given to it, though it is easy to see why it seems to have sense. For it is generally proper to inquire *of a particular belief*, whether its adoption is justified; and in asking this, we are asking whether there is good, bad, or any, evidence for it. In applying or withholding the epithets "justified", "well founded", etc., in the case of specific beliefs, we are appealing to, and applying, inductive standards. But to what standards are we appealing when we ask whether the application of inductive standards is justified or well grounded? If we cannot answer, then no sense has been given to the question.'[1] The explanation of what it is that makes philosophers dupe to their own senseless question undoubtedly carries with it a certain amount of appeal. But it does not bear close scrutiny. A philosopher like Russell, say, who has expanded on the point that to ask for the inductive grounds of induction is to involve oneself in a *petitio*, knows very well the difference between the philosophical question and a similarly phrased factual question. In fact, his own considerations make perspicuous the difference between them. The implication of Strawson's words is that a philosopher can cling to his mistaken notion about the intelligibility of a question despite his having been aware of distinctions which should prevent, and certainly remove, the mistaken notion. This recalls Moore's paradox,[2] which in the present context provokes the observation that it is easier to think that philosophers can remain lost in familiar territory than that their questions are vastly different from what they appear to be. That is why unrealistic explanations are given and why they are so easily accepted.

If we disengage ourselves from the continuing controversy and look at it from a distance, we shall become increasingly perplexed. The failure of philosophers after so much labour to discover an answer on which they could agree, together with their constant restatement and re-evaluation of the arguments clustering around the problem, will naturally suggest the Oxford tutor's notion as to where progress in the investigation of the problem lies. G. E.

---

[1] *Introduction to Logical Theory* (London: Methuen & Co. Ltd., 1952), p. 257.

[2] 'The strange thing is that philosophers should have been able to hold sincerely, as part of their philosophical creed, propositions inconsistent with what they themselves *knew* to be true . . .' ('A Defence of Common Sense').

Moore's well-known dictum that before we can hope to answer a question we must first try to get clear about what precisely the question is, may at first seem to provide an explanation of what has been taking place behind the debates of philosophers. This is that the problem is still in process of clarification and that we should curb our impatience for a definitive answer. But this is an idea from which we shall soon be disenchanted, if we attend to the kinds of turnings the debate has taken, and also to the attitudes of the debaters. Some practiced philosophical thinkers are convinced that there is a problem of justifying induction, that the words 'Can past experience ever provide good grounds for future expectations?' do actually express a question. Other practised thinkers are equally certain that there is no problem; and some of these think it makes no literal sense to ask for a justification of induction, while others think it is *unreasonable* to ask for this, that to do so is to 'cry for the moon'.[1] Still other philosophers are undecided about whether there is a problem. An oddity immediately forces itself on our attention. For what would enable a philosopher to decide that there is a problem, or that there is none, cannot be anything he is unaware of.

To continue with the catalogue of positions with regard to the problem, among those who take it to be genuine, some think it it has not yet been solved. Others are persuaded that it has been solved, but they are divided on what the solution is. This certainly is a bewildering variety of positions both with regard to the question and with regard to its correct answer, a variety which hardly suggests the presence of a disciplined effort to clarify a question. Indeed to imagine that the dispute is constituted by an attempt to clarify the question is to let fantasy take over. If anything, looking from a distance at the philosophical battlefield must soon create the impression of a battle that is waged in a thickening fog. The only hopeful idea which suggests itself is that the present problem is akin to the earlier problem about whether inductive inference is really deductive.

The mystery surrounding the problem deepens when we go on to consider the standard arguments, well known since Hume, that are brought to bear on it. For we find that there are striking and inexplicable differences of opinion amongst philosophers over

[1] F. P. Ramsey, *The Foundations of Mathematics* (New York: Harcourt Brace & Co., 1931), p. 197.

what the arguments show, how they are to be understood. Like the question itself, the argumentation appears to have a plastic character; it seems capable of presenting itself in different guises to different thinkers, and in different guises to the same thinker on different occasions. Ayer has described the problem of induction as one of finding a way to prove that certain empirical generalizations which are derived from past experience will hold good also in the future; and, following Hume, he states that there are two and only two approaches to the problem which could possibly lead to its solution. He writes: 'One may attempt to deduce the proposition which one is required to prove from a purely formal principle or from an empirical principle. In the former case one commits the error of supposing that from a tautology it is possible to deduce a proposition about matter of fact; in the latter case one simply assumes what one is setting out to prove.'[1] The conclusion he draws from this is that the problem is bogus. According to his assessment of the force of Hume's considerations, what they show is something about the nature of the problem. They are not the kind of considerations which isolate one of several putative answers and establish its truth.

Russell, as has already been noted, thinks that the arguments bear a different interpretation: this is that they show one of the traditional answers to be the true answer. In his judgment, Hume's arguments prove that induction is an 'independent logical principle'. To F. P. Ramsey Hume's reasoning appears to have a different outcome, which is that induction cannot be a logical principle: 'Since the time of Hume a great deal has been written about the justification for inductive inference. Hume showed that it could not be reduced to deductive inference or justified by formal logic. So far as it goes his demonstration seems to me to be final . . .'[2] As is well known, Hume's own assessment of his reasoning is that it shows the principle of induction to have no justification whatever, neither empirical nor *a priori*. But although he supposed himself to have shown induction to be entirely without foundation there is no indication whatever that he imagined his reasoning to show that the question is senseless. It is quite safe to say, instead, that, as against Ayer, he thought the question 'Can induction be justified?' to make perfectly good

[1] *Language, Truth and Logic*, p. 49.
[2] *The Foundations of Mathematics*, pp. 196–7.

sense and that the reasoning, far from showing the question to lack intelligibility, gave the correct answer to the question: 'Induction cannot be justified'. To sum up the different points of view with respect to Hume's reasoning: according to one assessment, it shows that there is no question; according to another, it shows the principle of induction to be *a priori*; according to still another, it shows that the principle is not *a priori*; and according to Hume's appraisal, it shows that the principle is without foundation and that no inductive inference can be justified.

What makes it possible for Hume's lines of reasoning to look so very different to different philosophers is a riddle which is not answered by saying that some philosophers have read them wrongly and that others have read them aright. For the argumentation is remarkable for its clarity and simplicity; and to suppose that philosophers divide, and remain divided, over what it shows is on a footing with supposing that mathematicians might divide over which one of a number of elementary theorems is implied by a certain demonstration. How rightly to understand the philosophical divisions of opinion remains a puzzle. On the surface they appear to be disagreements over what a line of reasoning shows, but the reality cannot be this. What the disagreements are about becomes even more puzzling if we look again at Hume's own words. For his central considerations are clear and are unmistakably directed toward showing the two things which are summed up in the following passage:

'What is possible can never be demonstrated to be false; and 'tis possible the course of nature may change, since we can conceive such a change. Nay, I will go farther, and assert, that [one] could not so much as prove by any probable arguments, that the future must be conformable to the past. All probable arguments are built on the supposition, that there is this conformity betwixt the future and the past. This conformity is a *matter of fact*, and if it must be proved, will admit of no proof but experience. But our experience in the past can be a proof of nothing for the future, but upon the supposition, that there is a resemblance between them. This therefore is a point, which can admit of no proof at all, and which we take for granted without any proof.'[1]

---

[1] *An Abstract of A Treatise of Human Nature*, reprinted with an Introduction by J. M. Keynes and P. Sraffa (Cambridge University Press, 1938), p. 15.

Hume's words make it evident that he wished to bring out in a perspicuous way a difference between entailment, or deducibility, and causation, i.e. a difference between the 'if, then' of logic and the 'if, then' which occurs in causal statements. When he states that 'it implies no contradiction that the course of nature may change, and that an object, seemingly like those which we have experienced, may be attended with different or contrary effects',[1] what he is doing is calling attention to the great difference between causal propositions, such as 'Friction generates heat' and 'A body submerged in a liquid is buoyed up by a force equal to the weight of the displaced liquid', and an entailment proposition such as 'Being a tree *entails* being a plant'. The proposition that heat is generated by friction does not imply that it is logically impossible for things to be in friction without heating; and the proposition that if a body is submerged in a liquid it will be buoyed up by a force equal to the weight of the displaced liquid does not entail the logical impossibility of a contrary state of affairs occurring. But the proposition that a thing's being a plant is logically necessitated by its being a tree entails the logical impossibility of anything being a tree and not a plant. In effect, what he remarks on and wishes to call to our special attention is a linguistic point: this is that causal terms do not fall into the category of entailment words and that in certain important respects they do not function in the language in the same way. And he achieves his aim by pointing out in the non-verbal mode of speech that the conjunction of the entailing concept with the denial of the entailed concept yields an 'impossibility of thought', i.e. a logical impossibility; whereas the conjunction of the cause-concept with the denial of the effect-concept does not yield a logical impossibility. It is something that is 'distinctly conceivable'. What Hume has done amounts to remarking the difference in use, in the language in which he makes his point, between causal descriptions and entailment expressions. The expression formed by the conjunction of the antecedent term with the negation of the consequent term in the one case has no descriptive function in the language, while in the other case it does function descriptively. In English, 'tree but not a plant' does not describe what does not exist. Instead, it has no descriptive sense, whereas the phrases 'in friction but not heating' and 'submerged but not buoyed up by a force equal to

[1] *An Enquiry Concerning Human Understanding*, Sec. IV, Pt. II.

the displaced liquid' have descriptive sense, although they describe what does not in fact happen.

The point that comes through quite plainly is that to distinguish between the way in which entailment expressions function and the way in which causation expressions function is to make perspicuous features of the use of 'logically implies', or 'entails', and the use of 'causes'. The sentence, 'Being in friction entails heating up', uses the word 'entails' improperly; for 'in friction but does not heat up' has descriptive use. And the sentences, 'Being a tree causes a thing to be a plant' and 'Being a mother is the cause of her having a child', use the word 'cause' improperly; for the expressions 'childless mother' and 'tree but not a plant' lack descriptive use. Hume's consideration simply makes us aware of criteria for the use of 'causes' and 'logically implies' which we all naturally employ. Parenthetically, it may be noted that philosophers who hold an entailment view of causation do not have an imperfect grasp of these criteria, which they themselves employ in everyday speech. The fact that they do not give up their view, despite what Hume and others have so often said, cannot, to use G. E. Moore's expression, be accounted a 'mere mistake'. Their view has to be understood as presenting in a veiled form of speech an academically stretched use of 'logically implies' and of 'entails', a use which is semantically empty, but which apparently gives some sort of satisfaction.

The first thing that Hume was concerned to show, to put the matter in Russell's way, is that 'the fact that two things have been found often together and never apart does not, by itself, suffice to *prove* demonstratively that they will be found together in the next case we examine':[1] the past is not a 'logical guarantee' for the future. The second thing which he sought to show is that such a fact could not even suffice to make it probable that they will be found together in a fresh case.[2] His main argument for this thesis rests on what appears to be an empirical investigation of attested

---

[1] *The Problems of Philosophy*, pp. 101–2.

[2] Thus he says, 'All probable reasoning is nothing but a species of sensation' (Bk. I, Pt. III, Sec. 8). According to Russell, part of Hume's view is that 'However many instances we may have observed of the conjunction of A and B, that gives no *reason* for expecting them to be conjoined on a future occasion . . .' (*A History of Western Philosophy*, p. 667). Hume's way of putting it is that from the repetition of a conjunction 'we can draw no inference . . . nor make it a subject of our demonstrative or probable reasonings . . .' (Bk. I, Pt. III, sec. 14).

causal occurrences, an investigation in which looking is represented as playing a decisive role. His famous report of the investigation he made was that observation discovers no tie between objects, nothing which transpires *between* them that could be identified as that feature in the action of the one which brings about the expected change in the other. We do not, in addition to seeing the action of the one and the change in the other, see the action producing the change. The outcome of his search for the tie of causation, or for what might be called productive causation as against mere joint occurrence, is that 'objects have no discoverable connexion together'. He wrote: ' . . . there appears not throughout all nature, any single connexion which is conceivable by us. All events seem entirely loose and separate. One event follows another; but we never observe any tie in them. They seem conjoined but never connected.'[1] The conclusion to be drawn from this, and it would seem so straightforward and unambiguous as to rule out the possibility of its being misunderstood, is that past experience, no matter how comprehensive, can furnish no ground for any inference with regard to future occurrences: 'Even after the observation of frequent or constant conjunction of objects, we have no reason to draw any inference concerning any object beyond those of which we have had experience.'[2]

According to Hume's description of his investigation, the careful scrutiny of conjunctions of occurrences which would normally be taken by everyone to be instances of a change brought about by one thing acting on another, e.g. the change brought about in water by the action of heat on it, brings to light the fact that the occurrences are conjoined but not connected. This is to say that what is revealed by observation is that they are independent of each other, the one occurrence having nothing to do with the existence of the other occurrence. Water is not made to boil by the flame but boils on its own concurrently with the fire burning. So to speak, they are cases of parallel action. Occurrences which happen together, no matter how much they may appear to be bound up with each other, turn out to be merely chance conjunctions of independent events. And as no series of known chance conjunctions of y's with x's can be counted as evidence for the proposition that a new x will be accompanied or succeeded by a y,

[1] *An Enquiry Concerning the Human Understanding*, Sec. VII, Pt. II.
[2] *A Treatise of Human Nature*, Bk. I, Pt. III, sec. 12.

just as no pure run of luck in a game of chance counts as evidence that the next bet will also win, the inductive principle is groundless. It is clear that the use of 'probable' makes it an impropriety of language to say, 'The frequent but wholly *accidental* conjunction of y with x, no exceptions having been observed, makes it probable that the next observed x will be accompanied by a y'. The statement, 'No number of occurrences of a known chance conjunction of y with x counts as making probable the occurrence of y, given x', in an oblique way tells us something about the use in the language of the word 'probable'.

Hume's investigation of causation has the air of an empirical investigation; and the language in which he couches his conclusion, 'So on the whole there appears not, throughout all nature, any single instance of connection which is conceivable by us', makes it look like a generalization that is founded on an examination of instances. A number of things, however, one being the fact that philosophers have been able to divide on what Hume's arguments show, suggest that the idea created by Hume's language may not correspond to what he was actually doing. Only two of these need be touched on here, one relating to an enigma of nature he alludes to, the other relating to the talk with which he surrounds his investigation and conclusion. The enigma to which he alludes concerns the regularities we daily observe around us, regularities which made Galileo declare, 'Nature is governed by immutable laws which she never transgresses'. Hume was impressed by the regularities in nature, but was satisfied (superficially at least) simply to dismiss them as inexplicable: in his own words, 'We cannot penetrate into the reason of the conjunction'.[1] He should, in conformity with his claimed findings and expressed view, have said, instead, that there is no reason to be discovered, that the conjunctions are and remain mere chance happenings, and that that is all there is to it. It just is a fact that we are everywhere surrounded in nature by prodigious improbabilities. But if this is what Hume really wished to hold he could not have failed to realize how vast was the probability that what he had looked for actually existed, despite his failure to find it. According to Russell's account, Hume's ' "real" argument is that, while we

---

[1] And also: '. . . that in the most usual conjunctions of cause and effect we are as ignorant of the ultimate principle, which binds them together, as in the most unusual and extraordinary' (*Treatise*, Bk. I, Pt. IV, Conclusion).

sometimes perceive relations of time and place, we never perceive causal relation. . . . The controversy is thus reduced to one of empirical fact: Do we, or do we not, sometimes perceive a relation which can be called causal? Hume say no, his adversaries say yes, and it is not easy to see how evidence could be produced by either side.'[1] If the controversy were as represented by Russell, i.e. about a matter of empirical fact, it is *easy* to see how evidence could be produced for one side and against the other. The evidence which no one could fail to have noticed would be the astronomical improbability of the regular concomitances we encounter everywhere in nature being pure coincidences. The words of an adventuress in a recent play sum up the point: 'I know that luck can only run a certain distance.' The probability of the claim that in addition to the conjunction of the occurrences there is the production of one occurrence by the other, would be so great as to make everyone, including Hume, laugh the counterclaim out of the court. And this throws the weight of evidence in favour of those who claim to perceive a causal tie, and against those who might claim that there is none to be perceived—providing, of course, that the dispute is empirical, about whether something is being perceived in occurrences or is only imagined to be there.

The second thing which goes against the idea that Hume's investigation and conclusion are empirical is the talk with which he links them. If we become attentive to this, a different picture from the one he himself apparently entertained begins to emerge. A phrase like 'seem conjoined but never connected' creates the impression that 'connected' is used to denote something in addition to what is denoted by 'conjoined': the phrases 'connected as well as conjoined' appears to mean something more than what is meant by 'conjoined'. And Hume's claimed discovery would seem to be that experience has shown that there are no instances denoted by the term 'connected', just as experience has taught us that there are no instances of the concept *unicorn*. But surrounding remarks he makes soon change this impression. Such observations as 'there appears not throughout all nature, any single connexion which is *conceivable* by us'[2] and 'we have no other *notion* of cause and effect, but certain objects which have been always conjoined together'[2], compel us to think that Hume, whether he was aware of it or not, supposed himself to have discovered an important

---

[1] *A History of Western Philosophy*, p. 669.   [2] Italics my own.

fact about the *concept* of cause, namely, that it is identical with the concept *constant conjunction*, and that 'connected as well as conjoined' does not express anything 'conceivable', i.e. does not denote a concept. The idea which these observations bring into focus is that some sort of *a priori* investigation is being conducted, behind the false façade of an empirical investigation of an empirical position. Elsewhere I have tried to show[1] that on Hume's own account his search for the tie of causation was a piece of unconscious humbug. It has to be said immediately, of course, that his search was bogus not in the sense that he pretended to look for something he did not find, but in the sense that the words he used to describe what he was doing in fact described no search but only imitated language which does describe one.

Hume gave expression to at least four different theories about causation: one of these, which if he did not state in so many words, he implied, is that nature works by hidden causes; another is that causation is nothing more than constant conjunction or unvarying sequence; another still is that there are no causes in nature, but only co-happenings; and finally, that 'cause', 'power', 'necessary connexion' are terms which have no literal sense. These views are, in fact, bound up with each other and, strange as it may seem, in the end come to the same thing. Here only the last two views will be considered. Take first the view, expressed by 'Nothing is ever the cause of anything; all conjunctions of occurrences are chance conjunctions; they are all loose and separate'. It is quite clear that anyone who asserts these words will not be made to give them up by any state of affairs to which we might call his attention. Cases of water coming to a boil on the gas flame, stationary billiard balls being activated by collision, or billiard balls having their direction changed by impact with other bodies, etc., which are of course already known to him, would be dismissed as not really being cases of something causing something else. They would be characterized, instead, as consisting of chance conjunctions of occurrences. No single conjunction of occurrences or any number of repetitions of the conjunction we might get him to examine would move him to give up his sceptical view, or tend to make him less assured of its truth. The ordinary variety of occurrence which we take to be causal he does not

---

[1] *Studies in Metaphilosophy*, pp. 202–11.

accept as in any way counting against his view.[1] And this is not because he somehow overlooks what we see in such occurrences. He sees what we see, behaves pretty much as we behave, and in his non-philosophical moments talks like the rest of us who are not at all in doubt about the existence and operation of causes. He does not see less in the causal picture than we see, any more than a person who declares da Vinci's *Last Supper* is not an arresting painting sees (or need see) less in it than others. This is mystifying, but there can be no denying that what counts with us as a case of causation (and also with him when he is not in one of his metaphysical moods) does not count as such in his philosophy. The view that 'Belief in the causal nexus is a superstition'[2] not only remains impervious to falsification by any of the occurrences we refer to, but is also impervious to theoretical falsification by any imagined occurrences we may describe. If we ask the sceptic himself to supply us with a description of an occurrence which if it existed he would accept as upsetting his claim, we find that he is in like case with us. He no more than we can describe any occurrence or set of occurrences, over and above those we encounter in science and in daily life, which, if they existed, would be taken to falsify the claim. And this can only mean that as he is using the words, 'All conjunctions of events are loose and separate, there is no causal nexus', they do not express a proposition which has a theoretical falsification.

It would thus seem either that he thinks these words, in their actual use, express an *a priori* proposition or else that as he, in some unfamiliar way, is using them they express one. These two ideas about the sentence, 'No conjoined events are causally connected; all co-occurrences happen by chance or accident', are not the same, but both are in accord with the fact that nothing, actual or describable, would be accepted by the philosopher as falsifying what it states. The first idea comes more naturally than the second, and it seems to square better with remarks like those already

---

[1] Philosophers who are led by metaphysical reasoning to deny the existence of a well attested phenomenon normally allow the existence of the corresponding appearance. Interestingly enough, Professor Brand Blanshard thinks that some metaphysicians would deny the existence of the appearances if consistency with a line of reasoning demanded this sacrifice. See his 'In Defense of Metaphysics', p. 348, in *Metaphysics: Readings and Reappraisals* (ed. by W. E. Kennick and M. Lazerowitz).

[2] L. Wittgenstein, *Tractatus Logico-Philosophicus*, 5.1361.

Q

noted, e.g. that there is in nature no conceivable instance of connection, which implies that causal connection is in principle inconceivable. If we adopt the first hypothesis, the sentence, 'No conjoined occurrences are causally connected; all conjunctions of occurrences are accidental', will be understood as stating that it is logically impossible for events to be related as produced effect to producing cause and that being a conjunction of occurrences entails being a chance conjunction or, what is the same thing, that it is logically impossible for there to be a non-chance conjunction of occurrences.

The question regarding the nature of logical necessity and logical impossibility is an important question to get clear on, but here no more can be said than that a sentence which denotes an *a priori* true proposition serves as a medium for placing before us a fact about the use of terminology in a given language.[1] It is a sentence which does not explicitly mention terminology but nevertheless has only verbal import; but to say this is not to say that the proposition it expresses is verbal. The sentence shares its outer form, i.e., the form of speech in which it occurs, with sentences which state non-verbal propositions; but it shares its content with sentences that express verbal propositions about usage. Without attempting an accurate description of the form and function of the sentence, we may say that it *exhibits* what the corresponding verbal sentence mentions: e.g. the sentence 'An uncle is someone's brother' exhibits the fact of usage about which the sentence 'Part of the meaning of the word "uncle" is being someone's brother' makes an explicit declaration. Like the Delphic oracle, a sentence denoting an *a priori* truth neither mentions nor conceals what it communicates. In the present connection the important thing to notice is that to a sentence which denotes a necessarily true proposition, p, there corresponds a sentence which expresses a true verbal proposition, such that anyone who knows that the first sentence denotes p knows that what the verbal sentence states is true.

On the hypothesis that the position of the sceptic with regard to causation comes to his advancing an *a priori* rather than a factual claim, will correspond to the sentence, 'There is no such thing as causal connection; events, by necessity, are loose and separate', the following verbal sentence: ' "Causal connection" has no

[1] See 'Logical Necessity' in *The Structure of Metaphysics*.

descriptive function in the language; the rules for the use of "loose and separate" dictate its application to whatever "conjoined occurrences" correctly applies to.' To say that the first sentence states a logical truth is equivalent to saying that the proposition about usage expressed by the second sentence is a matter of fact true. The first sentence might be said to exhibit the piece of verbal usage to which the second sentence refers. And on the assumption that the sceptic thinks the first sentence functions in the language to express a necessary proposition, it follows that he believes that the corresponding sentence makes a true declaration with regard to usage. We should have to think he has the idea that in the English language the term 'causal nexus' (and terms like 'produced' and 'made') have no more use than does 'unrelated siblings', and also that 'loose and separate' and such terms as 'chance conjunction' and 'accidental combination' apply, as a matter of usage, to all pairs of occurrences. But this is a notion which, apart from his philosophical view, is not to be taken seriously. So far as his grasp of everyday language is concerned, there is no doubt that he knows as well as anyone that 'caused occurrence', etc., has a perfectly good use and that usage does not dictate the application of 'chance conjunction' to everything denoted by 'conjunction of occurrences'. It is to take refuge in fantasy to say that he forgets usage or that he misdescribes usage while under the spell of philosophy. Bewitchment of some sort undoubtedly plays a part in the doing of philosophy, but it would be unrealistic to think he is under a spell which weds him to mistaken ideas about usage. Apart from his philosophical theory, he gives no indication of having wrong ideas about usage, and even while philosophizing he does not fail to use causal terminology in the correct, accepted way. The conclusion which forces itself on us is not that his mind is bewitched into adopting mistaken notions about usage but rather that he unconsciously changes terminology, stretches or contracts usage or banishes words from the language, for whatever gratifications such unconscious play with words brings him.

This, the second of the two hypotheses, although perhaps less natural and certainly less appealing than the first, is nevertheless the more plausible. This becomes clear if we consider with care the hypothesis that the philosopher autocratically uses the words to express a necessary proposition. The verbal counterpart of his philosophical utterance, e.g. the sentence, 'The expressions "causally connected" and "non-chance conjunction of occurrences" have no descriptive use', would then be understood, not as making a flagrantly false claim about conventions operating in ordinary language, but as describing conventions in a privately reconstructed language having a special, and, one may guess, subjective purpose. It is easily seen that this hypothesis makes understandable various mystifying features that are not explained by the first hypothesis. We can understand, for instance, how anyone who takes a sceptical position regarding causation can, without having to develop a bizarre kind of amnesia, resist correction of any sort, either by an appeal to ordinary language, which he of course continues to use correctly, or by an appeal to occurrences in the world. No state of affairs serves to correct him, and neither does a fact of verbal usage. The reason for this, provided by the second hypothesis, is that his view is neither about the world nor about actual language. The sceptic is not, to use Wittgenstein's description, 'a man out of his senses, a man who doesn't see what everybody sees'.[1] He is a man who introduces non-workaday changes in language, or it would be better to say, superimposes the changes on it; and he does this in such a way as to create a convincing illusion, an illusion realistic enough to make some people think that he sees more deeply into things or into language than the common man does.

The two hypotheses about the nature of the philosophical rejection of causation,[2] one representing the philosopher as describing actual usage, the other as in some way changing usage, have now to be brought into connection with the problem of justifying the principle of induction. It will be remembered that on the natural assumption that the rejection of causal agency was founded on observation, any number of observed conjunctions, however great, will have the status of a gambler's run of luck and cannot be used for calculating future chances. By way of a brief excursion, it is worth noting a puzzling argument which is sometimes brought against what may be called the pragmatic justification of induction, i.e. an objection to the contention that the use of the principle of induction is justified by its passing the test of

[1] *The Blue Book*, p. 59.
[2] This sometimes takes the form of a redefinition of the word 'causation'. See Hume's *Treatise*, Bk. I, Pt. III, sec. 14, especially the last part.

'success in practice'.[1] Russell expressed the objection in the following words:

'It has been argued that we have reason to know that the future will resemble the past, because what was the future has constantly become the past, and has always been found to resemble the past, so that we really have experience of the future, namely of times which were formerly future, which we may call past futures. But such an argument really begs the very question at issue. We have experience of past futures, but not of future futures, and the question is: Will future futures resemble past futures? This question is not to be answered by an argument which starts from past futures alone.'[2]

One plain implication of this argument is that past successful forecasts are not rational grounds for expecting equally successful predictions in the future, any more than a gambler's run of luck is rational ground for believing that his future bets will win. As Russell graphically epitomizes the situation, 'The man who has fed the chicken every day throughout its life at last wrings its neck instead'.[3]

There is a temptation to import into the argument metaphysical considerations about time, such as that the future is hidden from us because, being future, it does not yet exist and is not available for our inspection. These are considerations which are comparable to those created by the sign above the Checkerboard Inn in Yorkshire, 'Beer served free tomorrow'; and they only succeed in enshrouding the argument in unnecessary philosophical mystification. At one level of interpretation, the argument can be seen to be only another way of saying that we cannot look into the future, not because tomorrow is not today, but because all occurrences are independent, i.e. because those which are paired are paired by mere chance and so provide no data for an inductive reckoning of the future. In a world in which everything happens by chance the future is veiled, but not for the tautologous reason that what has not happened yet is not happening now.

As has been seen, the idea that the words, 'All conjunctions of

---

[1] A. J. Ayer, *Language, Truth and Logic*, p. 50.
[2] *The Problems of Philosophy*, p. 100.
[3] *Ibid.*, p. 98.

events are loose and separate; there is no causation or law in nature', state a proposition about the world turns out to be wrong. But taking them at face value, the words imply that the world is so constituted that the inductive principle does not apply to it. To put the point more concretely, the combination of statements, 'All conjunctions are accidental' and '*x*'s and *y*'s have frequently been observed together, the one never without the other,' does not imply that given an *x* it is probable that a *y* will occur. But the sceptic with regard to causation does not, despite his language, actually take the stand that it is an empirical fact, grounded in observation, that all conjunctions of occurrences are fortuitous. The way in which he expresses himself gives rise to the false picture that this is what he is doing and that with the help of observation he is demonstrating the inapplicability of induction to our world. Behind the façade of his form of speech he takes a different view. What this is often makes its appearance in the guise of an *a priori* proposition, to the effect that it is logically impossible, impossible in conception, for a conjunction of occurrences to be non-fortuitous, or for one occurrence to bring about another occurrence. Construed in this way the view implies that the inductive principle is logically inapplicable to the world. More specifically, it implies the logical impossibility of one event being causally dependent on another, or of a change being produced rather than just happening. And this in turn implies that regardless of how often *x*'s and *y*'s have been associated it is logically impossible for it to be probable that *x* and *y* are not independent. Restated so as to bring into plainer view the verbal point involved, the philosophical claim implies that it makes no literal sense to speak of non-accidental conjunctions of occurrences. The conclusion is that with regard to occurrences which have been constantly associated, it makes no literal sense to say that probably their association is not mere chance. It is hardly necessary to remark that in the English language it is perfectly intelligible to speak of the probability of conjunctions of occurrences not being accidental, and that everyone knows this.

The last hypothesis, like the one about the nature of the claim that inductive inference is really deductive, construes the Humeian position regarding causation and chance as presenting in a veiled form re-tailored terminology: a vacuously stretched use of 'chance' and 'accidental', which dictates their application to all conjunctions of occurrences, and a contracted use of 'cause of' which prohibits its application to any occurrence or thing. On this construction of what has been done with language, according to which the philosopher does not use terminology to describe fact or to exhibit a linguistic rule but to gerrymander with words, the problem of justifying induction has a dissolution rather than a solution. Correspondingly, the sceptic's position with respect to the problem has an explanation rather than a truth-value. Along with his contracted use of 'cause' and 'connexion', i.e. along with his academic deletion of these words, as well as with his stretched use of 'chance', he introduces a contracted use of the word 'probable' (and related terms). This word is academically shorn of at least part of its use, the use it normally has in such phrases as 'x is the probable cause of y' and 'probably y's following x is not mere chance'. This is what Hume's solution of the question, 'Can induction be justified?', comes to. His negative answer, i.e. his rejection of the inductive principle, sometimes expressed in the words 'the past can provide no standard for the future', is a statement which presents, in the fact-stating idiom, the pretended banishment of an important use of the word 'probable'. The question, Can the inductive principle be justified?, is not a request for factual information about the applicability or workability of a principle, but is a request, made in the spirit of a language game, for a redecision regarding one of the uses of 'probable'. The arguments which Hume adduced to back his verbal decision are themselves moves with terminology. The sceptical position and its supporting arguments constitute, under cover of the onto-logical form of speech in which the philosopher expresses himself, a complex verbal game that produces a dramatic effect. In part this is achieved by the mode of speech in which the game with words is played. And when the altered use of cause, chance, and proba-bility terminology is paraded against the backdrop of the language which remains in everyday use, the result is the intriguing picture of the sceptic looking behind the appearance of a world governed by immutable law and finding that it works only by accident and chance. Like the Platonic metaphysician who returns to the Cave from the realm of true reality to tell us that we, scientists and common folk, mistake shadows for things, the Humeian investi-gator of reality steps out in front of the curtain of illusion to tell us that the world we live in does not justify the use of induction.

The game Hume plays with the words 'chance', 'cause', and 'probable' appeals to many people. And when a philosopher accepts the arguments and declares their outcome inescapable, it means that he has made the game his own, for whatever satisfactions living under its spell may give him. Some philosophers, however, reject the game wholly or in part, or introduce modifications of their own. Ramsey, for example, has stated that what Hume showed was that inductive inference 'could not be reduced to deductive inference or justified by formal logic',[1] but this interpretation of Hume did not lead him to reject the inductive principle. Thus, he said:

'We are all convinced by inductive arguments, and our conviction is reasonable because the world is so constituted that inductive arguments lead on the whole to true opinions. . . . It is true that if any one has not the habit of induction, we cannot prove to him that he is wrong; but there is nothing peculiar in that. If a man doubts his memory or his perception we cannot prove to him that they are trustworthy; to ask for such a thing to be proved is to cry for the moon, and the same is true of induction . . . no one regards it as a scandal to philosophy that there is no proof that the world did not begin two minutes ago and that all our memories are not illusory.[2]

A number of shifts of terminology can be discerned in this passage, and some of these become visible in the comparison of the absence of a proof that the world was not created two minutes ago or that sense-perception is trustworthy with the absence of a proof that induction is reliable. The linguistic alterations which enter into the philosophical view that it is impossible for anyone to know that his senses do not deceive him are a contracted use of the word 'know', which confines its application to statements about an immediate experience, and the assimilation of statements denoting logical possibilities to the class of statements denoting physical possibilities. It is, of course, *logically* possible for a person to be constantly deceived by his senses, which is only a non-verbal way of saying that it makes *literal sense* to speak of his being constantly deceived. And in the philosophically refashioned way of speaking we can say we do not really know that we are not the

---

[1] *The Foundations of Mathematics*, pp. 196–7.   [2] *Ibid.*, p. 197.

dupes of our senses or that we are not being hallucinated by a Cartesian demon. In the same way, the assimilation of statements about the logical possibility of a break in the series of observed associations to the class of statements about physical possibilities, when conjoined with a suitably modified use of the word 'proof', gives rise to the philosophical complaint that we cannot prove the reliability of induction. The next step is to point out that no finite number of observed associations can prove, or logically guarantee, that the association has not been accidental, and that nothing short of an infinite number of observed associations with no known exceptions would establish this. All this delusively creates the picture of a goal that forever remains beyond our reach. In this atmosphere it seems a fitting rebuke to say that to ask for a logical guarantee is as unreasonable as to ask for the moon. But the theory, complaint, and rebuke are only in appearance a theory, a complaint, and a rebuke. A philosopher who adopts Ramsey's language game may later reject it, or he may accept it with part of his mind while rejecting it with another part of his mind. Something like the latter seems to have happened in the case of Ramsey. His remarking that it is not a scandal that there is no demonstration of the reliability of induction suggests that he plays the Humeian game with one part of his mind; but he does not take it seriously with another part of his mind.

However, what comes through more distinctly than this in Ramsey's words is his unwillingness to play part of Hume's language game. In the light of our understanding of the nature of Hume's theory, Ramsey's statement that 'the world is so constituted' that induction can on the whole be relied on is not to be taken as making a claim either about the constitution of nature or about the correctness or adequacy of a part of the language used to describe nature. Instead it is to be understood as an oblique expression of the decisions not to give up the word 'cause' and not to stretch 'accidental' so that it applies to whatever 'conjunction of occurrences' applies to. It is reasonable to take him to be rejecting part of Hume's terminological manœuvring, that part which eliminates one important word and stretches beyond their actual use other important words. It is much as if he were saying that on the whole he prefers not to engage in a philosophical game with the terminology of science. By accepting one of Hume's arguments, which he takes to show that inductive inference 'could not be reduced to deductive inference or justified by formal logic', he resists playing one game some philosophers play with induction terminology, viz. stretching 'entailment' to cover causal statements. And by rejecting another of Hume's arguments he resists still another game philosophers play with terminology, viz., stretching 'chance association' to cover cases of causation, on which hangs the philosophical denial of the validity of the inductive principle.

Ayer's position with regard to the problem of justifying induction is similar to Ramsey's. It is not unplausible to suppose that a philosopher who dismisses metaphysics on the ground that it is nonsense, who wishes to save philosophy from its excesses and restore its good name,[1] would like to see Hume's arguments given a different direction from the one Hume himself gave them. He would wish to see them directed against the philosophical question itself, rather than against the principle of induction. Thus we find Ayer thinking that Hume has been misinterpreted, that he has been charged with denying causation whereas he only sought to define it.[2] It is an interesting and curious fact that philosophical arguments often have remarkable adaptability and that it is sometimes the case that the same considerations will lead equally to antithetical views. To illustrate, the consideration which leads to the view that there are no things, but only processes, leads as well to the view that things are processes. And Hume's considerations can be seen to lead to the view which denies the existence of causal connections amongst happenings and also to the view which professes to explain the nature of causation, i.e., the view that a causal statement analyses into one which asserts an invariable conjunction of occurrences. Ayer elects the second path, in order, it would seem, to make room for induction and at the same time to discredit the philosophical notion that induction stands in need of justification. In his opinion Hume's answer to the question concerning what is meant by saying that one event is a cause and another its effect shows 'first that the relation of cause and effect was not logical in character, since any proposition asserting a causal connection could be denied without contra-

---

[1] Ayer's words, even out of their context, make this plain: '. . . if the philosopher is to uphold his claim to make a special contribution to the stock of our knowledge . . .' (*Language, Truth and Logic*, p. 51).

[2] *Language, Truth and Logic*, p. 54. 'He has been accused to denying causation, whereas in fact he was concerned only with defining it.'

diction, secondly that causal laws were not analytically derived from experience, since they were not deducible from any finite number of experiential propositions, and, thirdly, that it was a mistake to analyse propositions asserting causal connections in terms of a relation of necessitation which held between particular events, since it was impossible to conceive of any observation which would have the slightest tendency to establish the existence of such a relation'.[1] One thing that can be clearly seen in Ayer's words is that instead of using the first and third observations as reasons for banishing the word 'cause' he uses them as justifications for *redefining* the word. The redefinition, it is to be noticed, brings out a point of similarity as well as a point of difference between the use of 'conjoined events' and the use of 'causally connected events', or 'events related by a law': the similarity lies in the fact that the relations they refer to differ in *kind* from entailment, and their dissimilarity lies in the fact that between the relations they refer to there is a difference of degree. Russell's formulation of the inductive principle brings out this latter feature in the redefinition of 'cause'. He wrote that inductive evidence can 'make it nearly certain that A is always associated with B, and will make this general law approach certainty without limit'.[2]

It can be expected that the philosophical redefinition of 'cause' will be linked with a curtailed use of 'know', a use such that 'knows with certainty that ϕ is a law of nature' expresses what is logically impossible. Just as according to one view knowing with certainty that a physical object exists is impossible because an infinite number of sense tests would have had to be completed, so knowing that x and y are related by a law is impossible because an infinite number of conjunctions would have had to be observed. In this way of speaking, 'knows with certainty that ϕ is a law' has no application in any theoretical circumstance, which is to say that the phrase has no literal sense. In the usual way of speaking it does, of course, make perfectly good sense to say 'S knows that x is cause of y' and 'S knows that ϕ is a law of nature'. In non-philosophical speech it is correct English to say, 'The inductive principle helped us to discover causes and laws the existence of which has now been a long established fact'. But this is not the

[1] *Language, Truth and Logic*, pp. 54–5.
[2] *The Problems of Philosophy*, p. 105.

idiom of some philosphers. A philosopher who points out that causal laws are not analytically derived from experience, since they are 'not deducible from any finite number of experiential propositions', is informing us that he is redefining 'cause' and 'know'.

Without going into the complicated linguistic manœuvring involved, it may be pointed out that the inductive principle is so restated as to make it appear that the principle used in science had been given a more careful formulation, viz. a statement of a causal law is and remains a hypothesis which is made probable by observed instances of the law and is such that its probability can be made to approach certainty 'without limit'. This is not the way the inductive principle is understood in the *practice* of science. No practising scientist would say that further observations would continue to make, for example, 'Friction generates heat', even more probable. Only a philosopher of science indulges in this sort of talk. The philosophically reformulated principle, however, outwardly resembles the principle the scientist uses in his practice, and, moreover, is presented as a corrected version of the principle. We can see now, in the new verbal setting, how Hume's arguments could be construed as showing that the philosophical problem is fictitious, and how it could be maintained that the security of science, which uses the principle, does not hang on its solution.

It will be remembered that Ayer had the idea that the inductive principle is 'a proposition about matter of fact',[1] which is to say it is an empirical proposition, roughly expressible by the words 'the past is a reliable guide to the future'. What Ayer's idea suggests is that there is a philosophical problem of classifying the principle. Its denial, for one thing, does not imply a formal contradiction, one of the form $p.\sim p$; but, for another thing, it is not subject to disproof by appeal to experience. Thus, while certain features of the inductive principle incline Ayer to categorize it as empirical, other of its features incline some philosophers to categorize it as logical. And in a way that is typical in philosophy, each classification is achieved by artificially stretching words, in the present case, the words 'empirical' and 'logical'. Ayer's classification of the inductive principle, together with his idea of what Hume's arguments reveal about the nature of causation, opens the way to the position that Hume's considerations *really* show the problem of justifying induction to be fictitious. The

---

[1] *Language, Truth and Logic*, p. 49.

view that causation is nothing more than constant conjunction, unlike the view that no such thing as causation or agency exists, does not require the excision of 'non-chance conjunction' and the stretching of 'accidental conjunction'. It only requires readjustments in their definitions. Hence Hume's arguments are no longer to be construed as showing that induction is groundless; instead they are to be taken to show that the inductive principle is a *unique* empirical proposition, one which has no verification. So to speak, it becomes a 'higher order' empirical proposition, one which is about empirical propositions asserting the existence of a law of nature and cannot have the kind of evidence they have. The inductive principle thus becomes a kind of empirical proposition that is incapable of confirmation to any degree by induction but is somehow presupposed by particular inductive propositions: it is represented as a proposition which stands by itself amongst empirical propositions, one for which it is nonsense to demand justification or evidence. The manipulation of terminology that gives rise to this view can be seen to be extremely complex, involving the words 'empirical', 'chance', 'law', 'infinite', etc.; and here little more than a glimpse into its linguistic structure has been achieved.

Russell, whose position coincides with Ayer's at a number of points, disagrees both about the nature of the inductive principle and about what Hume's arguments establish. In one place[1] he remarks that the principle recommends itself on the ground of its 'intrinsic evidence', and in another place he characterizes it outright as not empirical, but as being a logical principle. He also disagrees with Ayer's type of position regarding what Hume's arguments show the character of the inductive principle to be. According to him they prove that it is 'an independent logical principle, incapable of being inferred either from experience or from other logical principles . . .'[2] These words have to be read in relation to the notions, (1) that Hume's arguments are to be reckoned as analytically laying bare the nature of causation, rather than as disproving its existence, and (2) that propositions declaring the existence of a law cannot be conclusively established. It also needs to be viewed in relation to the idea (3) that, because it can neither be rendered probable nor disproved by experience, the

---

[1] *The Problems of Philosophy*, p. 106.
[2] *A History of Western Philosophy*, p. 674.

principle of induction is not empirical. It then is possible to see in Hume's arguments an attempt to show that the inductive principle is an *a priori* axiom, or an independent logical principle. In the linguistic setting furnished by (1), (2), and (3), the arguments are to be understood as demonstrating that the inductive principle is not an empirical proposition and, inasmuch as its negation does not yield a formal contradiction, that it is not a tautology.

The remaining construction to be placed on the arguments is that they show it to be an *a priori* but not an analytic principle, one which is to be accepted on its 'intrinsic evidence'. In this connection Casimir Lewy has said some things that help us see what would lead a philosopher to describe the principle of induction as an *independent* logical principle, and what would make him look on Hume's arguments as supporting this idea. Lewy wrote:

'. . . it seems to me that the following proposition "whenever I have heard barking in the past there was always a dog somewhere near, I am hearing barking now, but I have no reason whatever to believe there is a dog in the neighbourhood" is *self-contradictory*. I cannot prove that this is so, but I should ask you to reflect on how we *use* expressions like "I have a good reason to believe", "It's probable", "It's very likely", etc. If you reflect on how these expressions are actually used, I am sure you will see that the proposition I've just stated is self-contradictory in the very same way in which it is self-contradictory to say "All men are mortal, Smith is a man but Smith is not mortal".'[1]

It will be remembered that according to Russell the 'real' question we have to ask with regard to induction is: Do *any* number of cases of a law fulfilled in the past afford evidence that it will be fulfilled in the future? And Lewy maintains that the affirmative answer to this question is guaranteed by its negation being a formal self-contradiction. His inability to *prove* that there is a contradiction in the statement, 'No number of cases of a law ϕ being fulfilled in the past affords evidence for or makes probable the proposition that ϕ will be fulfilled in the future', fits in with

[1] 'On the "Justification" of Induction', *Analysis*, Vol. 6, nos. 5 and 6, pp. 89–90.

Russell's claim that the inductive principle is a logical axiom, the truth of which cannot be demonstrated but which is self-evident. Lewy's direction for getting to see for ourselves the contradiction he sees is to pay heed to the *use in the language* of such terms as 'probable', 'likely', 'good reason for believing'. And indeed, if we become sensitive to the criteria for their use we see what might be called 'non-specific definitions'. That is, what we become aware of by following Lewy's direction are such linguistic facts as that an *unspecified* number of observed unbroken associations of x with y is *called* 'a good reason for believing that a fresh x will be accompanied by a y', 'ground for its being probable that . . .', 'makes likely that . . .', etc. The sentence, 'No number of correlations of y with x affords evidence for or makes probable that the correlation will continue', has a verbal import which goes against the use of 'is evidence' and 'makes probable'; it violates what we *mean* by these terms. But since no specific number is included in their definition, the sentence is not formally self-contradictory.[1] It nevertheless states a logical impossibility. The words, '*Some* number of constant associations of y with x makes it probable that x is a cause of y', express an *a priori* proposition but not a tautology. For since 'some' refers to no specific number, no statement of the form 'n associations have been observed, with no exceptions noted, but it is not probable that . . .' implies a formal contradiction.[2] What these considerations bring to our attention is that the sentence expressing the principle of induction is a *definition* of the word 'probable': it gives one meaning of the word in the language. And its being formulated in the non-verbal mode of speech explains in part its appearance of being an axiom of some sort. Its outer dress also makes it possible for other philosophers to view the definition as being about how the world works, and is part of the verbal material that is required for weaving various theories around the principle.

The philosophical problem of justying induction is not a problem of determining the validity of a basic scientific procedure. And the various positions put forward as solutions of it present in an unrecognized form academic manœuvrings with the lan-

[1] For a detailed discussion of this point, see Alice Ambrose, *Essays in Analysis* (London: George Allen & Unwin Ltd., 1966), pp. 200–2.

[2] It is this sort of fact which has led some philosophers to characterize the inductive principle as synthetic *a priori*.

guage of induction and have nothing to do with induction itself. We may justifiably wonder what it is about the philosophical tinkering with language that has continued to hold the attention of people for so many years. Psychologically speaking, it would be unrealistic to imagine that what absorbs them is just the game played with inference-vocabulary. To be sure, the verbal game brings to life the appealing illusion of the philosopher as a super-scientist who investigates the presuppositions of science; and this is an illusion which caters to the unconscious wish for omnipotence of thought. But there is more to it than this. It is reasonable to think that the profound spell is cast over his mind by something he perceives behind the verbal content of the game, a cluster of ideas he unconsciously associates with it. What invests the problem with the importance it has for the philosopher, what gives it its charge, are its 'subjective origins'. Unconscious ideas which he reads into the problem keep him thrall to it, and the special linguistic character of the problem makes it adaptable to the expression of subterranean mental contents. In sum, behind the appearance of attempts to solve a scientific problem is the artificial redistricting of the applications of induction-expressions, which produces the appearance; and below that, deep in the mind, are emotional problems which are given expression by the rearranged pieces of language.

We may permit ourselves a guess at one of the subjective determinants of the philosophical problem. It does not require much reflection to see the possibility of a link between the concern with the philosophical problem and a need to cope with a tendency to obsessional doubt. In connection with the problem of free will and determinism, which is an ingredient in the problem of justifying induction, Ernest Jones has written: '. . . there must be few serious thinkers who have not in some period of their life been perplexed by the antinomy that seems to inhere in every solution. The perplexity may even reach the intensity of the *folie de doute* of those afflicted with an obsessional neurosis, who endlessly oscillate between two opposite conclusions or decisions.'[1] In a Restoration play one character beautifully illustrates this tendency; he cries to his friend that while he is with his mistress he feels no uncertainty about her exclusive love for him, but the moment he is away from her doubt and suspicion set in.

[1] *Essays in Applied Psychoanalysis*, Vol. II, pp. 178–9.

To take up briefly one solution of the problem of justifying induction, namely, Hume's position that the past provides no rule for the future. This position can be seen to lend itself to the interpretation that it gives hidden expression to a disposition to doubt. Hume's view about what the past cannot teach us is not a theory about how nature works, rather it reveals a tendency in him to fall prey to doubt.[1] Proving his claim that the past is no guide for the future, which is a way of convincing himself that the tendency is 'natural', would then function psychologically as a reassurance formula: instead of suffering from a private affliction he satisfies himself that he participates in one that is common to all. He unconsciously consoles himself with the thought: I am not out of the ordinary, underneath we are all the same; it is the lot of everyone to fall prey to obsessive doubt. The well-known example which Russell used to show why we can never be certain that the next instance will be like its predecessors is that of the chicken that is fed every day but eventually has its neck wrung. The meaning of this is not overly concealed, and it tells us one of the ideas that is linked with anxiety and doubt.

[1] The following passage gives a clear indication of a tendency to what he called 'philosophical melancholy': 'The *intense* view of these manifold contradictions and imperfections in human reason has so wrought upon me, and heated my brain, that I am ready to reject all belief and reasoning, and can look upon no opinion even as more probable or likely than another. Where am I, or what? From what causes do I derive my existence, and to what condition shall I return? Whose favour shall I court, and whose anger must I dread? What beings surround me? and on whom have I any influence, or who have any influence on me? I am confounded with all these questions, and begin to fancy myself in the most deplorable condition imaginable, environed with the deepest darkness, and utterly deprived of the use of every member and faculty.' (*Treatise*, Bk. I, Pt. IV, Conclusion.)

INDEX